AF782625

Copyright © 2008 by Nova Science Publishers, Inc.

All rights reserved. No part of this book may be reproduced, stored in a retrieval system or transmitted in any form or by any means: electronic, electrostatic, magnetic, tape, mechanical photocopying, recording or otherwise without the written permission of the Publisher.

For permission to use material from this book please contact us:
Telephone 631-231-7269; Fax 631-231-8175
Web Site: http://www.novapublishers.com

NOTICE TO THE READER

The Publisher has taken reasonable care in the preparation of this book, but makes no expressed or implied warranty of any kind and assumes no responsibility for any errors or omissions. No liability is assumed for incidental or consequential damages in connection with or arising out of information contained in this book. The Publisher shall not be liable for any special, consequential, or exemplary damages resulting, in whole or in part, from the readers' use of, or reliance upon, this material.

Independent verification should be sought for any data, advice or recommendations contained in this book. In addition, no responsibility is assumed by the publisher for any injury and/or damage to persons or property arising from any methods, products, instructions, ideas or otherwise contained in this publication.

This publication is designed to provide accurate and authoritative information with regard to the subject matter covered herein. It is sold with the clear understanding that the Publisher is not engaged in rendering legal or any other professional services. If legal or any other expert assistance is required, the services of a competent person should be sought. FROM A DECLARATION OF PARTICIPANTS JOINTLY ADOPTED BY A COMMITTEE OF THE AMERICAN BAR ASSOCIATION AND A COMMITTEE OF PUBLISHERS.

Library of Congress Cataloging-in-Publication Data

Harnessing the service roundtrip over the Internet to support time-critical applications : concept, techniques, and cases / Allan Kang ... [et al.].
p. cm.
Includes bibliographical references and index.
ISBN-13: 978-1-60021-604-6 (hc : alk. paper)
ISBN-10: 1-60021-604-8 (hc : alk. paper)
1. Internet programming. 2. TCP/IP (Computer network protocol) I. Kang, Allan.
QA76.625.H365 2007
004.6'2--dc22

2007004864

Published by Nova Science Publishers, Inc. ✦ New York

CONTENTS

PREFACE

Although the Internet and World Wide Web (WWW) are popular as tools for convenient exchange of information, it is not easy to utilize the Internet for time-critical applications such as on-line remote diagnosis in telemedicine. It is a wish of the United Nations to bring e-health to every corner of the world via the Internet. This is easier said than done because the sheer size of the Internet implies unpredictable faults of all kinds. These faults are physically translated into communication and computation delays. Since these faults and delays have many contributing factors that can change suddenly, it is impractical to monitor them all for the sake of fault tolerance. For this reason the new concept of interpreting the channel dynamics by gauging its end-to-end behavior has emerged. The aim is to measure the changes of the average service roundtrip time (RTT) over time and interpret the possible signs of faults from these changes. If the length of the average service RTT is suddenly increased in an exponential manner, network congestion and widespread retransmission are indicated. Then, the Internet and/or the applications running on it should invoke fault tolerance measures to prevent system breakdown and partial failures. This concept of gauging the channel dynamics to prevent system failure is generally known as Internet End-to-End Performance Measurement (IEPM).

Other techniques to improve system fault tolerance and shorten the service RTT include the following: a) active queue management (AQM) to prevent congestion at the router/system level, b) user-level buffer size tuning to eliminate buffer overflow at the receiver end, and c) dynamic cache size tuning to maintain the given hit ratio at the proxy level to reduce the chance of remote information retrieval that involves the domain name server (DNS). The correctness and efficacy of these techniques in action, however, are determined by the ever changing Internet traffic pattern, which may be stationary or non-stationary at any time. Even when it is stationary it may change unpredictably from short-range dependence (SRD) (e.g. Markovian patterns) to long-range dependence (LRD) (e.g. heavy-tailed or self–similar) or vice versa. Previous experience indicates that the self-similar behavior, which involves traffic bursts, can seriously affect system performance and stability. These bursts can be monofractal (i.e. linear) or multifractal (i.e. non-linear) and intertwined in an unpredictable fashion. It is not unusual for these bursts to embed fractal breakdowns, which if persistent would lead to system failure. Therefore serious time-critical applications such as telemedicine should be equipped with the capability to detect the traffic pattern on the fly and use the detected result to reconfigure themselves accordingly to ward off any ill effects of the traffic. Ideally, there should also be some elements in the RTPD process that can proactively detect those fatal fractal breakdowns and circumvent their lethal ill effects. Real-time traffic pattern detection (RTPD) is a budding concept but the initial research results are solid and applicable already. The purpose of the book is to shed light on some of the novel practical fault tolerance techniques that can help shorten the end-to-end service roundtrip (RTT) time of a logical Internet channel. As a result the Internet can be harnessed for serious time-critical applications. Several practical cases will be presented to demonstrate how the effective harnessing can be achieved.

The first two chapters of the book discuss the issues associated with the Internet and provide a brief survey of relevant techniques that can help lower the average number of trails (ANT) to achieve successful transmission and thus shortens the client/server service roundtrip time. Then, the rest of the book is organized in the following order: a) Chapter 3 explains the origins of the ill effects of Internet traffic on system performance and stability; b) Chapter 4 introduces the novel concept of dynamic buffer size tuning (DBST) to prevent user-level buffer overflow; c) Chapter 5 introduces the concept of dynamic cache size tuning (DCST) that can maintain the given hit ratio and shorten the information retrieval RTT predictably; d) Chapter 6 highlights practical DBST and DCST application cases supported by the RTPD mechanism and empirical results and; e) Chapter 7 concludes with the contributions of these new techniques to successful time-critical applications and descriptions of some open issues from the DBST and DCST point of view.

The intended audience of the book includes: researchers in the relevant areas, designers/planners of time-critical applications to be run on the Internet, and final-year IT students (as a reference/text). On the professional level, the book is definitely useful because it was only in the mid-1990s that researchers (e.g. Teqqu and Paxson) concluded that systems designed for the Internet with preconceived mathematical models in mind, such as the traditional Poisson based engineering approach, would fail. Since the reason for such failures is the unpredictable nature of the Internet traffic, the systems running on the Internet ideally would need to be able to identify the current traffic pattern on the fly and reconfigure themselves as necessary to ward off the traffic ill effects. Until recently, research had concentrated mainly on offline traffic analysis, and this is good for understanding what had happened in the system. To remedy the traffic effects immediately, we need new techniques such as the RTPD presented in this book. The RTPD identifies traffic patterns in a spontaneous manner. The examples in chapter 5 will demonstrate how the RTPD mechanism detects traffic patterns on the fly for real-life problems, and how the detected result can be utilized by a running application to proactively counteract some Internet factors that cause system failures and poor performance.

AUTHOR INTRODUCTION

Allan Kang Ying Wong, Ph.D., is an Assistant Professor of the Department of Computing, Hong Kong Polytechnic University. His main research interest is telemedicine, which is intrinsically time-critical and therefore its success depends on how effectively the service roundtrip time over the Internet can be harnessed. He has to his credit over 100 refereed scientific journal and conference papers, more than half of which focus on how to shorten the service roundtrip time in real-time applications. Dr. Wong is also practising TCM (Traditional Chinese Medicine) in Hong Kong. For this reason his research effort on harnessing service roundtrip time effectively over the Internet is focused on TCM telemedicine applications. He has authored a TCM best seller.

Tharam S. Dillon, Ph.D., is Distinguished Research Professor in the Digital Ecosystems and Business Intelligence Institute at Curtin University of Technology in Western Australia. He is an expert in the field of software engineering, data mining, XML-based systems, ontology, and trust and reputation systems. Professor Dillon has published over 500 scientific papers in refereed conferences and journals, authored 5 books and co-edited 5. He is chair of the IFIP Working Group 2.12/12.4 on Web Semantics and Chair of the IEEE/IES Technical Committee on Industrial Informatics. He is co-editor-in-chief of three international journals.

Wilfred Wan Kei Lin, Ph.D., is a specialist in the area of dynamic buffer tuning for Internet application, and his other research interests include: Internet performance measurement, distributed fault tolerance, and real-time Internet traffic pattern detection. He graduated with his Ph.D. from the Department of Computing, Hong Kong Polytechnic University in 2005 and has more than 35 refereed conference and journal publications to his credit, with Dr. Allan Wong and Prof. Dillon. He has substantial experience in designing mobile medicine systems with Dr. Allan Wong (already deployed in Hong Kong) to help physicians treat patients in mobile clinics (vehicle-based). The aim is to make medicine and disease treatment to reach every corner of Hong Kong.

ACKNOWLEDGEMENT

This book is the outcome of the research team that includes Dr. Allan Wong, Prof. Dillon and Dr. Lin. Although this trio has contributed the manuscript of the book, the material also includes efforts of other team members in the past, especially in the aspect of empirical results. The authors thank Dr. Richard Sui Lun Wu who had provided useful information when Chapter 5 was written. Last but not least we also thank Ms. Patricia Hutton for her editorial work and professional opinions on how the material in the book should be presented for greater effect.

Chapter 1

INTRODUCTION

1.1. BACKGROUND

In recent times, we have seen the World Wide Web (WWW) and the Internet intrude into all aspects of human endeavor, including business and commerce, industry, community organizations, government and personal information. The pervasive nature of the Internet has made everyone in society increasingly dependent on it. The Internet itself is basically a loose connection of backbone networks that interact through the Internet Protocol (IP), as shown in figure 1.1. The actual interaction over the Internet involves a client (logical) that makes the request and a server (logical) that services this request. This interaction is represented by figure 1.2, which shows how the logical client's request goes through a logical channel that may consist of several intermediate nodes. Although there is a request queue buffer associated with the logical server in figure 1.2, there may also be buffer queues associated with the intermediate nodes through which the requests and responses are relayed. An important parameter that determines the Internet responsiveness is the service roundtrip time (RTT), which includes all the time delays (e.g. for transmission, queuing and service by the server) accrued in the period from the time a request was initiated to the point that the requested service is correctly returned. Generally, when the number of requests by the many clients on the Internet is not large, the buffer queues associated with both the intermediate nodes and the logical server queue are processed and serviced in an orderly manner. If, however, the number of requests reaching a particular node is too high, then the build-up of the request queue can lead to local buffer overflow. The result is loss of some transmitted messages or requests. Hence, the Internet is sometimes referred to as operating in a "send and pray" mode. The common method used for recovering the lost messages is retransmission. This, however, increases the average number of trials (ANT) for a correct transmission.

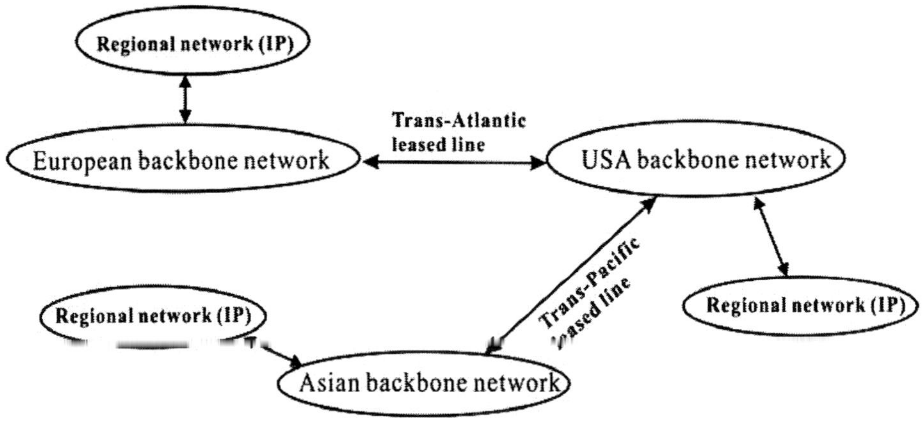

Figure 1.1. The Internet is basically a loose connection of backbone networks that interact with the Internet Protocol (IP).

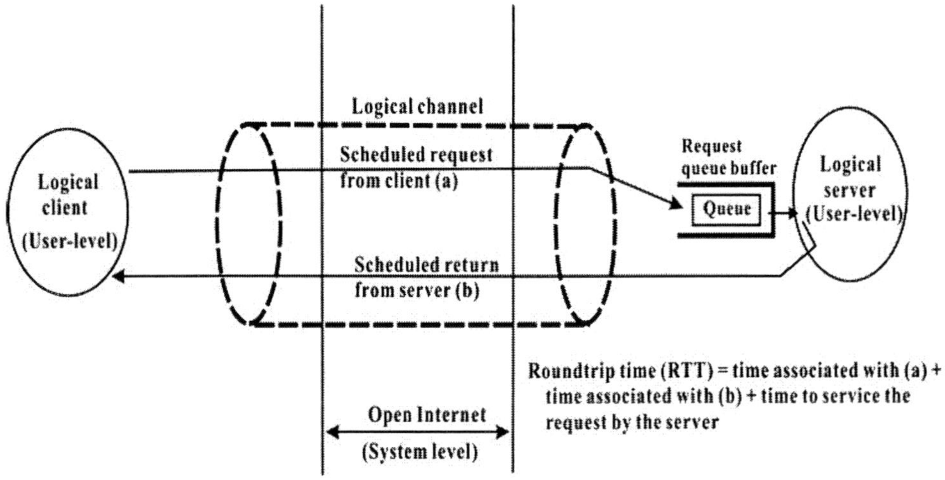

Figure 1.2. The logical end-to-end client server relationship.

The Internet today is operating on a "wired + wireless" (also known as "wireline + wireless") basis. It has practically provided a new platform for distributed computing. This platform differs from the previous ones that worked exclusively with a set of homogeneous nodes, for example, the PVM [PVM] and P4 [p4] systems. The differences are the following Internet attributes: a) its sheer size, and b) the heterogeneity of the underlying network.

Since its advent, the Internet has been growing relentlessly in complexity, particularly in terms of network size, structural heterogeneity, and information varieties. Information retrieval in the WWW is no longer heavily textual but leaning toward the multi-media side. It has been empirically measured [Wang1999] that the web page size has grown at a monthly rate of 15 percent, or more than 400 percent per annum. In contrast, the Internet backbone bandwidth improves by only 60 percent annually. If this continues, the Internet will become terribly congested and lose its appeal. Besides, according to Moore's Law [Moore], the VLSI (Very Large Semiconductor Integration) hardware speed may have conceptually reached the limits of physics. After that, the current VLSI technology would be unable to add further speed improvement until there is a new breakthrough.

1.2. Overview of Issues Associated with the Internet

The natural solution to transcend this limit is through distributed parallelism, the idea being to modularize a task into subtasks that can be executed in parallel processors over a network. In a large network, however, there are many factors that inevitably increase σ, the error probability that causes retransmissions, including hardware heterogeneity, possible congestion and partial failures. Therefore, the need to harness σ by counteracting the negative impact of these factors is more pressing than ever before because it would be impossible to run any serious time-critical applications on the Internet otherwise. The counteraction may have different views as follows:

a) Fault tolerance [Jalote1994] of a distributed system: The emphasis is on prevention, detection, and recovery, in this sequence. Firstly, measures are implemented to prevent the occurrence of system faults. If this fails, then the type of fault should be identified so that the appropriate mechanism can be invoked to rectify the fault and recover the system.
b) Quality of service (QoS) [Chao2002]: The aim of QoS is to deliver a contracted service correctly. Quality factors may tie in with different classes of service such as those for the ISO-OSI (International Standard Office – Open Systems Interconnection) transport layer [RFC793], where class 4 supports retransmission for channel failure recovery. Usually, timeliness of message delivery is an important QoS requirement, and this cannot be achieved without harnessing σ and network congestion effectively.
c) System dependability: This covers the following issues: a) system reliability, which deals with the trustworthiness of computer services; b) system availability, which deals with the readiness of a system for usage and its continuity of service; and c) safety, which deals with the effect of geographical location on a service [RFC1712].

If we scrutinize the contents of these views carefully, it is easy to identify various common factors. New views can be defined by including any of the appropriate factors that may be present within other existing views.

The structural complexity of the Internet does not come solely from the heterogeneity arising from loose interconnections of nodes of various brands brought together by the IP. The other contributors include incompatible protocols and the inclusion of wireless communications [Goldsmith2005]. As the Internet grows, new protocols emerge to cater for some immediate needs. Unfortunately, some of these protocols, such as the Asynchronous Transfer Mode (ATM) protocol, are not compatible with IP. The solution for overcoming the incompatibility is tunneling [RFC1853], which could introduce time delays and failure in the logical client/server communication process. The Internet is no longer "wireline" or wired only, but a complex structure made up of both wired and wireless portions. Wireless communication supports SFF (small form factor) device mobility. A SFF device or client could be a PDA (personal digital assistant), a mobile phone, or a computer notebook. When the SFF client moves from one wireless cell to another, it is still able to reconnect to the wired structure even after momentarily switching off. The reconnection capability is supported by the local base station that relays between the SFF client and the wired/wireline Internet component. The mechanism through which the Internet detects the location of a SFF client is called the location-aware capability [Patterson2003]. This capability is independent of the wireless protocol, which may be one of the following technologies: GSM (Global System for Mobile communications), UMTS (Universal Mobile Telephone Service), GPS (Global Positioning System), blue-tooth, e-911, cricket, and Infra-red. All these technologies have pros and cons and at this moment there is no dominant wireless communication technology [Goldsmith2005]. For example, GPS is good for communication only in an outdoor environment because walls block communication, and Infra-red communication performs poorly in sunlight.

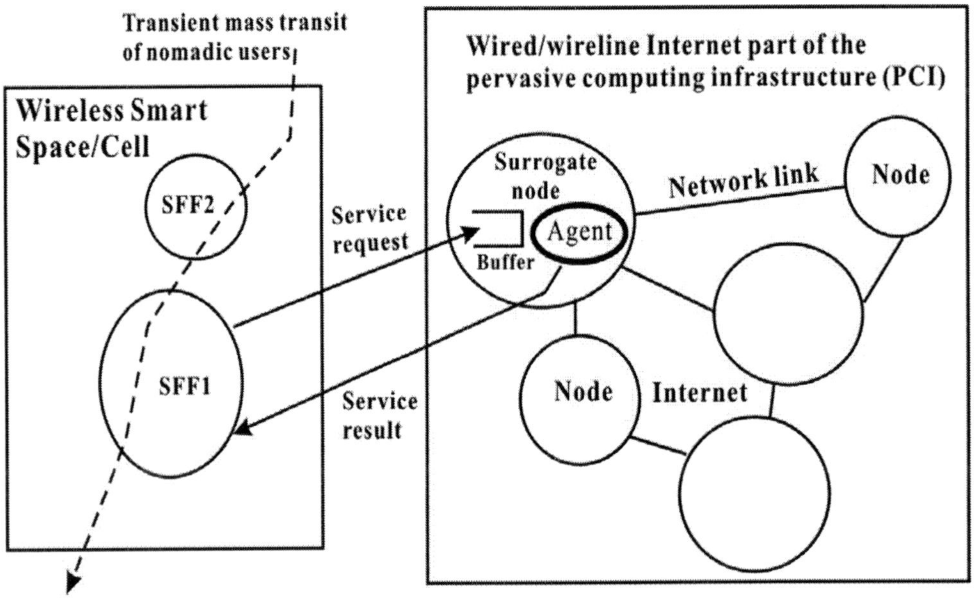

Figure 1.3. Pervasive computing infrastructure and surrogate node.

The complexity arising from the wireless and wired interconnections in the Internet has given it a very different character from its original wireline operation. It is therefore more appropriate to view the Internet today as a Mobile Distributed System (MDS) [Tseng2001]. If the capability to track user intent is added, then the MDS is a pervasive computing system [Patterson2003]. An example of tracking a user's intent is as follows: a) the user faxed a few important English language documents through its SFF device minutes before boarding a plane; b) he switched off the SFF device; c) the location-aware capability located the SFF client once the user had arrived at the Paris airport; and d) the Internet node (called the surrogate node) in the airport, which was assigned to serve the SFF client, automatically translates and prepares a French version of the faxed documents just in case. The system has traced the user's movement and tracked his intent by providing the French version of the documents because he is now in France. In fact, pervasive computing is still in the experimental stage, and some well known research projects include OXYGEN of MIT [OXYGEN] and Aura of Carnegie Mellon [Saty2001].

1.2.1. Pervasive Computing

The concept of pervasive computing is depicted in figure 1.3, which shows its two major components: wireless smart space (SS) and wired pervasive computing infrastructure (PCI). A node called the surrogate in the PCI is assigned to serve the SS. Assuming the SS is in an airport, then the SFF device SFF1 passes through with the flow of human transit traffic. The user of SFF1 switches it on temporarily to retrieve some useful local information. The request for information retrieval reaches the surrogate and queues there, waiting for service. The information retrieval RTT should be short to make the PCI set-up useful. To speed up the service, the logical server in the surrogate solicits help from other logical servers in the PCI. These servers collaborate among themselves or even seek help from other Internet nodes outside the PCI boundary, a process called cyber foraging [Patterson2003]. Conceptually, the logical server in the surrogate is trying to produce a service speedup. Cyber foraging can effectively shorten the service RTT when the transit traffic has grown exponentially and increases the number of SFF requests sent to the surrogate proportionately. We cannot, however, rely on cyber foraging to alleviate the problem of a sudden surge in the number of requests into the queue of the logical server. If the queue buffer has a static size, then overflow may occur during voluminous request periods. Two of the effective solutions for resolving the problem of transient queue buffer overflow at the user/server level are:

a) Dynamic buffer size tuning (DBST) [Lin2005]: The aim is to tune the buffer size on the fly with the adjustment computed from some chosen network parameters.
b) Dynamic cache size tuning (DCST) [Wong2003]: The aim is to maintain a given hit ratio for the logical server in the surrogate by adjusting the cache size in a dynamic manner with respect to selected parameters. If the logical server can return the requested data immediately without even involving cyber foraging, then service roundtrip time is automatically shortened. DCST is useful in information retrieval applications.

The complexity of the modern Internet "wired and wireless *(WandW)*" structure, which is fundamental to mobile and pervasive computing [Saty2001], has led to unpredictable traffic patterns. In fact, some researchers empirically confirm that any systems designed with a preconceived mathematical model in mind (e.g. Poisson) would fail over the Internet because of this unpredictability [Paxson1995]. In fact, the Internet traffic can change suddenly, for example, from short-range dependence (SRD) (e.g. Poisson) to long-range dependence (e.g. self-similar or heavy-tailed) or multifractal over time [Molnar1999]. Provided that a system possesses the ability to adapt its operation on the fly, it would be able to ward off the ill effects of traffic on its performance due to sudden pattern changes. A prerequisite for this success is that the system should have real-time traffic pattern detection (RTPD) capability. The concept of RTPD is novel [ATNAC], and the few cases shown in this book demonstrate how RTPD can be utilized effectively.

1.2.2. Interaction among Logical Entities

Applications running on the Internet are naturally object-based and logical objects interact by message passing. The Internet (or *Internetworks*), which is a collection of different interconnected networks, provides two basic protocols for inter-object communications and interactions: the connectionless UDP (User Datagram Protocol – RFC768) and the connection-oriented TCP (Transmission Control Protocol – RFC793, RFC1122 and RFC1323). These two protocols make use of the IP (Internet Protocol) layer underneath for network-wide communications. In figure 1.4, the relationships among UDP, TCP and IP are shown as two separate Internet protocol layers, "Internet Layer 1" and "Internet Layer 2". Internet Layer 1 corresponds to the transport layer in the 7-layers protocol hierarchy defined by the ISO-OSI reference model. Conceptually, communication via a virtual circuit/channel in the transport layer is end-to-end. The seven layers in the OSI peer-to-peer protocol hierarchy are: application (highest layer), presentation, session, transport, network, data link and physical (lowest layer). Internet layer 2 corresponds to the OSI network layer. The UDP data unit is a packet, which is basically a data structure with an 8-byte header followed by the payload. The header specifies the source and destination *ports*. UDP segments are not sequenced and the communication has no flow or congestion control. In contrast, TCP segments are sequenced (with sequence numbers). Unlike UDP, TCP does not support multicasting or broadcasting. TCP uses the sliding window mechanism for flow control, and it allows the sender to alleviate network congestion by using Jacobson's *slow start* approach [Jacobson1988]. The core idea of this approach is that a congestion window is dynamically maintained by the sender (more details are given in Chapter 2).

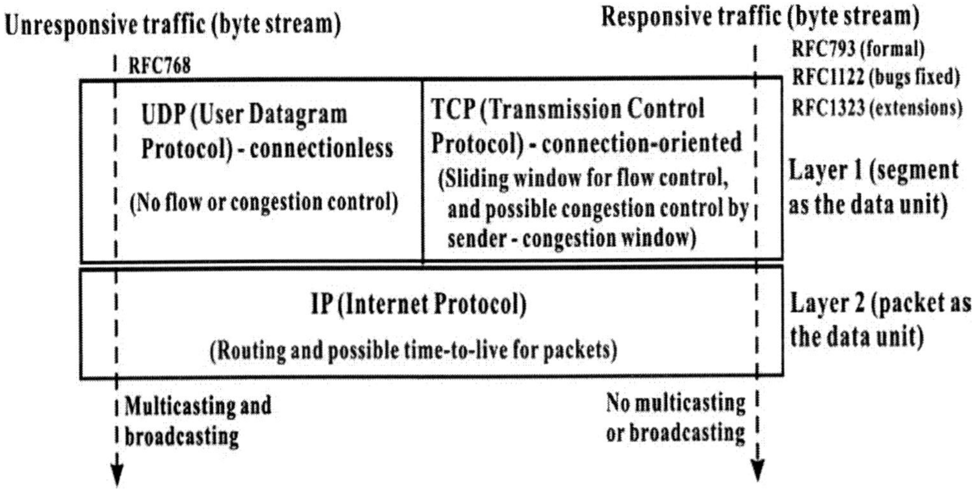

Figure 1.4. The relationship among UDP, TCP and IP.

The UDP traffic is unresponsive because the sender sets the rate of transmission and this rate would not be adjusted for the sake of congestion control. The TCP traffic is responsive because the sender's flow control (i.e. sliding window) and the congestion prevention (i.e. congestion window) together regulate the transmission rate adaptively to prevent network congestion. In the process, all the TCP senders consciously reduce their transmission rates. Unfortunately, the bandwidth freed from the responsive traffic can be usurped by the unresponsive traffic producers (e.g. video streams) because they would aggressively make use of any available bandwidth. Therefore, AQM (active queue management) mechanisms such as Black are useful in preventing any lopsided bandwidth usage [Chatranon2004].

1.2.2.1. Interaction by Transmission Control Protocol (TCP)

TCP is connection-oriented and the end-to-end communication is conceptually through the virtual channel (VC), which has to be explicitly established. In the establishment process, the segment size for data communication has to be negotiated and decided. The end points of a VC are the sockets. Every socket in a host has a unique number made up of two parts: "TP address + port". The port is an entity local to the host and has a 16-bit identification. Normally, the port numbers up to 1024 (i.e. well-known ports) are reserved for standard services (e.g. port 21 is for the FTP (File Transfer Protocol) operation). A pair of remote sockets can support multiple VC (figure 1.5), and the binding of the VC ends to the corresponding sockets is carried out by the locally forked daemon at each end. The forked daemon is a child process of the local "supervisory daemon", which is commonly referred to as *inetd* (Internet daemon) in UNIX. The supervisory daemon attaches itself to multiple ports and then listens and waits. When a connection call occurs, it forks a child process and executes the appropriate daemon in it to handle the necessary communication. Although TCP communication is usually a "store/buffer and then forward" operation that can incur significant transmission delay, it allows the sender to set the PSH bit in its header to indicate "PUSHed" data. As a result, the intermediary receivers expedite and relay the data immediately upon its arrival until the destination is reached.

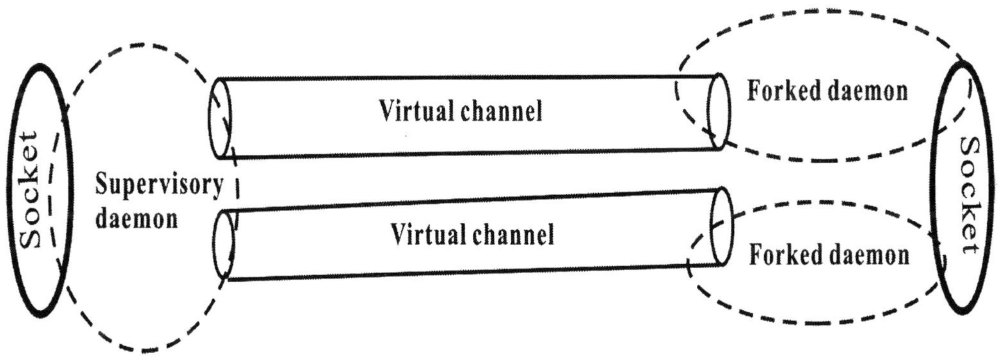

Figure 1.5. TCP virtual channel, daemons and sockets.

The end-to-end (E-E) TCP communication is peer-to-peer, and the inclusion of the sockets, which are supported by their operating systems at both ends, gives the impression that the connection is point-to-point (P-P). With respect to the ISO-OSI reference model (figure 1.6), P-P connections are specific to the data link layer, and the transport layer should be E-E by nature. Peer-to-peer means that every data unit has two basic portions: the header and the payload. For example, the header of the APDU (Application Protocol Data Unit) has source and destination indications. When the APDU is passed to the presentation layer, the PP (Presentation Protocol) header is added with the APDU as the payload of the PPDU.

When this PPDU from host A has reached the presentation layer of the remote host B, the PPDU header is stripped and the APDU is passed on to the receiving application. The whole process of passing data units downward to the physical layer in the sending host and then upward in the receiving host to the destined layer is peer-to-peer data communication. The same layers are involved in both the sender and the receiver. The Internet operation basically follows the ISO-OSI concept except that it does not support the presentation and session protocols. In the Internet, the ISO-OSI data link and physical layers are called the host-to-network layers (figure 1.6). The Internet subnet boundary conceptually consists of three ISO-OSI layers: network, data link and physical. Within a subnet, these layers have their own internal protocols, and each is capable of communicating with the rest of the Internet via its router(s) with IP.

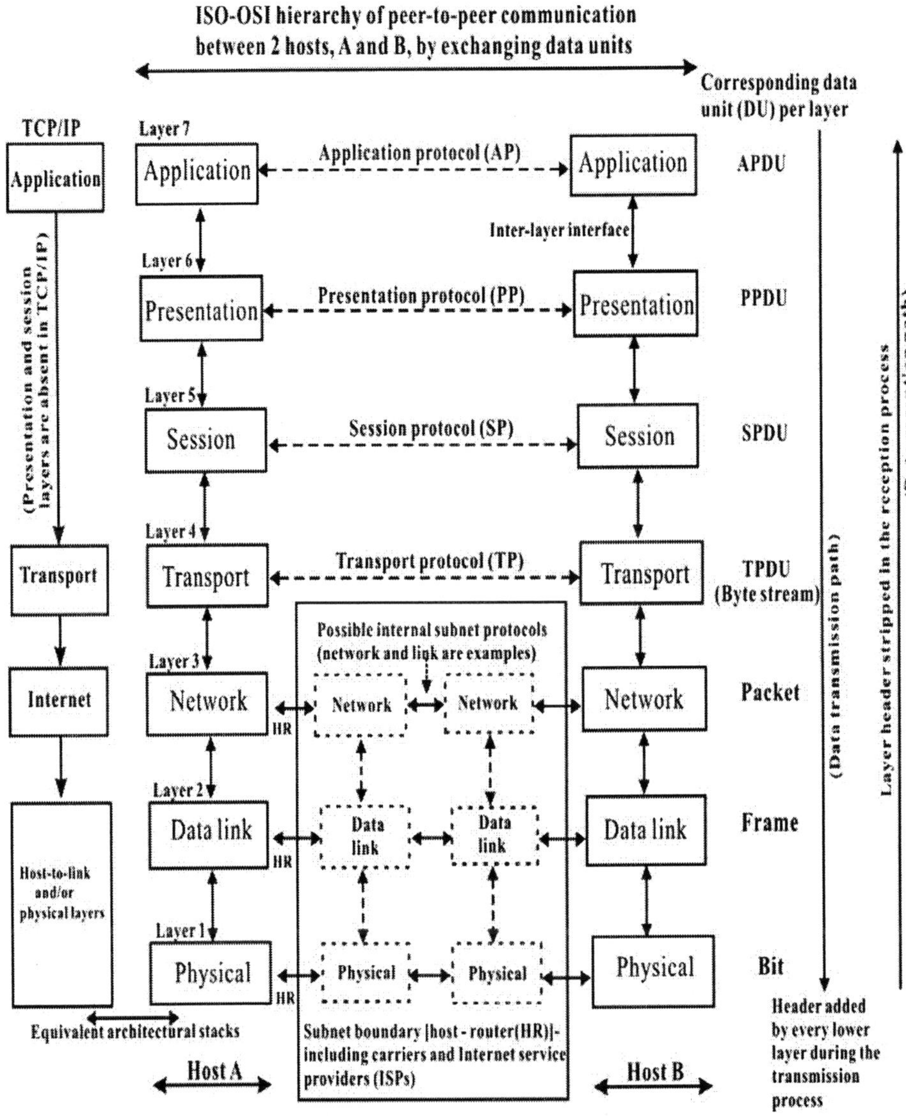

Figure 1.6. ISO-OSI protocol hierarchy reference and the TCP/IP stack equivalence.

Figure 1.7 depicts TCP communication over a fully duplex virtual circuit or channel, which supports byte streams. The data unit sent by the TCP is a segment, and its size is limited by the following: a) the 64000 bytes IP payload, and b) the maximum transfer unit (MTU) of the local network (e.g. 1500 bytes is the Ethernet payload size). Therefore, a segment may be fragmented (i.e. the fragmentation process) into the appropriate packet size so that it can be routed. The receiver then has to reassemble packets into the original segments. That is, a big file to be sent by TCP is broken down into sequenced segments, which may be fragmented into packets. With the correctly received segments, the receiver could reconstruct the original file. In fact, fragmentation may also occur at the data link layer because the size of their data frames for inter-link communication is even smaller. All the Internet hosts, however, must support the TCP segment size of 576 bytes, which include up to 24 bytes for the header.

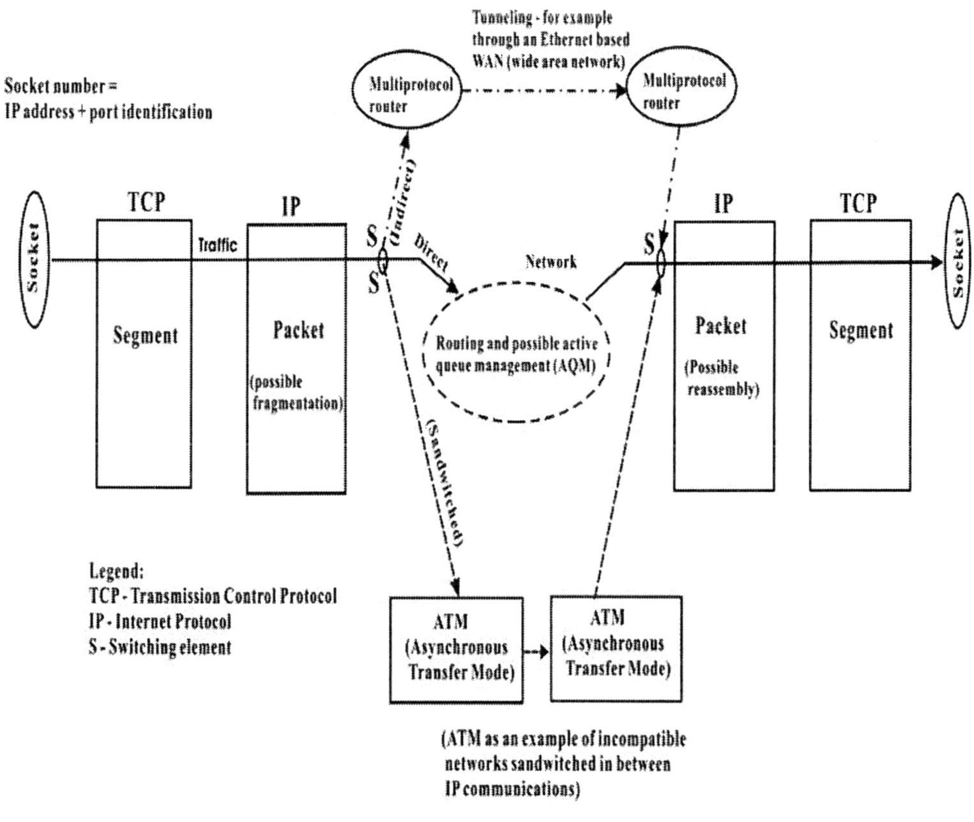

Figure 1.7. TCP peer-to-peer communication with tunneling.

In the TCP communication path, data units may pass through different incompatible local networks such as the ATM (Asynchronous Transfer Mode). This requires the conversion of a data unit from one format to another, and the translation operation may be repeated many times along the communication path with continual and repeated fragmentations (breaking down a large data unit such as a packet to smaller ones) and reassembly (putting the fragments together to make the original large data unit) taking place. The operation that ensures the correct passage of a TCP segment across different network boundaries, which involves format matching and translation, is generally referred to as the tunneling technique (as shown in figure 1.7). Successful tunneling, however, means that the source and destination network should be the same type. Many different tunneling schemes are available in the field for different operational conditions and requirements [Wang2001]. Figure 1.8 generalizes the peer-to-peer communication concept by using the TCP segment to IP packet conversion as an example. When the data is passed down from a higher level OSI layer to the lower one, the data unit from the high layer becomes the payload of the lower. The lower layer adds its data unit header, which will be stripped by the corresponding higher layer (peer) at the reception side.

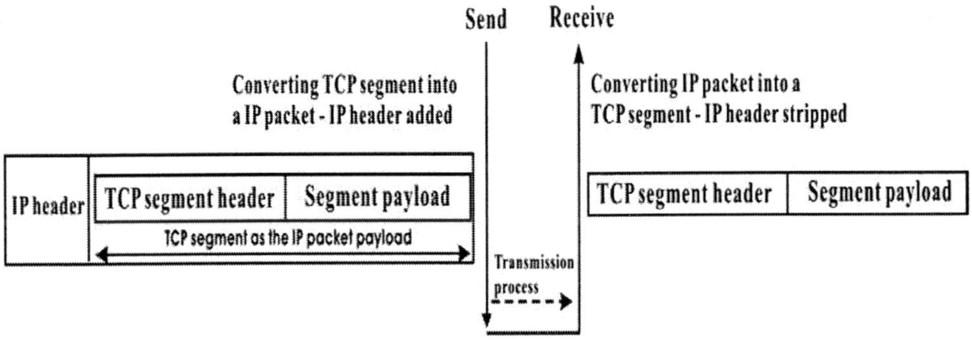

Figure 1.8. Peer-to-peer transmission process (from TCP segment to IP packet).

The maximum TCP segment size is established by negotiation at the stage of virtual channel establishment. The actual size is determined by the lower bid of the two negotiating partners. The sliding window management in TCP differs from the norm of most data links that equate window size to the number of data units. For example, in non-Internet cases, if the negotiated sliding window size during linkage establishment is ten data units, then the maximum number of units or frames (by OSI concept) that can be sent by the link layer without waiting for acknowledgements is ten. Even though the actual payload in a frame (i.e. number of bytes) may be less than the maximum allowed, the window size decreases by one after each successful transmission. This implies wastage in actual buffer utilization. In the TCP transmission policy, the segment management is more efficient because it allows the receiver to advertise the rest of the unused buffer space as the new window size. For example, if the receiver handles a 2048-byte buffer (i.e. maximum segment size) and has received a 1024-byte segment, it can advertise the next window size as 1024 bytes.

1.2.2.2. Interaction by Internet Protocol (IP)

The IP is an unreliable protocol that has the basic similar packaging and routing mechanism as in the ISO-OSI network layer. Every node (host or router) in the Internet is identified uniquely by at least a 32-bit IP address. At present, over half a million networks are connected to the Internet. Each of these networks is identified by a unique network number managed by the nonprofit organization, the Internet Corporation for Assigned Names and Numbers (ICANN). The ICANN assigns different address spaces to various regional authorities so that they can distribute IP addresses to organizations and ISPs (Internet service providers). The IP protocol was accepted by the OSI Standards Committee as one of the choices for layer 3, the Network Layer (but the IP address length is made into a variable length instead of the 32 bits or four bytes). Another choice for layer 3 is the HDLC (High-level Data Link Control), which supports the X.25 for packet switching. Normally, the IP address has two portions, network and host, and it is customarily written in *dotted decimal* format. For example, the IP address can be "192.70.70.09" (4 bytes), and in such a way every host in the Internet can be identified and entered into the routing table. The interpretation of the IP address depends on the address class. For example, the class A address format may have one byte for the network portion and three bytes for local host identifications. Similarly, the class C address format would have three bytes for network addresses and one byte for the local hosts.

An IP packet can have a payload of 64,000 data bytes, but the actual packet size is determined by the carrier at the lower level. The minimum, however, is 576 bytes. An IP packet has a header between 20 to 24 bytes long and the rest is payload. The header contains important information such as the following:

a) Version number – to help correct IP operation.
b) Total length – to indicate the total length of the whole packet in bytes.
c) Fragment control – to help the receiver reassemble fragmented packets.
d) Time to live – to prevent network congestion by setting the interval for a packet to exist while being routed.
e) Protocol – to identify which protocol is being used above IP, ICMP, TCP or UDP.
f) Source and destination addresses – to enable correct routing.
g) Checksum – to detect erroneous transmission and help data recovery.

The IP operation is capable of "Source Quenching", which means slowing down the sender. This is achieved by sending ICMP (Internet Control Message Protocol) choke packets. ICMP is actually a control system within the IP protocol to support different message types, including the following:

a) Echo Reply: A *ping* operation to determine whether a remote host is reachable.
b) Source Quench: An operation to send choke packets (usually by the router) to throttle a runaway sender, which sends too many packets in a short time and potentially congests the system.
c) TimeStamp request: A system that allows the server/receiver to drop the request so as not to waste valuable CPU time in producing a useless result (useful for real-time implementations where time is critical).
d) TimeStamp reply: A system that enables the receiver to drop the overdue service to avoid deleterious effects.

The previous IP version (e.g. IPv4) did not support mobile hosts because the limitation is in the addressing scheme itself. If the IP address is "192.70.70.09" with 192.70 as the network address and 70.09 identifying the particular host in this network, then the routing table in every router would have this unique combination. For routing a packet destined to the 192.70 network, every router uses the same line. Now if the 70.09 host is mobile, then the packet has to be relayed by the 192.70 network. To resolve this problem, the IETF (Internet Engineering Task Force) developed the new IPv6 version (RFCs 2460 to 2466) or mobile IP, which is actually a combination of two proposals [Deering1993, Katz1993]. Called the

Simple Internet Protocol Plus (SIPP) by IETF, it is not compatible with IPv4 but works with auxiliary Internet protocols such as TCP, UDP, ICMP and IGMP (Internet Group Management Protocol). It caters for the following:

a) The mobile host can use its home IP address (e.g. 192.70.70.09).
b) Most packets for the mobile host would not be detoured on the way.
c) No overhead for adopting the mobile scheme is incurred if the host is at home.

The major differences between IPv4 and IPv6 are as follows: a) the IPv6 address is 16 bytes long to provide an unlimited Internet address; and b) IPv6 has a more simplified header to shorten routing time. Intrinsically, the IPv6 version caters for the wireline based (hardwired) Internet infrastructure. As a matter of fact, the Internet has evolved and now it is "mobile" and strives to support wireline and wireless interactions at the same time in a seamless manner. Therefore, there are two basic classes of mobile hosts as follows:

a) Nomadic/tethered hosts
   - They work in the wireline fashion by plugging into a wired network (through a jack or a connector) anywhere and any time.
   - They are tethered by the wired points for attachments.
   - They are not truly ubiquitous like the mobile hosts capable of wireless communications.

b) Mobile hosts
   - They communicate with the wireline Internet infrastructure by wireless means and move from one wireless cell to another to continue interacting with the same partner seamlessly.
   - They exist in both mobile and pervasive computing environments based on the "wireline + wireless" infrastructure (figure 1.3). The main difference between the two environments is that pervasive computing tracks the user's intent. The publication by Garlan et al [Garlan2002] provides a comprehensive description of this difference.
   - The cells on the host's moving path may be supported by different wireless technologies (e.g. GSM (Global System for Mobile Communication – popular in Europe and some parts of Asia) and AMPS (Advanced Mobile Phone System – popular in North America)). Seamless operations among different wireless technologies rely on interoperability among them.
   - The IMT2000 recommendation by ITU (International Telecommunication Union) tries to unify different wireless technologies for interoperability. IMT2000, also known as FPLMTS (Future Public Land Mobile Telephony System), provides a vision for the convergence of different wireless access technologies.
   - While mobile hosts are traveling, their current locations can be identified by the location-aware and context-aware technologies [Peterson2003].Yet, the connection between a wireless cell and the wireline Internet infrastructure needs the support of a point-to-point protocol. For example, the Shiva PPP (peer-to-peer protocol) middleware, which should be installed on the wireline

infrastructure side, supports and bridges wireless and wireline communication and data exchanges.

With proper hardware support, communication among hosts, mobile or not, should be user transparent. These hosts under IPv6 interact seamlessly and freely in the WandW environment. The interaction between a static host and a mobile one can be summarized in five steps as shown in figure 1.9. These hosts can locate anywhere in the Internet, which is separated into different domains for the sake of effective network management. For example, each domain may have one or more SNMP (Simple Network Management Protocol [Case1996]) agents that monitor the working condition of every node. The SNMP agent gathers different information related to loading, security and the power on-off frequencies of the nodes. SNMP agents in different network domains collaborate to enhance the Internet operation by, for example, locating a mobile host quickly. In contemporary SNMP setups, mobile agents are used to make the network information gathering process more effective [Knight1999]. Rather than exchanging large volumes of information across the open Internet, a mobile agent is sent from one SNMP domain to another to interact locally with the SNMP entity. Since the mobile agent works on the local data and sends back only the necessary results, this approach frees backbone bandwidth, which would otherwise be consumed in a brute-force massive information exchange process.

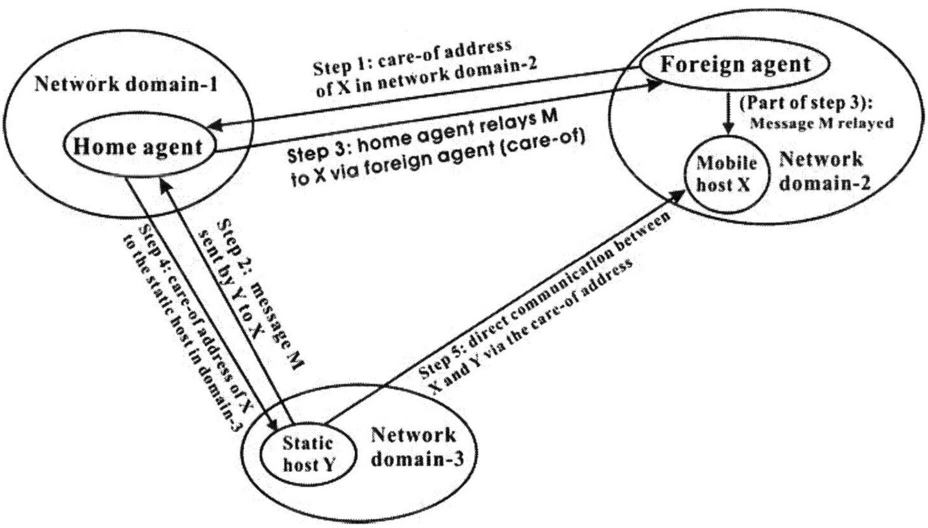

Figure 1.9. Interaction between a static host and a mobile one.

To support mobile hosts, every domain in the Internet has two special agents, home and foreign. The home agent monitors all the local hosts, which are identified by the unique home IP addresses. If a mobile host has moved from one network domain to another, it is still uniquely identified by its home IP address. When a mobile host has reached a new domain, it registers with the local foreign agent, which monitors all the outsider hosts by giving them care-of addresses. Figure 1.9 shows the interaction between a static host in network domain-3 and the mobile host X, which has migrated from network domain-1 to domain-2. The interaction between the static host Y and the mobile host X can be summarized into the following steps:

a) Step 1: The foreign agent of domain-2 sends the care-of address of the newly arrived mobile host X to X's home agent.
b) Step 2: When the static host Y sends the message M to the mobile host X (no longer in his home domain), a relay process is necessary.
c) Steps 3 and 4: The X's home agent relays M to the mobile host X via its care-of address. Meanwhile, this care-of address is also sent to the originator of M.
d) Step 5: The static host Y then communicates directly with the mobile host X using this care-of address.

Effective use of mobile hosts is an important contemporary issue for successful distributed computing. The appropriate interconnection of a mobile host to the wireline Internet infrastructure requires the following elements: location-aware or context-aware capability (the latter is an improved version of the former [Peterson2003]); point-to-point protocol (PPP) (e.g. the Shiva PPP middleware), which bridges the radio link and the wired link; and mobile support system (MSS). Figure 1.10 provides a concise picture of how these elements work together to form the mobile Internet architecture.

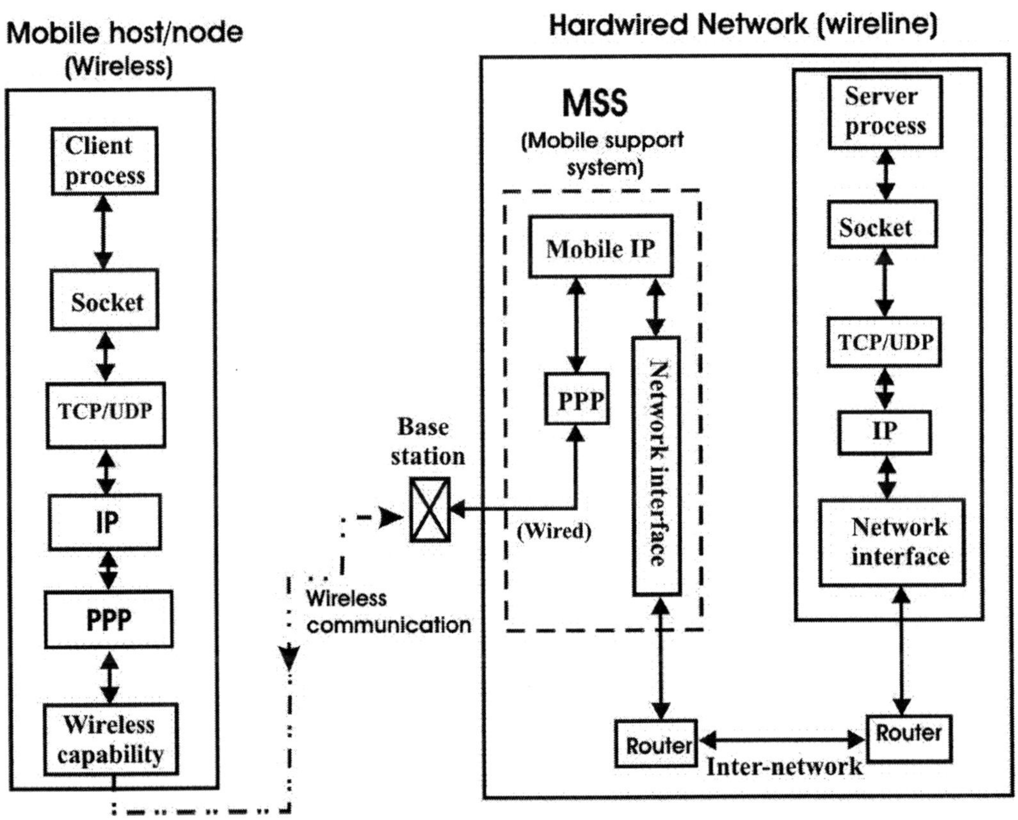

Figure 1.10. Backbone of the mobile Internet architecture with mobile-IP support.

A distributed program or software on the Internet is basically object-based. These logical objects run on different nodes/hosts and collaborate to produce the final result. Among the many advantages of distributed computing, the most sought after is the speedup produced by the distributed parallelism. From the distributed computing point of view, systems can be tethered, untethered, or a mixture of both. Figure 1.11 provides a concise taxonomy in this light, where a PPP middleware (e.g. Shiva) can be used to unify different networks into a single platform. The use of an appropriate PPP middleware is especially important for interconnecting mobile hosts in ad hoc networks which do not have an infrastructure.

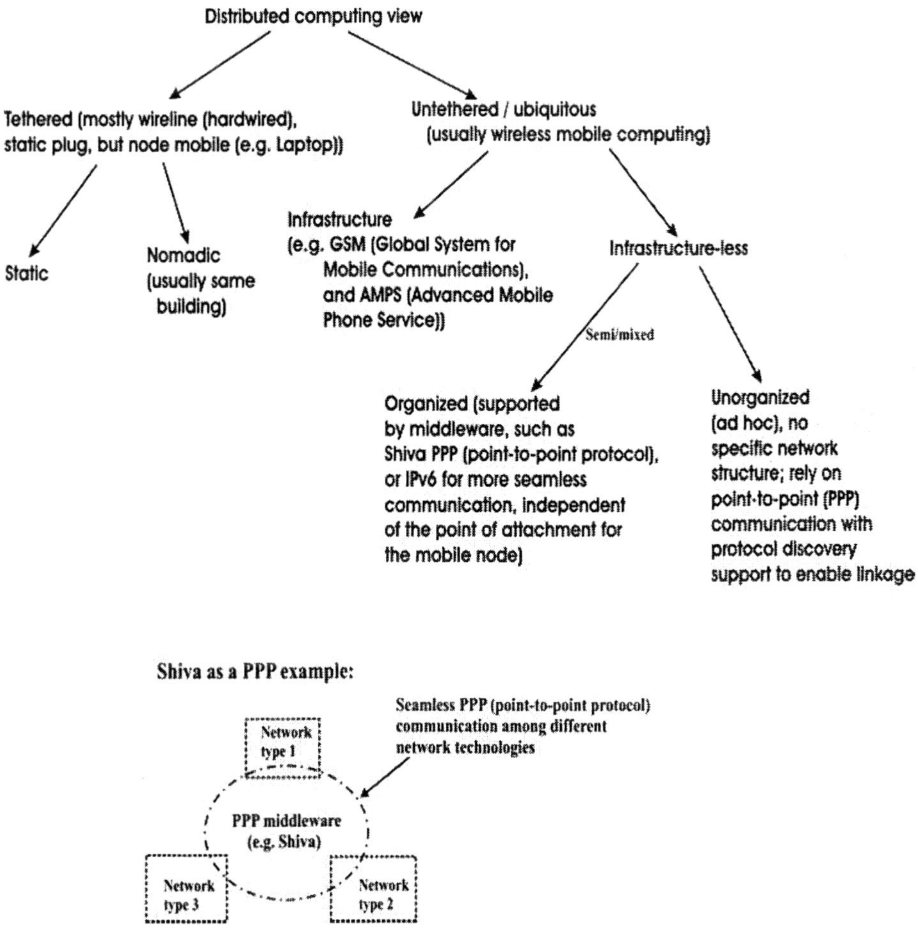

Figure 1.11. A concise taxonomy of distributed computing involving mobile hosts.

1.3. ESSENCE OF ROUTING

The Internet (or *Internetworks*) is basically a large network formed by interconnecting heterogeneous networks. These networks are heterogeneous because they work with different technologies and protocols, a protocol being a set of communication rules. Figure 1.12 illustrates the interconnection of three home networks by a subnet. Namely, network 1, network 2 and network 3 are foreign to one another and may operate with different internal protocols. They communicate through the appropriate routers that are capable of translating one protocol to another. These routers are known by different names for example, gateways and multiprotocol routers, and interact by radio (wireless) and/or wired (wireline) links. A home network usually has at least one router and many hosts. A commercial subnet, which is a network managed by a carrier operator or a commercial ISP (Internet service provider), however, may have no hosts. A router in a home network can be private or rented from a commercial subnet, which is normally interconnected to the rest of the Internet.

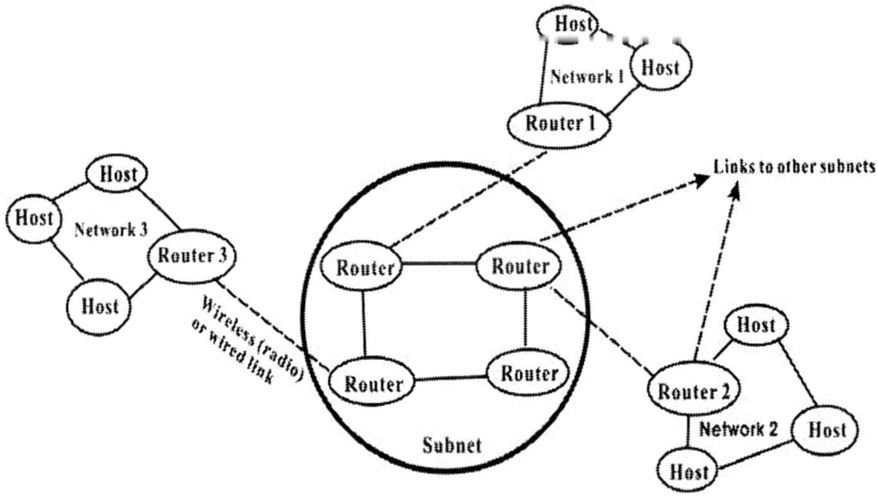

Figure 1.12. Home networks and subnet.

Home networks, which vary in size and purpose, can be divided into three basic types:

a) WAN (wide area network) that serves a country or even a continent.
b) MAN (metropolitan area network) for a city (e.g. cable TV network or high-speed broadband wireless Internet access network – IEEE 802.16/WiMax family of standards for the physical layer (i.e. below the data link layer) of the protocol stack..
c) LAN (local area network) for the same building or office (e.g. token ring, Ethernet, and wireless – IEEE 802.15 (Bluetooth)) and IEEE 802.11/WiFi family of standards for the physical layer of the protocol stack. For example, the 802.11 family involves different technologies as follows: 802.11/Infrared, 802.11/FHSS (Frequency Hopping Spread Spectrum), 802.11a/OFDM (Orthogonal Frequency Division Multiplexing), and 802.11b/HR-DSS (High Rate Direct Sequence Spread Spectrum).

The 802.11 and the 902.16 families of standards associate with the WiFi and WiMax industrial consortiums. Although both 802.11 and 802.16 were designed with the aim of achieving high-bandwidth wireless communications, they serve different purposes. The 802.11 technologies cater to mobile computing in which computer nodes are mobile and move from one communication cell to another continuously. Every cell has limited expansion and does not require high-energy radio signals and full-duplex communication to keep costs low. In contrast, the 802.16 is not aimed at dealing with mobile computing (of computer notebooks), but instead supports intercommunication among static buildings within a city. Therefore, it would try to cover an area of many kilometers with full-duplex communication. This needs high-energy radio signals and incurs high costs. The long-distance communication relayed by base stations of varying perceived power can easily increase the 802.16 signal-to-noise ratio and reduce its reception quality. Due to the open nature of the client/server communication and the need to traverse a long distance, the requirements for signal modulation schemes, security and privacy are more stringent for IEEE802.16. Typically, the 802.11 operates in the unlicensed ISM (industrial, scientific and medical) signal spectrum from 800 MHz to 6 GHz. This spectrum varies from one country to another. The more popular ISM band is around 2.4 GHz, which is widely used for wireless LAN operations (e.g. Bluetooth). The signal frequency for 802.16 is higher and typically between 10 to 60 GHz [Ghosh2005]. The 802.16 needs this bandwidth to support a movie network for different families within the coverage enabling them to watch movies of acceptable resolution at the same time. It is very unlikely for mobile nodes to jam a cell or smart space through the watching of movies at the same time. Therefore, the 802.11 and 802.16 fulfill very different purposes even though they could be linked together through base stations. This explains the differences between what 802.11 and 802.16 are trying to achieve. In the process, they have to address the same issues in a different manner. These issues include: operating costs, cell size, signal energy, band spectrum, modulation concepts, spread spectrum techniques, user requirements, signal-to-noise ratio, and the degree of signal interference. All of these can be simply expressed as the difference between two needs, mobility of the user and the cell size.

An interesting point in the wireless era is the lack of the interoperability among different vendors. Wireless products keep appearing and claim to operate in the 802.11 and 802.16 spectral ranges. Yet, these products inevitably have interoperability problems, typically in the medium access control (MAC) and physical (PHY) levels. To alleviate the problem of interoperability, the IEEE802.11 and IEEE 802.16 working groups and their associated industry consortiums, WiFi and WiMax create operation profiles. The rationale is that adherence to these profiles by vendors would provide the necessary interoperability.

In the Internet, the IP protocol interconnects different types of networks via the routers and the key to the success of this process is a good routing table. For example, when a host in network 3 sends a packet to the designated receiver in network 2 (figure 1.12), it entails hop-to-hop routing. Basically, all the hosts in the Internet are uniquely identified by their IP addresses, and each is made up of two parts, the unique network address and the local host identification (*port*) in the network. A host can keep a local routing table of two types of entries for fast action: hosts in the home network and routers that provide entry to other foreign networks. An aging strategy, which keeps only the most frequently used addresses, prevents the local routing table from overflowing. The local host can send data to a remote host by finding the appropriate remote router in its local routing table. If the remote router address is absent, it passes the data to the local router (e.g. router 1 in figure 1.12), which liaises with the subnet routers and locates the remote router for the host to update its local routing table. In fact, every router maintains its own routing table and works in the same fashion in the routing process. Since a router may be connected with many others, a decision is required when choosing the next router or hop. The effective decision making process depends on the routing algorithm.

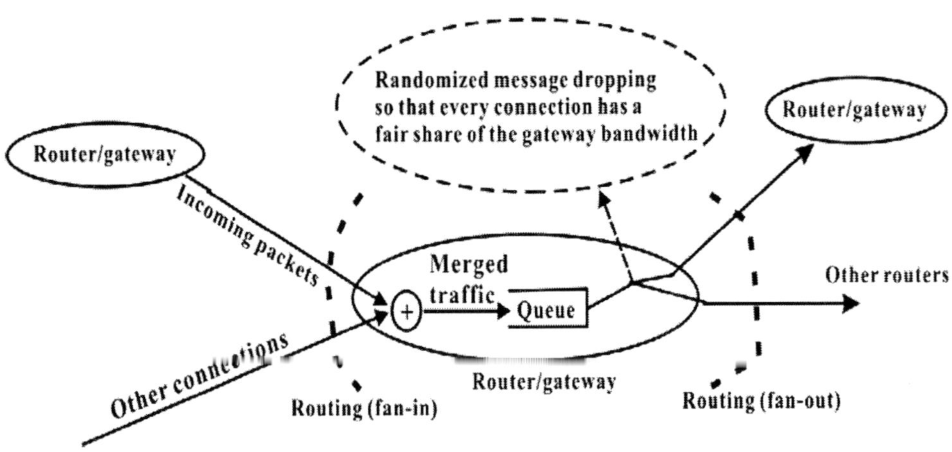

Figure 1.13. Hop-to-hop routing with fan-in and fan-out packets.

During the routing process, the forwarded data may pass through several routers. Each router makes the decision about which remote router the data should go to next. Therefore, the path/route in each routing case is event driven, real-time and stochastic in nature. Figure 1.13 shows the router/hop, which receives incoming packets from its collaborating routers in all directions. The packet traffic pattern and the inter-arrival time (IAT) of each incoming stream are unpredictable. The traffic pattern can be short-range dependence (e.g. Markov such as Poisson), long-range-dependence (e.g. self-similar or heavy-tailed) or multifractal [Molnar1999] and change suddenly. The traffic streams that merge into the router queue may surge into the expanding queue and overflow its buffer. In congested situations, the router ensures smoother passage of those packets already queued for service by dropping the new incoming packets. The deleterious effects of this dropping action are possible widespread retransmissions and network congestion [Lakshman1997, Paxson1995, Paxson1999]. Massive retransmissions would lengthen the service roundtrip time (RTT) in a client/server interaction.

1.3.1. Real-Time Systems, RTT Character and Effect of Distributed Parallelism

Any application that has a timeliness concern is real-time [Stankovic1998]. There are three basic types of real-time systems: hard, soft and firm. Strict timeliness is an absolute requirement for hard real-time systems because any delay can lead to disaster. Soft real-time systems can tolerate occasional deadline slippages, and for firm real-time systems service results are meaningless if they are returned after the deadline. The key for shortening the client/server RTT over the Internet is to reduce ANT, defined by the expression, $ANT = \sum_{j=1}^{k\to\infty} jP_j$. The parameter P_j is the probability of success at the jth trial. It is defined by $P_j = \sigma^{j-1}(1-\sigma)$, where σ is the error probability that causes retransmissions. That is,

$ANT = \sum_{j=1}^{k\to\infty} jP_j$ can be rewritten as $ANT = \sum_{j=1}^{k\to\infty} j[\sigma^{j-1}(1-\sigma)]$, which can be further simplified to $ANT \approx 1/(1-\sigma)$. Since only one trial is needed for a transmission success for $\sigma = 0$, the key to controlling RTT timeliness is to harness σ. Therefore, reducing or eliminating σ is essential for enhancing the success of time-critical applications.

Applications running on the Internet are naturally object-based and gain speedup from the intrinsic distributed parallelism. From the Markovian queuing model this speedup (S) can be visualized as $S = W_1/W_n$. W_1 and W_n are the response times of the M/M/1 and M/M/n (M for Markov and *n* for the number of parallel servers) models respectively. W_1 by a single server is defined by the expression $1/\mu(1-\rho)$. It is normally longer than W_n defined by $1/\mu(1-\rho/n)$, and this yields a speedup of $S = W_1/W_n = (1-\rho/n)/(1-\rho)$, where ρ is the system utilization, which is the ratio of average input rate (λ) over average output/service rate (μ) (i.e. λ/μ). The S expression shows how the system speedup scales with *n* for a high ρ [Lewis1996]. It does not, however, relate RTT to the real-time nature of the application. Having a large *n* in a M/M/n setup cannot guarantee that the application will satisfy the required execution deadline unless the average client/server RTT in the application is low.

1.4. Service Roundtrip Time and Dynamic Solutions

The Internet and the World Wide Web (WWW) have provided several new opportunities for people to extend their horizon of knowledge, to communicate quickly and effectively, and to set up e-business. In fact, the Internet-based distributed systems are a key factor in the achievement of economic gains for many companies. Firstly, it is common for company employees to interact with buyers and suppliers via the Internet in field operations. Secondly, business transactions such as buying a birthday present in Hong Kong and having it sent to the receiver in Canada can be conducted quickly and accurately in an electronic manner (i.e. e-business). Thirdly, up-to-date background information can be obtained immediately, via a mobile device (e.g. PDA and PMDA) [Patterson2003] to back up a time-critical decision such as trading stocks right at the airport minutes before boarding a plane. Fourthly, opportunistic data acquisitions can be conducted in a pervasive manner to prevent disasters proactively [Hightower2001]. For example, a pedestrian encounters a terrorist act in progress and videos the scene with her mobile phone. Then, the short video is immediately transmitted to the police so that the latter can assess the situation quickly to save the victim(s).

In the above situations, the service response time, which is the interval between sending a request and getting the correct result, is important. The sheer size and heterogeneity of the Internet make it difficult to control and guarantee the prescribed response deadline unless special techniques are employed. This difficulty is aggravated by the fact that the Internet nowadays is basically a "wired and wireless" setup, which involves different incompatible protocols that require the technique of *tunneling* to link them [Tanenbaum2003].

Since short roundtrip time is an important QoS attribute, many research activities have been dedicated to finding effective solutions. Among them the following dynamic solutions are promising:

a) Dynamic buffer size tuning (DBST): The aim is to eliminate buffer overflow by tuning the buffer size adaptively on the fly. As a result, it contributes to reducing σ and thus ANT.
b) Dynamic cache size tuning (DCST): The aim is to maintain a given proxy hit ratio, which represents the expected caching performance by the user. Information retrieval over the Internet involves two "legs". The first leg is between the client and the proxy server. The second leg, which usually needs more time and involves the Internet DNS (domain name server/system), is between the proxy server and the remote data source (e.g. web server). A high hit ratio reduces involvement of the second leg and thus shortens the service roundtrip time. For example, if the following are assumed, the first leg takes T time units, the second legs takes 10T and the hit ratio being maintained is 0.7 (70%), then the speedup S by caching in this case is $S = {(T+10T)}/{[T+(0.7*0+0.3*10T)]} = {11}/{4} = 2.75$.

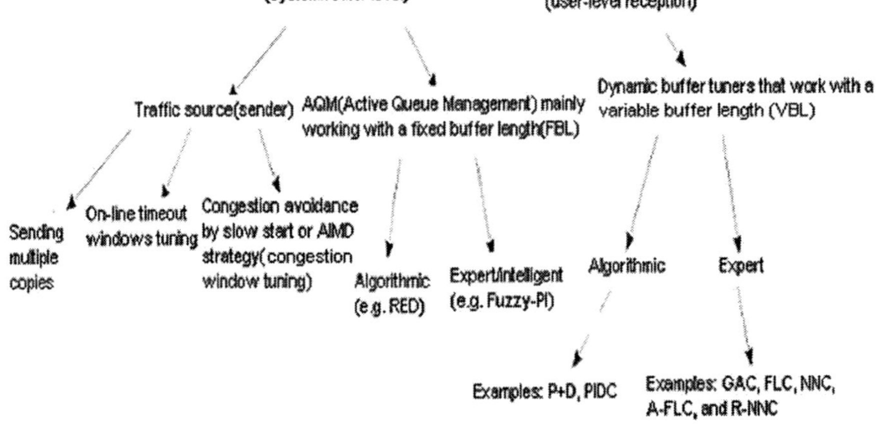

Figure 1.14. A brief taxonomy of different queue buffer management techniques.

A literature search will show that there are only a few dynamic buffer size tuners in the field, including the PIDC ("Proportional + Integral + Derivative" Controller), the GAC (Genetic Algorithm Controller), the FLC (Fuzzy Logic Controller) and the NNC (Neural Network Controller) [Wong2002, Lin2005, Wu2005]. Similarly, the literature indicates that there is only one basic model published so far for dynamic cache size tuning, the MACSC (Model for Adaptive Cache Size Control) [Wong2003]. Figure 1.14 shows a concise taxonomy of the different queue buffer management techniques in the field. The novel dynamic buffer tuners and their variants represent all the research done in this area to date. Figure 1.15 summarizes the different categories of techniques relevant to caching. The MACSC framework and its variants represent only the beginning of the important area of dynamic cache size tuning.

Interestingly, the researchers in both these areas came to the conclusion that the stability and accuracy of dynamic solutions are affected by the ill effects of Internet traffic patterns. The Internet traffic pattern can be short-range dependence, (e.g. Poisson) long-range dependence (e.g. self-similar and heavy-tailed) or multifractal and may change without warning. Therefore, detection and identification of the exact Internet traffic pattern on the fly is vitally important for the tuners in order for them to use the detected result in reconfiguring themselves adaptively to ward off any negative impact on their performance. This led to the proposal of the novel real-time traffic pattern detection (RTPD) framework [ATNAC]. The RTPD mechanism was successfully incorporated into the following frameworks: a) the FLC - to produce the more powerful Reconfigurable FLC (R-FLC) dynamic buffer tuner, and b) the MACSC - to create the highly adaptive RTPD/MACSC dynamic cache tuner. Different dynamic buffer size tuning and dynamic cache size tuning schemes will be elaborated in later chapters.

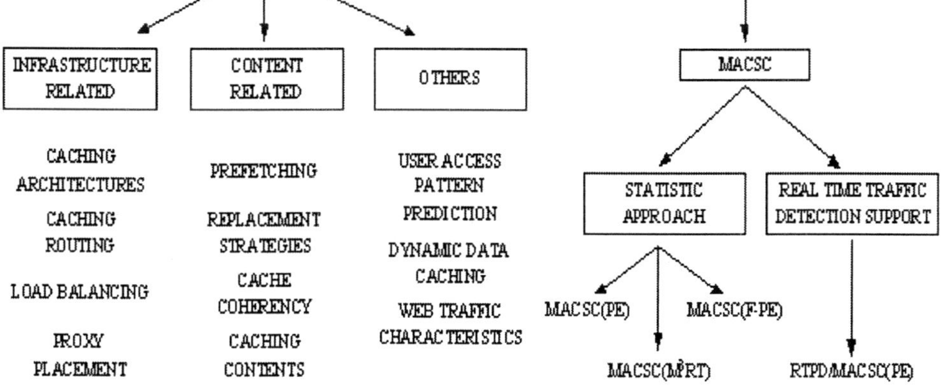

Figure 1.15. A brief taxonomy of existing techniques relevant to caching.

1.5. THE FOCUS OF THE SUBSEQUENT CHAPTERS

The focus is on how the following two novel, powerful mechanisms, namely dynamic buffer size tuning and dynamic cache size tuning, help shorten the service roundtrip time over the Internet. These mechanisms can work independently or together as the situation requires. Dynamic buffer size tuning ensures that the buffer always covers the queue. As a result, the possibility of buffer overflow is eliminated, leading to a reduced ANT value. This is the direct consequence of a smaller σ that encapsulates the error probability of user-level buffer overflow.

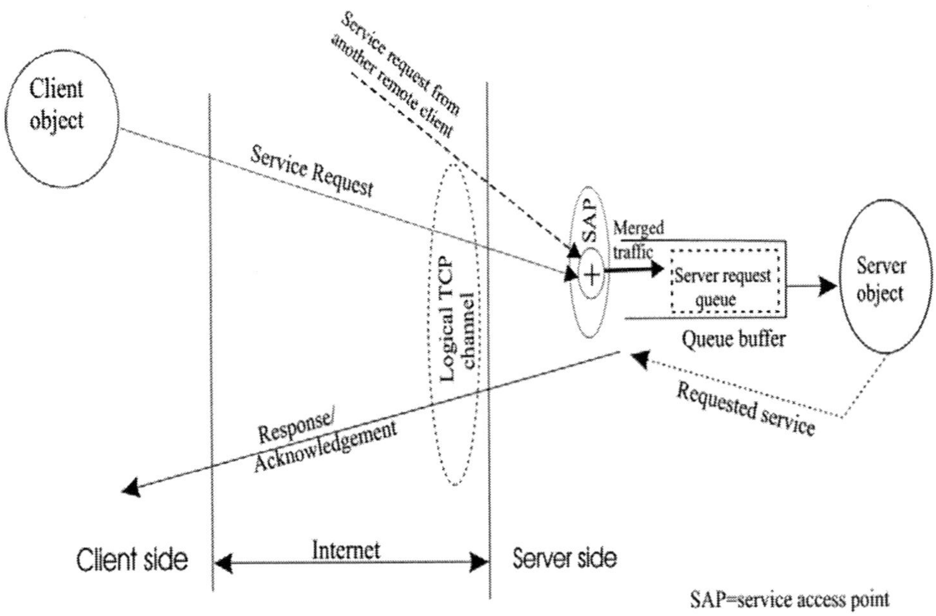

Figure 1.16. Merged Traffic into the server queue at the user level.

Dynamic buffer size control at the user-level prevents wastage of the resources already used to alleviate network congestion at the system or router level. The major mechanism at the system level used to prevent router buffer overflow is throttling. If a router feels that its request buffer is likely to overflow because the senders are sending too much in a short period, it throttles the runaway senders to voluntarily slow down transmissions. If the throttling fails, then the routers drop the incoming requests in a pre-defined manner. The "throttle first and then drop" operation is generally known as active queue management (AQM) [Floyd1993]. The relatively well-known examples include the algorithmic RED (Random Early Detection [Braden1998]) and the expert Fuzzy-PI algorithms [Li2002]. Effective AQM cannot prevent overflow at the user level because of the one-server-to-many-clients relationship (i.e. asymmetric rendezvous). In this relationship, as shown in figure 1.16, the unpredictable requests from different client sources merge at the service access point (SAP) of the server before entering the request queue. The merged traffic pattern is unpredictable for several reasons as follows:

a) Different stream traffic patterns: The IAT (inter-arrival time) patterns of the various request streams differ.
b) Sudden change in stream traffic pattern: The IAT pattern of a request stream can change without warning, for example, from SRD to LRD or vice versa.

The unpredictability of the pattern of the merged traffic can easily inundate the scheduling mechanism or the server [Paxson1995].

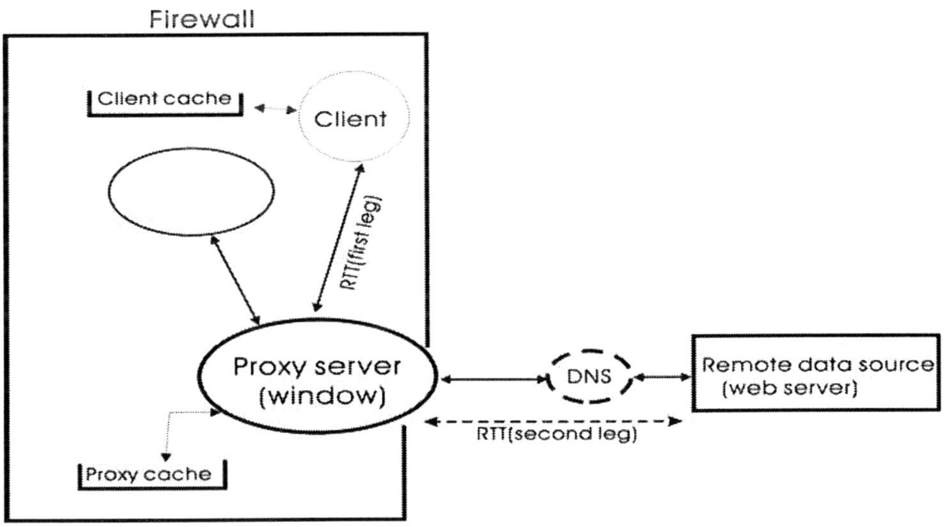

Figure 1.17. The proxy server as the firewall's window to the outside world.

Dynamic cache size tuning deals with a different problem because its aim is to maintain a given cache hit ratio φ . In the process, the information retrieval time over the Internet is shortened by consistently reducing the DNS (domain name server) involvement. Figure 1.17 shows a proxy system in which the proxy provides the window for the client processes, which are protected by a firewall, to communicate with the outside world. If the proxy maintains a server hit ratio of 0.6, then 60% of the time the clients would find the needed information from the proxy cache. The miss ratio of 0.4 means that 40% of the time the proxy server has to enlist help from the DNS to locate the needed data in remote web servers. Therefore, information retrieval over the Internet is a "2-leg" operation. The first leg is the roundtrip between a client and the proxy, and the second is that between the proxy and the remote web server. Assuming the average RTT for the first and second legs are RTT_1 and $RTT_2 = 10RTT_1$ respectively, then the speedup by caching, assuming a 0.6 cache hit ratio, can be computed by the following equation: $S_{cache} = {(RTT_1 + 10RTT_1)} / {(RTT_1 + 0.4 * 10RTT_1)} = 11/5 = 2.2$. The fringe benefit of caching is that less remote data will be transferred across the network because 40% of the time that RTT_2 is obviated. This frees up more backbone bandwidth to be shared publicly as a fringe benefit and thus improves the overall network throughput.

The potential benefits of caching have inspired different related areas of research. For example, one of the most researched topics is replacement strategy, which deals with ways to keep as much hot data as possible in the proxy cache. While the algorithms can produce a high hit ratio, they cannot necessarily maintain it because they work exclusively with a static cache size. Leveraging more parameters to produce a high hit ratio can be counterproductive because heavy parameterization leads to high complexity and longer computation delay. Undesirable or deleterious effects can result from such a delay because the true problem will have disappeared by the time the remedy has been computed. Correcting a spurious problem can result in grave consequences. Dynamic cache size tuning differs because it strives to maintain a given hit ratio (i.e. a consistent S_{cache}) under all conditions with the minimum number of parameters possible.

Figure 1.18 summarizes the relationship among the three common terms, namely fault tolerance, quality of service and dependability. Service roundtrip time is a factor, which is common to these terms, is vital to the success of time-critical applications. Therefore, the drive to reduce service RTT, especially in a sizeable network such as the Internet, is ever-increasing at both the system and user levels.

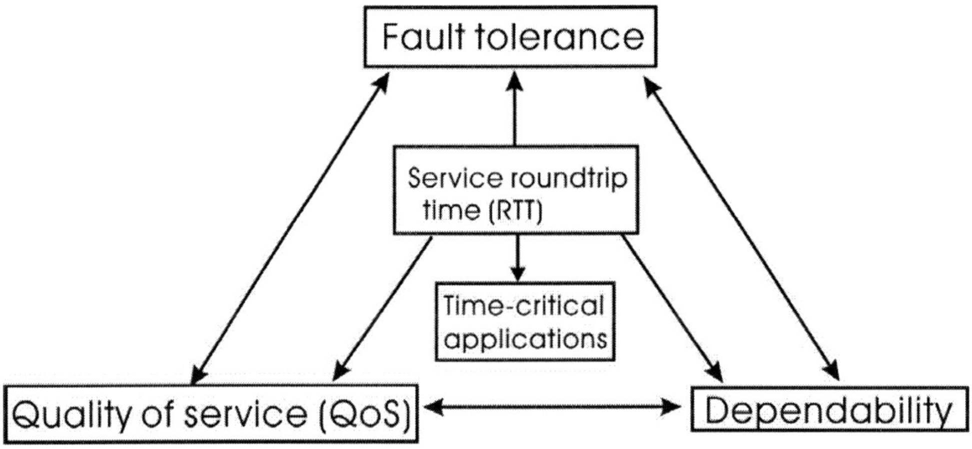

Figure 1.18. Relationships among fault tolerance, dependability and quality of service.

1.6. Summary

This chapter provides an overview of the Internet in terms of the following:

a) Architecture: A collection of heterogeneous networks that are loosely interconnected by IP.
b) Protocol hierarchy: The TCP/IP hierarchy is compared with the ISO-OSI reference model.
c) The transport protocols: The connection-oriented TCP and the connectionless UDP are concisely introduced.

d) The "*Internetworks*": The unreliable connectionless IP and its relationship to UDP and TCP are explained.
e) Mobile Internet: This contemporary Internet definition indicates that the infrastructure combines both wireline and wireless communications and enables interactions in a relatively seamless manner. To support mobile hosts the IPv6, which is incompatible with IPv4, is needed.
f) Service roundtrip time (RTT): RTT is an important QoS parameter for time-critical applications. Many techniques have been proposed for shortening the service RTT, including popular solutions such as caching and active queue management (AQM).
g) Dynamic solutions: Analyses of the existing caching and buffer overflow prevention techniques indicate that dynamic solutions are seemingly the appropriate answer. In this light, two new schools of thought have emerged: dynamic buffer size tuning and dynamic cache size tuning. They will be discussed in detail in this book.
h) Real-time traffic pattern detection (RTPD): This is an effective mechanism to help Internet-based systems to ward off the ill effects of the unpredictable and changing traffic patterns. It makes the Internet more suitable for time-critical applications.

1.7. Key References

[ATNAC] Wilfred W.K. Lin, Richard S.L. Wu, Tharam S. Dillon and Allan K. Y. Wong, A Novel Real-Time Traffic Pattern Detector for Internet Applications, Proceedings of the 2004 Australian Telecommunication Networks and Applications Conference(ATNAC), Sydney, Australia, December 2004, pp. 224-227

[Braden1998] Braden et.al., Recommendations on Queue Management and Congestion Avoidance in the Internet, *RFC* 2309, April 1998

[Chatranon2004] G. Chatranon, M.A. Labrador and S. Banerjee, A Survey of TCP-Friendly Router-based AQM Schemes, *Computer Communications,* 27(15), September 2004, 1424-1440

[Deering1993] S.E. *Deering, Simple Internet Protocol, IEEE Network Magazine,* v.7, May/June 1993, 16-18

[Garlan2002] D. Garlan, D. P. Siewiorek, A. Smailagic and P. Steenkiste, Project Aura: Toward Distraction-free Pervasive Computing, *IEEE Pervasive Computing,* 1(2), April 2002, 22 – 31

[Ghosh2005] A. Ghosh, D.R. Wolter, J.G. Andrews and R. Chen, Broadband Wireless Access with WiMax/802.16: Current Performance Benchmarks and Future Potential, *IEEE Communications Magazine,* February, 2005, 129-135

[Hightower2001] J. Hightower and G. Borriello, Location-Aware Systems for Ubiquitous Computing, *IEEE Computer,* 34(8), August 2001, 57-66

[Jacobson1988] V. Jacobson, Congestion Avoidance and Control, *Proc. of the ACM SIGCOMM'88 Conference,* 1988, 314-329

[Katz1993] D. Katz and P.S. Ford, TUBA: Replacing IP with CLNP, *IEEE Network Magazine,* v.7, May/June 1993, 38-47

[Lakshman1997] T. Lakshman U. Madlow, The Performance of TCP/IP for Networks with High Bandwidth-Delay Products and Random Loss, *IEEE/ACM Transactions on Networking,* 5(3), June 1997, 336-350

[Lin2005] Wilfred W.K. Lin, Allan K.Y. Wong and Tharam S. Dillon, Application of Soft Computing Techniques to Adaptive User Buffer Overflow Control on the Internet", *IEEE Transactions on Systems, Man, and Cybernetics* – Part C: 2005

[Patterson2003] C.A. Patterson, R.R. Muntz and C.M. Pancake, Challenges in Location-aware Computing, *IEEE Pervasive Computing,* 2(2), April-June 2003, 80 – 89

[Patterson2003] C.A. Patterson, R.R. Muntz and C.M. Pancake, Challenges in Location-aware Computing, *IEEE Pervasive Computing,* 2(2), April-June 2003, 80 – 89

[Paxson1995] V. Paxson and S. Floyd, Wide-Area Traffic: The Failure of Poisson Modeling. *IEEE/ACM Transactions on Networking,* 3(3), June 1995, 226-244

[Paxson1999] V. Paxson, End-to-end Internet Packet Dynamics, *IEEE/ACM Transactions on Networking,* 7(3), June 1999, 277 -292

[RFC1853] W. Simpson, IP in IP Tunneling, *RFC1*853, 1995

[Saty2001] M. Satyanarayanan, Pervasive Computing: Vision and Challenges, *IEEE Personal Communications,* August 2001, 10-17

[Wong2002] Wong, Wilfred W.K. Lin, May T.W. Yip and Tharam S. Dillon, Genetic Algorithm and PID Control Together for Dynamic Anticipative Marginal Buffer Management: An Effective Approach to Enhance Dependability and Performance of Distributed Mobile Object-Based Real-Time Computing over the Internet, *Journal of Parallel and Distributed Computing,* vol. 62, 2002, 1433-1453

[Wu2005] Richard S.L. Wu, Allan K.Y. Wong and Tharam S. Dillon, E-MACSC: A Novel Dynamic Cache Tuning Technique to Reduce Information Retrieval Roundtrip Time over the Internet", *Computer Communications,* 2005

Chapter 2

PREVIOUS STRATEGIES FOR REDUCING THE SERVICE ROUNDTRIP TIME (RTT)

2.1. INTRODUCTION

In the last chapter, we examined several functions of Internet systems including wireless and wireline. We noted that service roundtrip time (RTT) was a QoS parameter for timely applications. In this chapter, we provide an overview of various aspects that relate to harnessing the RTT over the Internet. We examine several approaches that can effectively shorten RTT, maximize bandwidth usage and reduce network congestion. They include: scheduling, sharing of dependable communication links, fair bandwidth usage, transmitting multiple copies of the same message, neutralizing traffic ill effects in a real-time manner, preventing denial of service attacks, caching, and stifling buffer overflow. The methods and techniques discussed in this chapter include those that have previously appeared in the literature as well as some of our own methods. They play an important part in the successful running of time-critical applications over a sizeable network such as the Internet. This success relies on how well the service RTT can be harnessed. In fact, operations over a network intrinsically involve asynchronous interactions by message passing. The supposedly parallel tasks, however, may not run truly in parallel, and this is the innate character of distributed parallelism. To facilitate the discussion, we begin by introducing a single illustrative example, namely the Master/Slave example, in the next section.

2.2. THE MASTER/SLAVE SYSTEM EXAMPLE

We consider an example that shows how distributed parallelism works. In this example, the master coordinates the six independent slaves by barrier synchronization via six communication channels as shown in figure 2.1. The master SW communicates with the slaves using dedicated channels, namely, C1, C2,…., C6. The average service roundtrip time for every channel is RTT_a. When a new barrier synchronization pass begins, the master signals all the slaves to start at the same time. In reality, these slaves do not really start in parallel due to delays from various causes such as network congestion and overloaded hosts where some of the slaves are located. The asynchronism among the different slaves is depicted by figure 2.2. The RTT for every master/slave interaction is marked by R (e.g. R1, R2, etc.) Assuming the degree of overlapped parallelism is β then the actual collective RTT_{ac} is defined by equation (2.1), where N is the number of slaves. The physical meaning is that for a highly parallel distributed system with a large β value RTT_{ac} is equal to $RTT_a * N^0$ or $RTT_{ac} = RTT_a$. For a small β value, which represents considerable sequential processing (i.e. lower degree of overlapped parallelism), the RTT_{ac} value can be calculated by equation (2.1). For a fully sequential system RTT_{ac} is equal to $RTT_a * N^1$ for $e^{-\beta} \approx e^{-0} \approx 1$.

$$RTT_{ac} = RTT_a * N^{e^{-\beta}} .....(2.1), \; \beta_{sequential} \le \beta \le \beta_{fully-parallel}$$

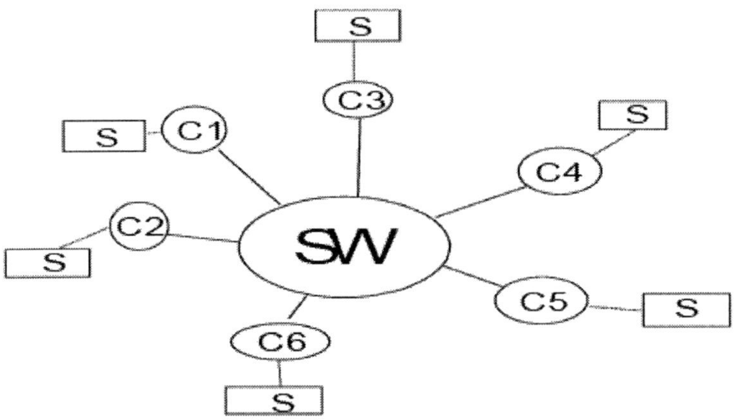

Figure 2.1. A master/slaves application with one master and six slaves.

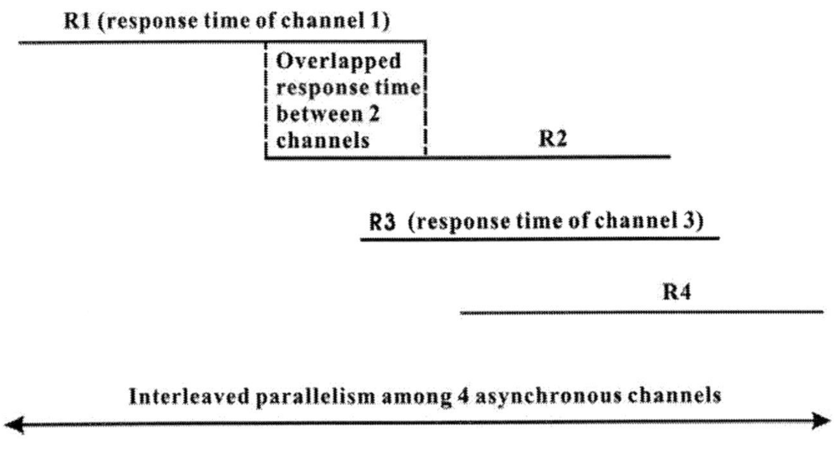

Figure 2.2. Interleaved distributed parallelism among slaves (equation 2.1).

It is essential to harness the service RTT to improve the channel response timeliness for time-critical applications. The ultimate aim logically is to achieve $RTT_{ac} = RTT_a * N^0$. In fact, there are many extant methods that try to achieve this aim. Some of the newer approaches are adaptive by leveraging the chosen metrics on the fly. For example, real-time traffic pattern detection (RTPD), dynamic buffer tuning, and dynamic cache size tuning are among these approaches [Wong2001A, Wong2001B, Wong2000, Lin2004]. In fact, equation (2.1) covers the spectrum of parallelism embedded in the Flynn's classification scheme as follows:

a) SIMD (single instruction / multiple data stream): The collaborating processors execute the same instruction to process their typically different incoming data streams. The executions of the same instruction by the processors are synchronized to produce *intrinsic* parallelism. This is basically the $RTT_a * N^0$ phenomenon.
b) MIMD (multiple instruction / multiple data stream): The collaborating processors execute different instructions to manipulate their different data streams. The resultant parallelism can be intrinsic or distributed (asynchronous) in a network environment. In the latter case, the networked collaborating processors form a *multicomputer* architecture, which is characterized by $RTT_{ac} = RTT_a * N^{e^{-\beta}}$ for a finite β value.
c) MISD (multiple instruction / single data stream): This is systolic computing and the collaborating processors can be tightly-coupled for intrinsic parallelism or loosely-coupled for distributed parallelism. That is, $RTT_{ac} = RTT_a * N^{e^{-\beta}}$ for $0 \leq \beta < \infty$.
d) SISD (single instruction / single data stream): This can be a component in an intrinsic MIMD architecture or a standalone (e.g. a personal computer (PC)). That is, $RTT_{ac} = RTT_a * N^{e^{-\beta}}$ for $\beta \rightarrow 0$.

2.3. SCHEDULING

Scheduling is the first approach discussed here to effectively harness RTT. In the client/server interaction model schedules are present on both the client and server sides. The client scheduler helps prioritize the messages/packets to be sent, and the server scheduler collaborates by allowing urgent requests to be served first. This scheduling collaboration indirectly shortens the average RTT (figure 2.3) so that the chance of service results by the server being received by clients before the deadlines is enhanced. In the scheduling process, however, it is inevitable for some requests to miss their deadlines because it is difficult to have 100% global optimum [Floyd1995].

Schedules may be supported by algorithmic or heuristic strategies such as the following: a) FIFO (first in first out) – algorithmic, b) EDF (earliest deadline first) - heuristic [Zhu2001], and c) SJF (shortest job first) – heuristic. Finding an optimal scheduling strategy, however, is a NP-hard problem [Karp1975]. But, by appropriately mixing heuristics and timing-utility functions, very efficient schedulers [Jensen1985, Wang2004, Locke1986] can be produced.

The term utility abstracts the usefulness and benefit produced by a scheduling operation. It has a range between 0 and 1.

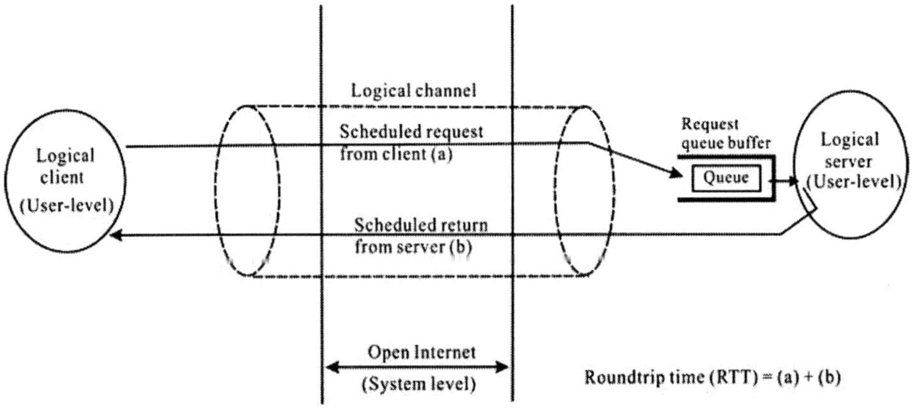

Figure 2.3. Client/server interaction over the Internet.

In the time-utility concept, a scheduler has a utility value for every finished task (i.e. task utility) to quantitatively indicate the benefit that the scheduler produced for this particular task. The total utility for the scheduler is the sum of all the task utilities in the specified period. For example, the task utility produced by the scheduler side for a real-time task is zero if the service result reaches the client after the deadline. In reality, such overdue results are useless and possibly detrimental [Stankovic1998, Zhu2001].

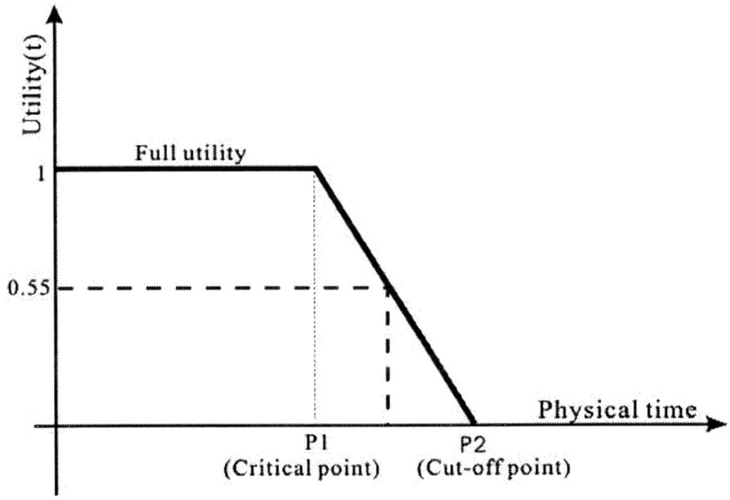

Figure 2.4. a time-utility (TU) function example.

Figure 2.4 is an example of using a time-utility function for the server side of a channel (figure 23) to schedule real-time service requests. In actuality, this time-utility function should be plotted with past utility data for the channel. The Y axis is the utility value, which can change from 1 (at the critical point P1) to 0 at the cut-off point P2 on the X axis, which represents the Δ delay variable. The following parameters are relevant to figure 4:

a) The sender sent request R at t_S (physical time).
b) The physical deadline (i.e. physical time) for the service result from the server to be received correctly by the client is t_D.
c) The server schedules the request to be served at t_Q (physical time).
d) The Δ delay is the instantaneous sum of "service time required by R and the communication delay for the server to return the service result to the client".

The scheduling algorithm on the server side should consider the following:

a) For $[t_D - (t_Q - t_S)] \geq \Delta$ schedule R and, if the condition is not satisfied, then discard R to save server time because the service result would not be returned to the client before the deadline.
b) For $\Delta \geq P2$ discard R because, from empirical experience, the utility value under such a scheduling condition would be zero, which indicates that the return service result would not reach the client before the deadline t_D.
c) For $\Delta \geq P1$ scheduling of R may start depending on whether there are better cases (that yield a utility of 1) waiting to be scheduled. This selective process ensures that high utility cases will be served first to improve the system throughput.

For the above algorithm to work properly, it is necessary to synchronize the physical clocks on both the client and server sides [Millis1995]. Scheduling harnesses the RTT by making sure that no bandwidth is wasted in transmitting useless information through communication channels. It maximizes bandwidth usage and lessens the chance of network congestion. As a result, the number of possible retransmissions due to congestion is reduced. This leads to shorter RTT because of a lower average number of trials (ANT) to get a transmission success. The σ parameter in $ANT \approx \frac{1}{(1-\sigma)}$ is the error probability that causes transmission.

2.4. Sharing of Dependable Communication Links

This is the second approach to harnessing RTT effectively. This is important in real-time applications that run over multihop networks in which a message is relayed forward in a stochastic manner [Han1998, Shin2000, Kim2001]. The stochastic routing process traces the operation path of a message from one node to another (i.e. a hop in between) in an event-driven manner. The final traced route is usually unpredictable, especially in a large network such as the Internet. The overwhelming number of factors at work in the Internet can lead to transient or persistent partial network failures. The result is widespread retransmission that lengthens the service roundtrip time (RTT). This makes the Internet unsuitable for serious time-critical applications. One of the approaches that can resolve this problem and enhance QoS (quality of service) is methodical resource sharing [Krishna2003].

Transient failure usually means infrequent loss of messages or packets in the process of being routed. The causes include random drop that alleviates buffer overflow [Floyd1999] during network congestion. Persistent failures are caused by hardware and/or software faults, which need repair and a lengthy recovery process. For example, the TCP is a best-effort communication approach to provide highly reliable end-to-end communication. It can handle the transient, but not the persistent, failures. So far, the only known approach in the literature for handling persistent failures is *dependable connection* (DC) [Gartner1999]. It aims at satisfying some real-time distributed fault-tolerance requirements. In the DC scheme, every primary connection is backed up by a permanent, dedicated secondary one. If the primary connection fails, the secondary takes over immediately and seamlessly. A strict implementation of the DC concept is expensive because it needs hardware and software duplications. Besides, this strict implementation is practically impossible for the Internet because the heterogeneous nodes in the network collaborate through the clustering principle. That is, every node contributes only what it can afford for public sharing. Therefore, the practical alternative is to share secondary backup connections by timely multiplexing, exemplified by the following:

a) Reservation based [Kandlur1994]: Schemes in this category ensure that the rate of failed message delivery in a real-time channel is lower than the predefined threshold. The necessary resources to achieve this are requested and reserved by the system, for example, by using the Resource Reservation Protocol (RSVP) [Zhang1993].
b) Backup multiplexing: Several primary channels time-share one or a set of secondary channels in this scheme.
c) Segmented backup: This scheme tries to maximize the use of resources by segmenting a primary connection/path. Each segment is then supported by an independent backup.
d) Primary-backup multiplexing: In this scheme, a primary channel and the backup share some links in a dynamic, timely manner. The shared links are sometimes insecure because of possible contention. But, this sharing approach supports flexible usage of network resources in a time-shared manner.

The implementation of the above examples needs the following support [Han1998]: a) a mechanism to back up the primary channel in a dedicated or shared manner; b) a mechanism to detect network failures; c) a method to immediately switch from a primary path to its backup; and d) a scheme for effective and efficient resource management to support all the backup activities. An efficient backup scheme would reduce the chance of retransmissions and timeouts and thus shorten the service RTT to satisfy the timeliness requirements of time-critical applications.

2.5. FAIR BANDWIDTH USAGE

Bandwidth arbitration is the third approach to harness RTT effectively. The aim is to distribute bandwidth fairly among different users to gain high Internet throughput. If the operation is at the system/router level, it is usually paired with network congestion prevention such as AQM (active queue management) [Braden1998]. Figure 2.5 shows an end-to-end TCP (Transmission Control Protocol) channel, which basically has two levels: system/router and user. The system level includes all the activities inside the logical TCP channel that operates on top of the IP (Internet Protocol) layer. The user level includes all the sender/receiver operations outside the TCP channel. Traditional Internet applications that use the connection-oriented TCP include FTP (file transfer), TELNET, SMTP (email) and World Wide Web (WWW) information retrieval (HTTP). Other applications such as audio/video streaming over the Internet involve wireless communication and the connectionless UDP (User Datagram Protocol) [RFC768].

The TCP traffic flow is responsive because the router can throttle a runaway sender by choke packets. The throttled sender reacts by voluntarily cutting down its transmission rate to avoid inundating the router reception. Any inundation as such can cause buffer overflow and loss of messages, leading to widespread retransmission. If the throttling fails, the router drops the incoming packets as a last resort to prevent network congestion [RFC896]. This message dropping strategy, however, does not apply to the UDP and the wireless communications. In these two cases, the sender retransmits immediately to compensate for the loss rate. If these immediate retransmissions occur throughout the network, they would worsen the network congestion to the point of producing a total network breakdown. This failure phenomenon is called congestion collapse [Floyd1999].

In contrast to the responsive TCP communication, both UDP and wireless traffic are unresponsive. If the aggressive unresponsive traffic it is not effectively regulated and arbitrated, it can easily usurp the bandwidth saved by the TCP congestion prevention effort [Braden1998]. The result is long service roundtrip time (RTT) for TCP channel because of throttled transmissions. This would make the Internet lose it appeal as the universal platform for information exchange and e-commerce [Wu2003]. The location of the arbitration process is very important. If the immediate router that serves the clients directly can arbitrate the bandwidth consumption between responsive and unresponsive traffic, then the resultant retransmissions are limited within the locality. This prevents local congestion from invading the other parts of the network, thereby creating new router bottlenecks.

There are many TCP variants in the field including Tahoe, Reno, Vegas, and Sack [Jacobson1990, Stevens2001, Mathis, Brakmo1994]. The basic unit of transmission in a TCP channel is a data segment. In these TCP variants, a timeout and a choke-packet is a sign of network congestion. If the sender side has implemented the AIMD (Additive Increase/Multiplicative Decrease) capability [Jacobson1988], it can be immediately invoked to proactively alleviate the congestion. Figure 2.6 shows how the AIMD scheme works. Firstly, the congestion window is set to one segment and it doubles for every correctly returned acknowledgement until it hits the threshold predefined for the first cycle (i.e. the first-cycle threshold in figure 2.6). This first phase is called *slow start*, and thereafter the second *congestion avoidance* phase commences by incrementing the congestion window size linearly by one segment every time. The largest congestion window is limited by the advertised window, which is the current capacity of the TCP channel. If a timeout has occurred or a throttling choke packet is received, then the increment threshold is set to half (i.e. first-cycle threshold to second-cycle threshold) and the size of the congestion window "slow starts" with one segment again.

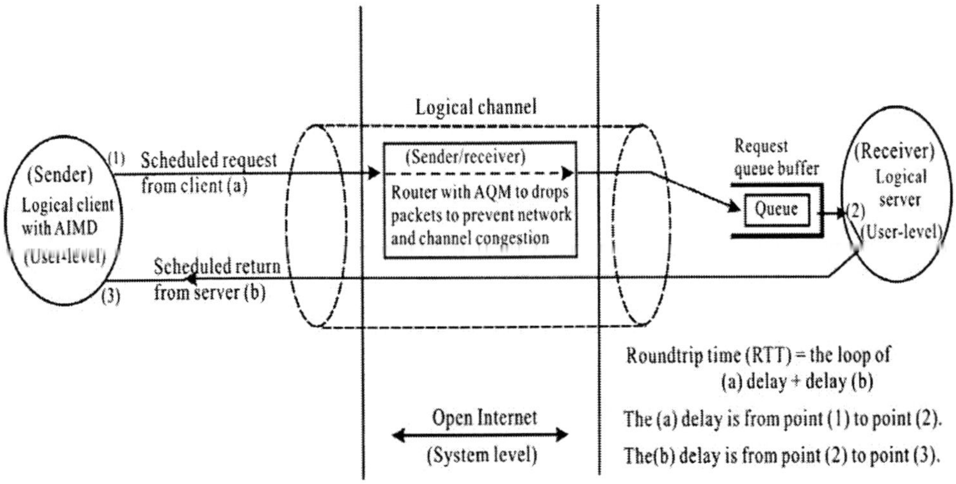

Figure 2.5. Network congestion prevention and fair bandwidth distribution by arbitration.

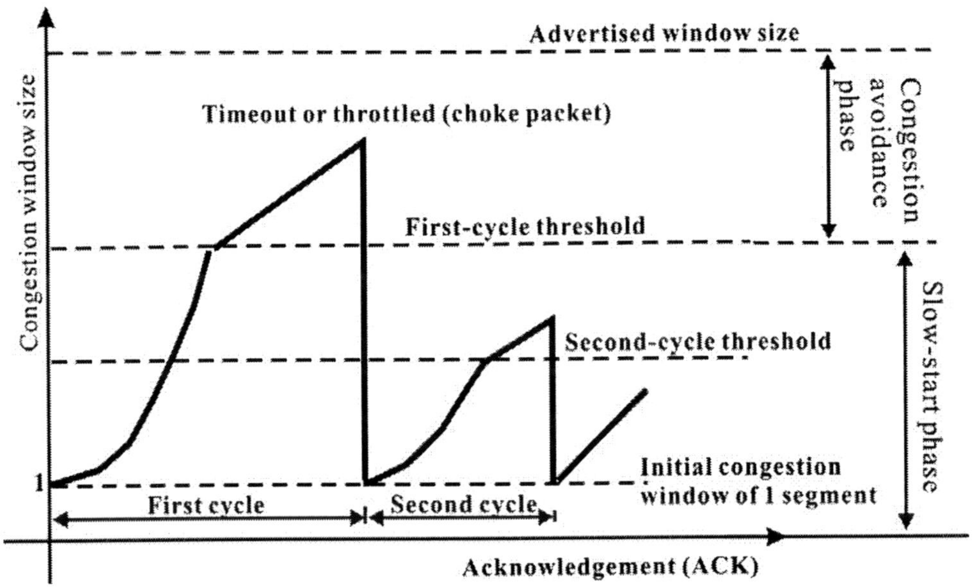

Figure 2.6. Two cycles in the AIMD scheme.

The choke packet ties the sender-controlled AIMD operation and the AQM (active queue management) mechanism by the router. Any effective AQM strategy has to competently deal with unresponsive traffic simultaneously. Therefore, it needs to derive per flow information from the traffic so that those flows that are likely to deplete the bandwidth will be punished. Therefore, different possible punitive actions are administered, for example, by limiting the transmission rate [Jacobson1990]. Those AQM schemes that require full per-flow state information (e.g. LQD [Lakshman1996], FRED [Kim1998] and BRED [Anjum1999]) are difficult to deploy for practical purposes. Those AQM schemes that require no full per-flow state information are easier to implement. They include the CHOKe [Pan1999] and SRED [Ott1999] models. All the AQM strategies basically operate in two steps: a) a router first throttles a sender to slow down transmission voluntarily; and b) if the throttling action has failed, then incoming packets are dropped. There are many packet dropping strategies available for smooth operation [Braden1998]. The drop-in-front strategy [Lakshman1996], which drops the incoming packets, can accelerate retransmissions to shorten the service RTT.

To achieve successful arbitration of responsive and unresponsive traffic streams, an AQM strategy needs real-time support. The supporting system should have two basic elements: a) an equitable, mathematically tractable throughput reference; and b) a throughput index to show fair bandwidth sharing by both responsive and unresponsive streams.

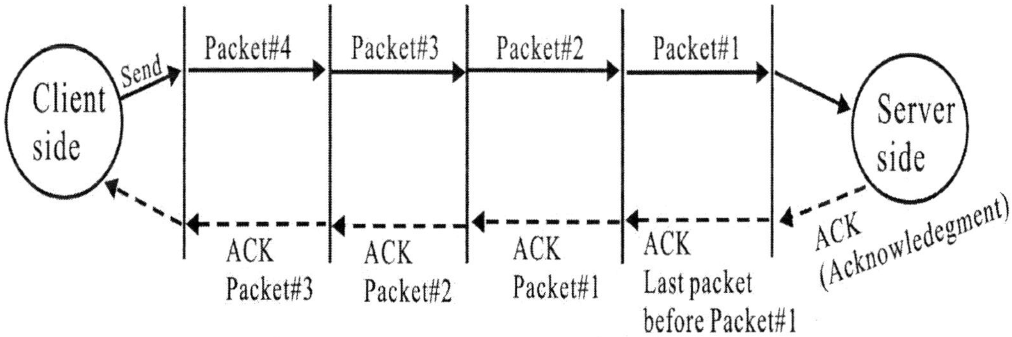

Figure 2.7. Sending packets with corresponding acknowledgment at the steady state.

An effective, traceable way to define equitable throughput reference is by analytical techniques. First, the following are assumed for the AIMD system figure 2.6:

a) The average congestion window size is W.
b) The router's buffer is infinite.
c) The average drop rate is γ.
d) The average RTT per packet is RTT_{av}.
e) The segment size is Sz bytes.

With these assumptions, the outcome will be:

a) For every timeout or choke packet, the congestion window will be reset to one segment.
b) Sending $W/2$ packets needs $(W/2)RTT_{av}$ delay at the steady state as shown by figure 2.7.
c) The AIMD operation can be represented by the saw wave in figure 2.8.

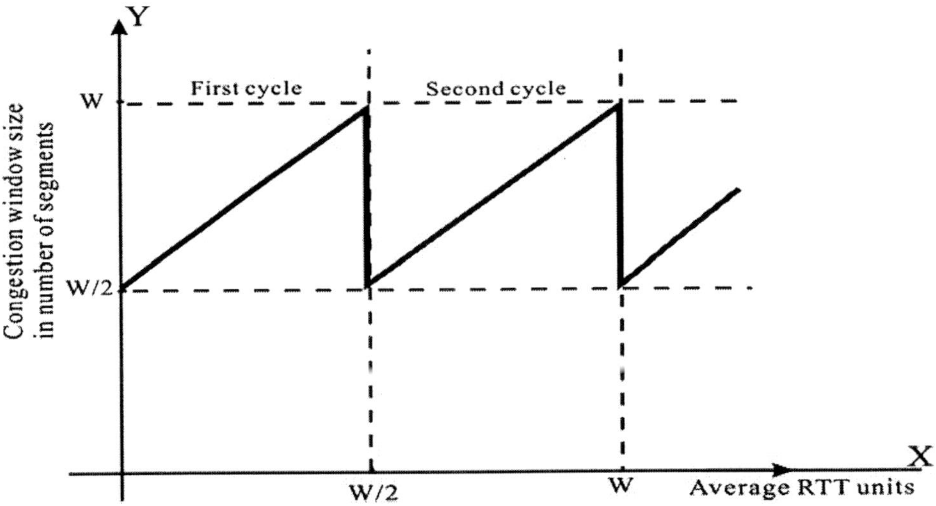

Figure 2.8. Saw-wave representation of the AIMD operation.

At the steady-state operation, a timeout or choke packet after W segments may occur, where W is the average congestion window size (figure 2.8). The $W/2$ mark on the Y axis differentiates the slow-start phase (below) and the congestion avoidance phase (above) in figure 2.8. From figure 2.7 it is clear that at the steady state sending a segment happens in parallel with acknowledgement (ACK) of the previous one. The total number of segments sent (P_T) per cycle is equal to the area under the saw tooth wave or

$$P_T = [(W/2)^2 + 1/2(W/2)^2] = 1.5(W/2)^2.$$

Since the drop rate γ is bound by one in $1/P_T$ or $8/(3W^2)$, $W \leq \sqrt{8/3\gamma}$ holds. This implies the throughput T_C defined by equation (2.5.1). Using the method described in [Padhye1998] that takes the finite size of the receiver into account, equation (2.5.2) can be refined as equation (2.5.2).

$$T_C = \frac{P_T}{(W/2) * RTT_{av}} = \frac{(\frac{3 * Sz * W^2}{8})}{RTT * (W/2)} = \frac{Sz / \gamma}{RTT_{av}\sqrt{2/3\gamma}} = \frac{1.5 * Sz * \sqrt{2/3}}{RTT_{av}\sqrt{\gamma}} \text{..........(2.5.1)}$$

$$T_{CR} = \frac{1.5 * Sz * \sqrt{1/3}}{RTT_{av}\sqrt{\gamma}} \text{.........(2.5.2)}$$

Once the drop rate γ and RTT_{av} are correctly estimated with Sz predefined, the T_C and T_{CR} values of a system can be calculated. These values can be used as the equitable throughput reference. If the system throughput has suddenly and significantly dropped below these values, unfair depletion of the bandwidth by the unresponsive flows is indicated. The system can adaptively correct the unfair situation by limiting the unresponsive flows. Different AQM strategies, however, produce different outcomes in arbitrating the bandwidth usage between responsive and unresponsive traffic streams. Some may over-punish the unresponsive flows and others may under-correct the situation. As a result, the unresponsive flows may be unfairly advantaged or disadvantaged. There is no way of telling exactly which AQM algorithm would perform more fairly than another unless their fairness can be measured and compared under the same conditions. Some researchers proposed to achieve this by devising fairness indexing schemes. One of them is called the Jain's fairness index f_{idx} [Jain1999], which is represented by the equation (2.5.3). z_j is the jth throughput measured by the sampling process. Simulation results by different researchers indicate that f_{idx} can be used for comparing the fairness performance among different AQM schemes. For example, the BLACK AQM scheme ($f_{idx} = 0.9905$) is fairer than CHOKe AQM approach ($f_{idx} = 0.9721$) [Chatranon2004]. A fair bandwidth usage arbitration system reduces the chance of network congestion and thus retransmissions. As a result, the client/server service RTT is shortened.

$$f_{idx} = \frac{(\sum_{j=1}^{n} z_j)^2}{n\sum_{j=1}^{n} z_j^2} \quad ....(2.5.3)$$

2.6. Transmitting Multiple Copies of the Same Message

The fourth approach to harnessing RTT effectively is by sending multiple copies of the same message. By doing so, the reception is speeded up [Ramanathan1992]. This scheme is applicable to both the system and the user levels. The argument is based on the $ANT \approx 1/(1-\sigma)$ concept, where σ is the collective channel error probability that causes retransmissions. If the sender sends multiple copies consecutively and immediately one after another, the σ value would be reduced. In effect, sending n immediate, consecutive copies of a message yields a new channel error probability of σ^n. This produces the effect of $ANT_n \approx 1/(1-\sigma^n)$ and a speedup because $\sigma > \sigma^n$. The argument is that the chance of at least one of a number of multiple copies reaching the receiver is higher than sending a single copy. The *sending consecutive multiple copies* (SCMC) scheme is *proactive* in light of fault-tolerance but speculative in the performance context. The speculative factor is that only "one" correct message is kept by the receiver. This factor is expensive because the sender solicits resources to send the multiple copies at the expense of other users. The SCMC scheme could consume excessive local memory and cause task suspensions by the operating system due to lack of recyclable memory. The operation may also deplete transmission bandwidth leading to low system throughput. Therefore, the suitability of this speculative scheme for time-critical applications is debatable [Wong2000]. The potential SCMC benefit is the speedup by $S_n = ANT / ANT_n$. For example, for $\sigma = 0.3$ and $n = 5$ the speedup is $S_{n=5} = [1-(0.3)^5] / (1-0.3) \approx 1.425$. The speedup S_n depends on σ and n, and for a given σ the effect of n tapers off asymptotically. For example, $\sigma = 0.3$ and $n = 10$ yield $S_{n=10} \approx 1 / (1-0.3) \approx 1.428$, and this is not much better than $S_{n=5} \approx 1.425$ for $n = 5$. In reality the σ value changes over time because of the dynamic nature of a large network such as the Internet. The SCMC scheme is *proactive* and timeout based retransmission is *reactive*.

The potential SCMC power can be fully realized if a corrective mechanism is present. This mechanism should be adaptive and capable of determining the number of appropriate copies of the same message (i.e. n) to be sent on the fly [Wong2000]. This can be achieved by measuring σ in a dynamic manner explicitly or implicitly. Implicit measurement means leveraging some parameters that can quickly and accurately reflect the σ changes. One of the useful parameters for such a purpose is the service roundtrip time (RTT) between the client (sender) and the server (receiver) [Wong1999]. The sender can trace the RTT values and maintain a window of size W_{scr} to scrutinize the current RTT samples within. For example, if the sender wants to determine the appropriate n values at time Td (figure 2.9), then the current time window W_{scr} is scrutinized so that the following parameters can be calculated and leveraged:

a) The average RTT within W_{scr}: It provides the scale or proportional (P) control by comparing the difference between the average value being used and the new value computed on the fly for W_{scr}.
b) The rate of RTT change in W_{scr}: It is the derivative (D) control based on the current $dRTT / dt$ value.

The historical trend of change in RTT should be used as the feedback for the current W_{scr}. This forms the integral (I) control to dampen the possible noise embedded in the RTT samples and alleviate the perturbation in the final mean RTT calculations.

How the P, D and I control elements are used depends on the controller design. These elements may be used alone or combined in various ways. One combination is "P+D+I" or PID controller [Karray2002], which can be represented by the following expression: $PID \cong \alpha RTT + \beta \frac{dRTT}{dt} + \int_{W_{scr}} RTTdt$, where $\cong$ denotes equivalence. For easier application, the PID output is normalized to 1; $0 < (\alpha RTT + \beta \frac{dRTT}{dt} + \int_{W_{scr}} RTTdt) \leq 1$. This range can be calibrated for different n values so that the sender can send the predefined number of copies corresponding to the instantaneous PID output. The advantage of this adaptive SCMC approach is that more than one copy is sent only when necessary. This lessens the chance of network congestion.

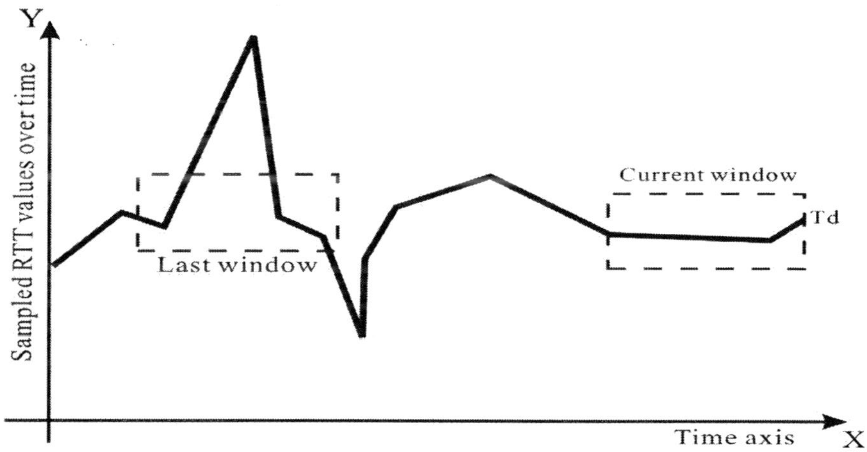

Figure 2.9. Leveraging the RTT trend to determine n in SCMC.

Designing an effective integral control for a real-time application is no easy task because the computation should be accurate and quick in preventing deleterious effects. These effects would cause the computed remedy to correct a spurious problem, which has long disappeared due to the computation delay. The report by Ip [Ip2001] shows how effective integral control for real-time application is achieved by using the Convergence Algorithm (CA) [Wong1999], also called the M^2RT (mean message response time) algorithm. The version for real-time application is the M^3RT (micro mean message response time) [Ip2002]. The CA/M^2RT/M^3RT approach belongs to a contemporary school of thought, Internet End-to-End Performance Measurement (IEPM) [Cotroll1999], the core of which will be discussed in Chapter 3.

2.7. Neutralizing Traffic Ill Effects in a Real-Time Manner

This is the fifth effective approach to harness the Internet RTT. It was observed repeatedly that the Internet traffic patterns can cause system instability [Wu2003, Wu2004] and lead to system failure [Paxson1995]. The conclusion from these observations is that Internet applications should be adaptive in regard to traffic pattern changes. The R^2-FLC (Real-time Reconfigurable Fuzzy Logic Controller) dynamic buffer tuner is an example. It adjusts its internal parameters with respect to different traffic patterns on the fly. As a result, it is more stable and outperforms its predecessors. The prelude to this success is the incorporation of the real-time traffic pattern detection capability as a R^2-FLC component.

The Internet follows the power or hyperbolic laws and its traffic pattern changes inevitably over time, for example, from short-range dependence (SRD) to long-range dependence (LRD) or vice versa [Medina2000, Molnár1999, Paxson1997, Willinger2003]. SRD traffic includes the Markovian traffic patterns and LRD traffic can be heavy-tailed or self-similar. A self-similar traffic trace can be monofractal by having a single dimension throughout. If it embeds different dimensions, then it is multifractal. A traffic trace (in the form of a time series) is stationary provided that it has independent increments. A stationary time series has its Hurst (H) effect/value in the range (0,1). The $0 < H < 0.5$ range indicates SRD and $0.5 < H < 1$ is for LRD. The value of 0.5 indicates white noise [Willinger2003]. In fact, traffic self-similarity may have a heavy-tailed origin, but "heavy-tailedness" is not necessary for self-similarity as reported by Ryu et al [Ryu1996].

Internet traffic patterns can seriously impede system operation and performance. They should be an important parameter to be leveraged for better system performance in real-time applications. This point is well demonstrated by the system perturbations caused by traffic patterns to the MACSC (Model for Adaptive Cache Size Control) dynamic cache size tuner, which strives to maintain a given hit ratio on the fly [Wu2004]. The performance data indicate that changes in traffic patterns would cause data loss in the cache and steep hit-ratio drop. Therefore, there is a need to detect the current traffic pattern (i.e. SRD or LRD) in a real-time fashion so that the tuner reconfigures with respect to the detected traffic result in order to ward off the traffic ill effects. The MACSC works by computing the ratio of two consecutive standard deviations measured on the fly. This "popularity ratio" as it is called, provides the basis for dynamic cache size adjustment. The MACSC(PE) is the MACSC version that is supported by the statistical point-estimate (PE) method for computing the necessary standard deviations. More details can be found in Chapter 5. Figures 2.10 and 2.11 show the average data sample misses and average hit ratio respectively versus the inter-arrival times (IAT) among the data points.

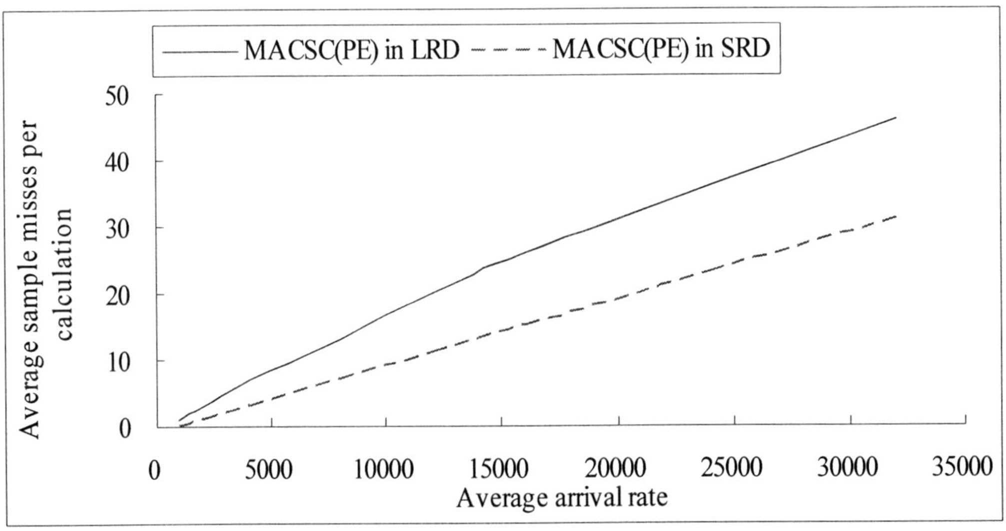

Figure 2.10. Data loss (missed data) of MACSC(PE) versus IAT for the LRD and SRD traces.

The first step in alleviating or even eliminating traffic ill effects on the system performance and stability [Paxson95] is effective traffic analysis. The available methods for such analyses so far cater mainly for off-line applications that work on pre-collected data traces [Molnár1999]. The only exception is the Convergence Algorithm (CA), which will be discussed in detail below. Therefore, the present methods other than CA are good for understanding what has happened in the Internet in the past. They lack the capability of helping any running applications to react immediately to prevent failure due to the ill effects of traffic.

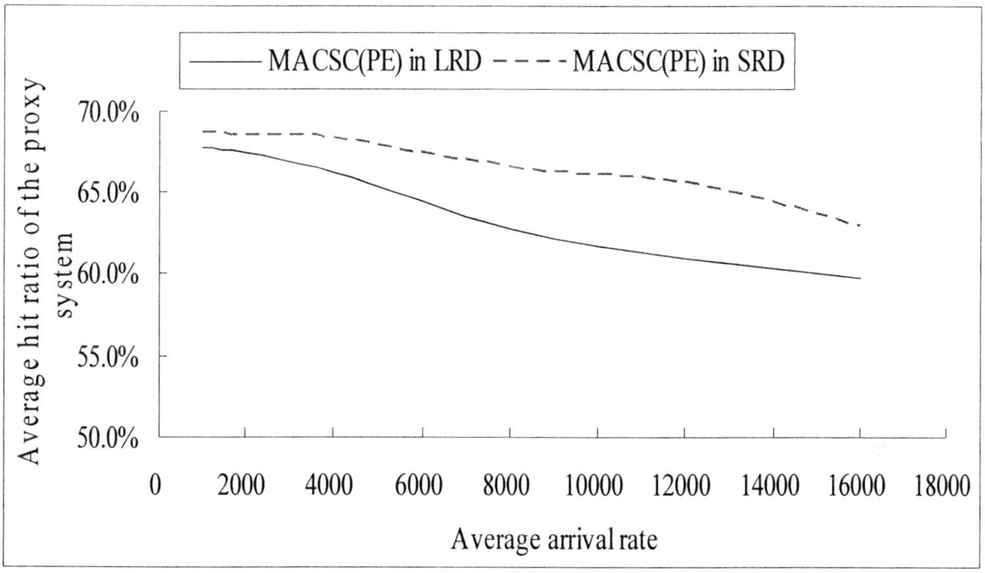

Figure 2.11. Hit ratio of MACSC(PE) versus IAT for the LRD and SRD traces.

Table 2.1. Comparison of some common IEPM tools (N/A for Not Applicable)

	AMP	pchar	PingER	Skitter	Surveyor	CA
Platform	FreeBSD	FreeBSD and Solaris	Not Specified	FreeBSD	BSDI	Internet
Parameters	Packet loss, RTT, Connectivity, On-demand throughput	Bandwidth, Latency, Loss of links	Packet loss, RTT, Reachability, Predictability, Quiescence	RTT, Routing data	Uni-directional delay, Packet loss, Routing data	Any single parameter (as a waveform)
Language	N/A	C++	Perl and Java	N/A	N/A	Java
Datagram Protocol	ICMP	UDP/ICMP	ICMP	ICMP	UDP	TCP/IP
Limitations	Aims at HPC sites	Needs super-user access	N/A	N/A	Need to install GPS for synchronizing clocks	None
Visualization tool	Yes	No	Yes	Yes	Yes	Yes

Two types of approaches can be identified for traffic analysis from the literature: Internet End-to-End Performance (IEPM) analysis and traffic pattern identification. The aim of the IEPM approach is to gauge the channel end-to-end behavior by monitoring and measuring its mean RTT over time [Cotrell1999]. Therefore, the mean RTT connotes the moving average. There are two kinds of IEPM tools: macro and micro. The macro tools must be installed at the nodes that represent the two ends of a channel for effective operation. A few well-known examples include the following: AMP [Amp1, Amp1999], pchar [Mah2001, Matt2001], PingER [Matt2000], Skitter [Alex2001], Surveyor [Sunil1999] and CA [AJWong2001] (also known as the M^2RT [Wong2001B]) and their characteristics are summarized and compared in table 2.1.

The macro CA/M^2RT is the predecessor of the micro M^3RT, which is designed for real-time applications. Being micro, a tool should exist independently as a logical entity that provides service anytime anywhere when invoked by message passing. It treats a traffic pattern simply as a waveform. The speed and accuracy of the CA is independent of the waveform type because it is derived from the *Central Limit Theorem* (CLT). The CA /M^2RT/M^3RT operation is summarized by the equation, (2.7.1) and (2.7.2).

$$M_i = \frac{M_{i-1} + \sum_{j=1}^{j=F-1} m_j^i}{F} \quad .....(2.7.1)$$

$$M_0 = m_{j=0}^{i=1} \quad ....(2.7.2)$$

In equation (2.7.1) the estimated mean M_i in the ith prediction cycle is based on the F (*flush limit*) number of data samples. It is called the prediction cycle because of the following CLT characteristics: a) plotting enough sample means $\bar{x}$ (usually 10 or more) would produce a bell-shape curve, and b) the mean $M_{\bar{x}}$ of this curve indicates where the true mean M_{true} of the x population is ($\bar{x}$ is the mean of a collection of values for the x variable). The "telltale" behavior is predictive, and M_i has the same effect as $M_{\bar{x}}$ [AJWong2001]. It was repeatedly confirmed by many previous experiments that the optimal region/range for fast M_i convergence is $9 \le F \le 16$, and F=14 is the fastest [AJWong2001]. The terms and parameters in the equations (2.7.1) and (2.7.2) are: a) M_{i-1} is the feedback of the last predicted mean to the current M_i prediction cycle, b) m_j^i is the jth data point sampled in the ith M_i cycle, $j = 1,2,3,....,(F-1)$, and c) M_0 is the first data point sampled when CA had first started. Figure 2.12 shows the M_i distribution predicted by M^3RT over time with RTT samples from a real-life TCP channel. In this particular case M_i always settles to the value of 480ms at the steady state. The M^3RT mechanism contributes to shortening of the service RTT because it can be incorporated as a component in other mechanisms such as the EMACSC dynamic cache size tuner [Wu2004]. With the help of the M^3RT element, which is part of its construct, EMACSC maintains a high cache hit ratio more effectively and consistently. As a result, the high hit ratio reduces the chance of the proxy server having to access remote web servers for the required data. This reduction is translated into a shorter RTT for information retrieval over the Internet. As a fringe benefit, more backbone bandwidth is released for public sharing because less data needs to be transmitted across the open Internet.

In fact, different timing analyses with the Intel's VTune Performance Analyzer [VTune] indicate that the average M^3RT execution time is 255 clock cycles [Ip2002]. This can be converted into the physical time T_{phy} with respect to the hardware platform on which M^3RT is running; $T_{phy} = CLK / SPD$, where CLK is the measured clock cycle and SPD is the speed of the hardware platform. If M^3RT is running on a platform operating at 100 megahertz, then the execution time is $T_{phy} = 255/(100*10^{-6}) \approx 2.55$ micro seconds. This short execution time makes the M^3RT immensely suitable for real-time applications due to the decreased possibility of deleterious effects. The CA is natural for Internet applications because it is derived from the *Central Limit Theorem* and therefore is independent of any waveforms.

The present traffic pattern analysis techniques are mostly off-line [Molnár1999] and new techniques for real-time applications have started to emerge only recently [Lin2004]. In general, off-line traffic analysis with a trace provides some understanding of how the system performed at the time. Real-time traffic analysis not only fulfils the same role but, with the detected result, also enables a real-time system to reconfigure on the fly and neutralize any traffic ill effects in a timely manner. The details of traffic analysis and how real-time traffic pattern detection (RTPD) can help enhance system performance will be presented in later chapters.

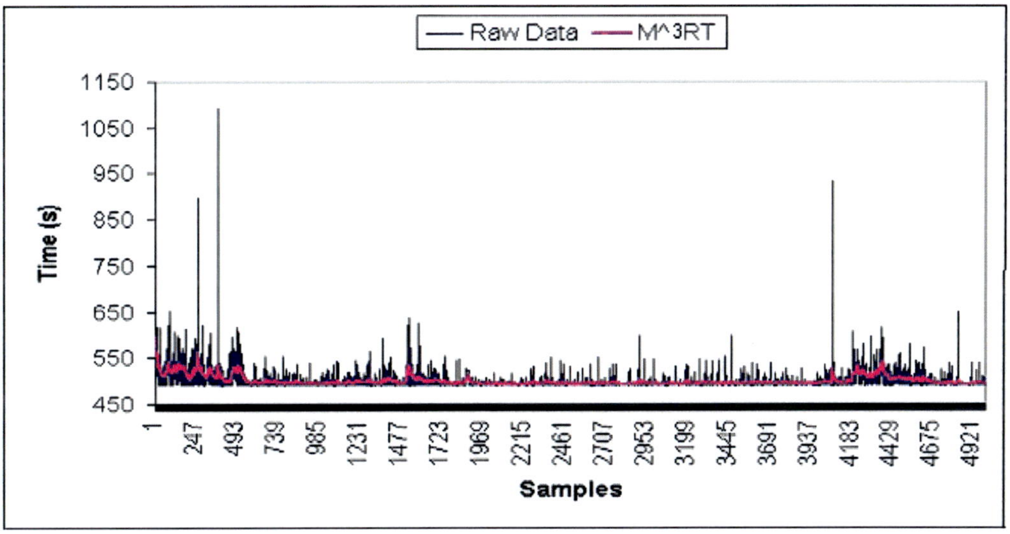

Figure 2.12. M_i prediction by M^{3}RT for a TCP trace (M^3 means M^3).

2.8. PREVENTING DENIAL OF SERVICE ATTACKS

Preventing denial of service attacks (DOSA) over the Internet is the sixth important approach to help reduce the RTT. DOSA increase the system utilization maliciously. First, let us assume the following: a) the average input rate of requests to the server asking for service is λ; b) the average rate of servicing the queued requests by the server is μ ; c) the system/server utilization is $\upsilon = \frac{\lambda}{\mu}$; d) both the inter-arrival times among requests and the service time per request are random (i.e. Markov [Jain1992]); and e) the M/M/1 model (M for Markov and 1 for one server) yields a queue length defined by $L = \frac{\upsilon}{1-\upsilon}$. From these assumptions the queue length L will grow asymptotically to infinity as υ approaches 1. The net effect of DOSA is to maliciously increase υ by increasing λ exponentially, and this eventually leads to severe system congestion and breakdown. The malicious attacker usually bombards the server with spoofed messages continuously until it is overwhelmed.

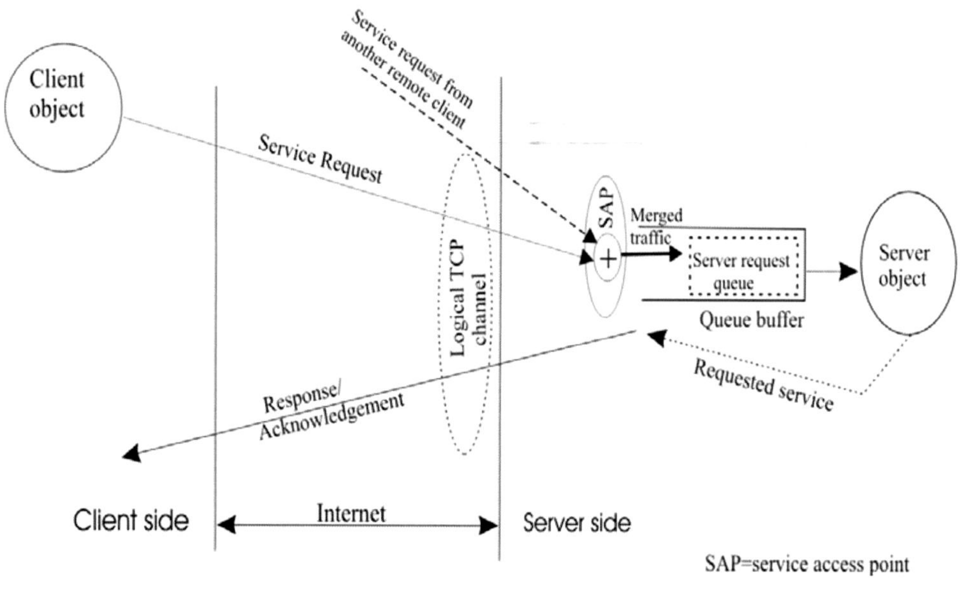

Figure 2.13. The asymmetric rendezvous client/server interaction.

The congestion caused by DOSA can propagate to other parts of the network. For this reason, it is essential to nullify the ill effects from DOSA by the following steps: a) the first step is to detect their presence; b) the second step is to identify the specific DOSA pattern or signature; and c) the third step is to invoke the "antidote" to nullify the malicious effects. DOSA can have different origins, for example, they may come from the operating system (OS) level or the communication level (e.g. TCP and UDP [Jonckheere2002]). Most of the reported DOSA cases, however, have come from the TCP level [CERT]. The common attacking strategy is to steal victims' identities (e.g. IP address) and use them to send spoofed messages. In this way, it would be difficult for the system to trace the original attacker. At the

TCP level, DOSA occurrences easily cause channel congestion and increase the channel probability error σ to cause widespread retransmissions. These occurrences inevitably increase the number of timeouts as well as the ANT to get a transmission success, and this means prolonged client/server RTT.

Under normal circumstances, it is difficult to differentiate DOSA from normal communication traffic. As shown in figure 2.13, the asymmetric rendezvous has the many-clients-to-server relationship. The bursts of requests from different clients merge at the server's service access point (SAP). If the queue buffer is not effectively managed, any sudden surge in the merged traffic can overflow the server queue and lead to widespread retransmission. One technique that can detect DOSA cases effectively under certain circumstances is the Bloom filter [Jonckheere2002]. Its rationale is summarized as follows:

a) A set of key elements (i.e. a_i for $i = 1,2,..,n$) is chosen, and this set is represented as $A = \{a_{1,}a_2,....a_n\}$.
b) A set of hash functions (i.e. h_i for $i = 1,2,..,k$) is chosen, and this set is represent as $H = \{h_{1,}h_2,....h_n\}$.
c) A working vector $v[m]$ of m bits long and for $m \geq n$ is assigned separately to every hash function. All the bits in $v[m]$ are set to 0 initially.
d) If all the hash functions in set H work on the same key element in A, each function produces a private vector, which has all the hashed positions in $v[m]$ set to 1. In effect, $v[m]$ contains all the private vectors for $A = \{a_{1,}a_2,....a_n\}$ superimposed. It is possible for a "1" in $v[m]$ to be shared by different private vectors.
e) To answer the query "if the given element b belong to A (i.e. $b \in A$?)" all the functions in H will hash b. If the resultant vector does not match any in $v[m]$, then $b \in A$ is false.

The probability of a false hit is defined by the equation (2.8.1). P_{0-hit} is the chance that a particular bit in the private $v[m]$ vectors is still 0 after the n keys are hashed. The probability $1/m$ indicates an equal chance for all m positions to get the value of 1. The important issue in the Bloom filter application is to accurately determine the "falsehood" or "truth" probability for a query. The same probability $P_{f/t}$ can represent falsehood or truth depending on the domain of application. This probability, which is represented by the equation (2.8.2), can be defined in terms of P_{0-hit} [Fan2000]. For example, it can confirm that the query $b \in A$ is true if all the hashed positions in the $v[m]$ vectors are 1s. Inside the brackets "[ ]" of equation (2.8.2) is actually a geometric function in the cumulative binomial form of $F(kn) = 1-(1-(1/m)^{kn}$, where "kn" is the variable, "$1/m$" connotes the "probability of success", and "m" is the average of the geometric distribution. This binomial function can be crudely approximated by the cumulative exponential function $1-e^{-(kn/m)}$ for $1/m$ represents a rare event as well as the rate of decay. Therefore, the equations (2.8.2) and (2.8.3) have the same meaning for rare events. From equation (2.8.3) the useful relationship that correlates k and the m/n ratio can be derived by assuming $k = \ln 2 * m/n$. With this assumption $(1-e^{-(kn/m)})^k$ yields $(1-e^{-\ln 2})^k \approx (\frac{1}{2})^k$. In fact, $(\frac{1}{2})^k \Rightarrow (\frac{1}{2})^{(\ln 2)*(m/n)}$ means $[(\frac{1}{2})^{(\ln 2)}]^{m/n} = (0.6185)^{m/n}$, and thus the $(\frac{1}{2})^k = (0.6185)^{m/n}$ relationship in the equation (2.8.4). From this relationship effective Bloom filters can be designed by selecting the appropriate values for k, m and n.

$$P_{0-hit} = (1-1/m)^{kn} \quad ----(2.8.1) \qquad P_{f/t} = [1-(1-1/m)^{kn}]^k \quad ------(2.8.2)$$

$$P_{f/t} \approx (1-e^{-(kn/m)})^k \quad -----(2.8.3) \qquad (\frac{1}{2})^k = (0.6185)^{m/n} \quad -----(2.8.4)$$

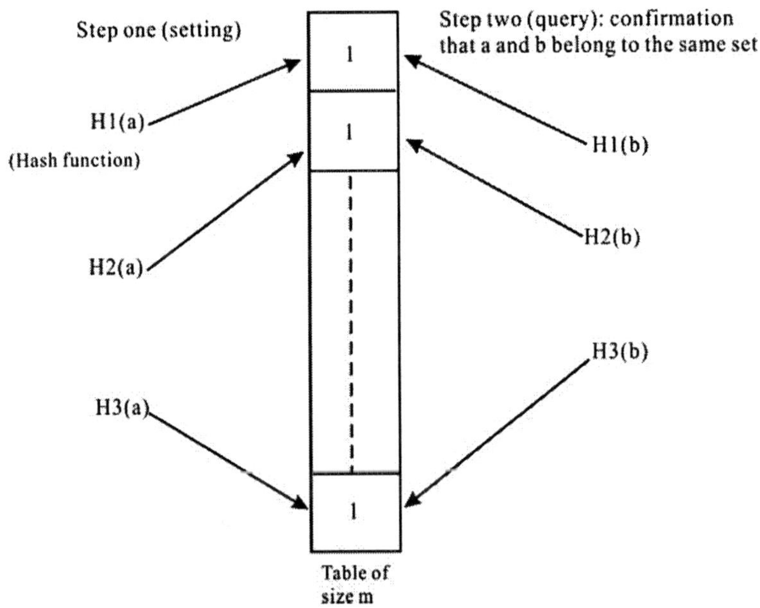

Figure 2.14. The Bloom filter confirms $(a,b) \in A$.

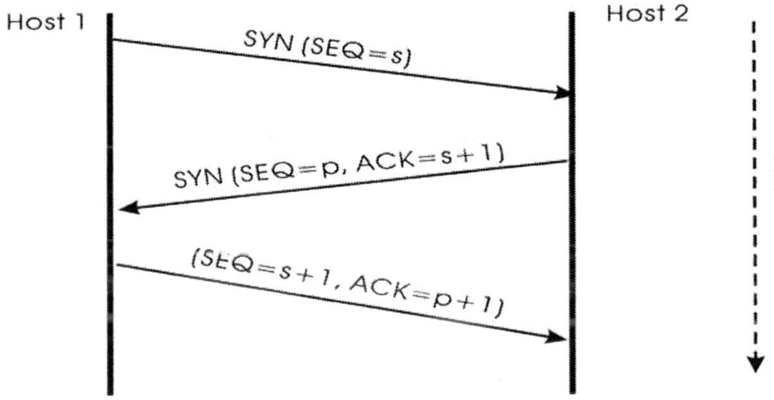

Figure 2.15. Three-way handshake in TCP channel establishment.

The following example shows how the Bloom filter is applied to detect DOSA in the TCP three-way handshake. Figure 2.15 shows a TCP connection establishment in a normal case. Host 1 passes its connection request by sending a SYN (synchronization) control packet via the local edge router that registers all the IP addresses in its domain. In the Bloom filter these IP addresses correspond to the key elements in set A, $A = \{IP_{1,} IP_2, \ldots IP_n\}$. After receiving the SYN packet the interested Host 2 returns the SYN packet with the proper ACK. If everything is fine, then Host 1 sends back an ACK packet to confirm the channel establishment. The connection of Host 1 and Host 2 has conceptually included the IP address of Host 2 in A. For example, Host 1 and Host 2 may be considered equivalent and hashing the IP address of Host 2 would produce the same effect as hashing Host 1.

It is assumed that the Bloom filter in the edge router in this example hashes only those IP addresses that represent successful TCP connections. Then, all the corresponding hashed bit positions in all the private vectors would be set to 1 provided that the IP address belongs to A or as equivalent of belonging to A (e.g. Host 2). Now, if a malicious agent tries to send messages to an unconnected IP address, its DOSA intention would be blocked because the edge router would hash the recipient IP address. If it is not connected, some of the hashed bit positions would have 0 values. Many network operations make use of the edge router to resolve DOSA [Cisco].

2.9. CACHING

This section introduces caching as the seventh effective means to shorten the service RTT. Without caching, the Internet can become terribly congested and lose its appeal as the platform for sharing information globally. As was pointed out by Jia Wang [Wang1999], the static size of a web page grows at the rate of approximately 15% per month but that of the backbone bandwidth increases approximately only 60% annually. This trend spells trouble for the Internet unless a technique such as caching is used to compensate for the difference [Bharat]. The basic advantage of caching is to let the client fetch as many of the needed data objects as possible from the proxy server. This implies that the proxy should maintain a local cache with a high hit ratio. The corollary is that the proxy should keep a high number of hot or popular data objects in its local cache.

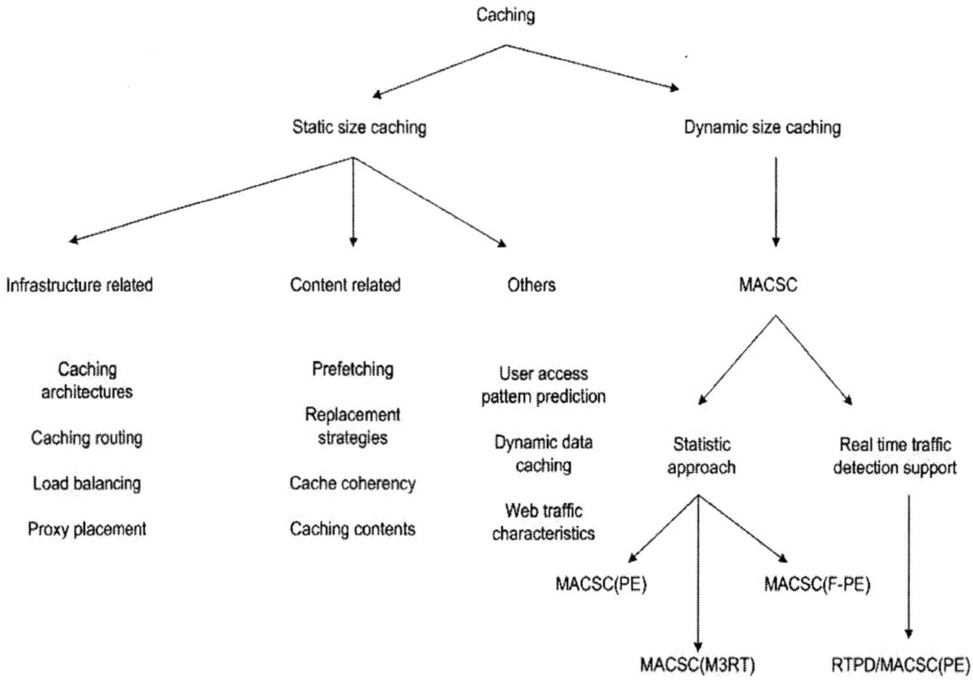

Figure 2.16. Existing techniques relevant to caching (figure 1.14).

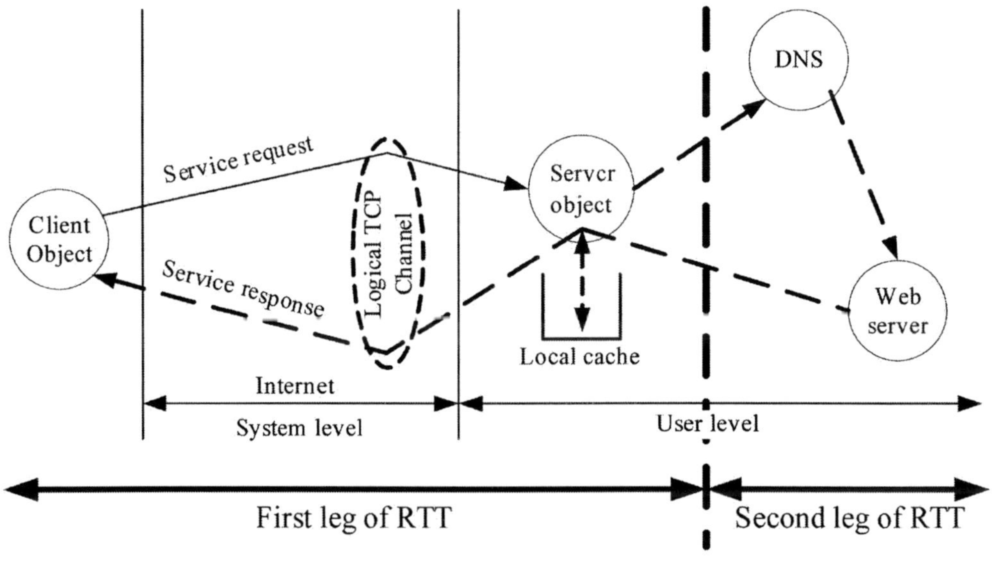

Figure 2.17. The relationship between the client and the proxy server.

There are many possible strategies for achieving a high cache hit ratio as illustrated by figure 2.16. These strategies can be divided into two categories: a) static size caching in a traditional manner, and b) *dynamic caching size* caching in which the cache is changed adaptively on the fly. The main difference is that static size caching, which uses a fixed-size cache, can produce a high hit ratio under certain conditions, but may not necessarily maintain it. In contrast, the dynamic caching size approach maintains a given hit ratio under all operational conditions. This approach can work with any replacement strategies, which push out relatively "colder" data objects from the cache to make room for the new, hot incoming ones. At this moment, the only published framework for dynamic cache size tuning is the MACSC (Model for Adaptive Cache Size Control) [WMW2003], the details of which will be presented in Chapter 5.

Static size caching can be divided into three main categories [Podlipnig2003] that address different issues, as shown in figure 2.16: a) infrastructure related issues such as caching architectures, caching routing, and proxy placement; b) content related issues such as prefetching, replacement strategies, cache coherency, and caching contents; and c) others that include user access pattern prediction, dynamic data caching, and web traffic characteristics. Normally, the overall average service roundtrip time (RTT) in information retrieval consists of the average RTT_1 for the first leg and average RTT_2 for the second; $RTT=RTT_1+RTT_2$. As shown in figure 2.17, if the requested data can be found in the proxy server's cache then $RTT_2=0$ holds. Locating the requested data object in a remote web server involves the Internet Domain Name Server (DNS) and data transfer over the open Internet. This usually makes RTT_2 much larger than RTT_1. The speedup produced by installing a cache in the proxy server can be depicted by the following example. Assuming $RTT_2 = 10RTT_1$, the speedup S by a cache of hit ratio 0.6 (60%) is:

$$S = {(RTT_1 + RTT_2)} \Big/ {[RTT_1 + (1-0.6) * RTT_2)} = 11 \Big/ (1+4) = 2.2$$

The fringe benefit, in addition to the information retrieval speedup, is less data to be transferred across the network. As a result, backbone bandwidth is freed for public sharing, and this reduces the chance of network congestion.

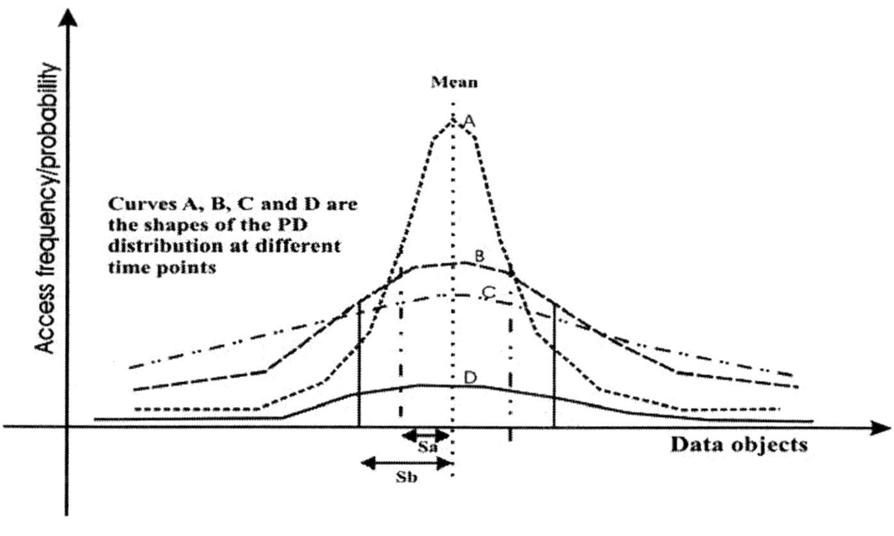

Figure 2.18. Relative popularity of a data set at three different time points.

The main difference with dynamic cache size tuning is that it succeeds in both objectives: yielding *and* maintaining a high cache hit ratio in a dynamic manner. It also accommodates any replacement algorithms in principle. The aim of replacement is to keep as many hot data objects in the cache as possible. Replacement strategies are usually either LRU (least recently used) or LFU (least frequently used) based. The problem of a fixed-size cache is that it cannot accommodate changes in the relative popularity among the data objects. This popularity changes with time and can be expressed in terms of the data object access frequencies. Figure 2.18 shows the access frequencies for the same set of data at three different time points (A, B, and C). The highest access frequency is the centre point.

From figure 2.18, it becomes obvious that one needs the right cache size to yield a hit ratio within one standard deviation. Using a fixed-size cache to match the standard deviation Sa yields a lower hit ratio when the standard deviation has changed to Sb in a dynamic manner. If the cache size can be adjusted to ensure "one standard deviation" (assumed) on the fly, it is dynamic cache size tuning. This is the rationale of the MACSC tuner. In fact, extant techniques for static cache size have the following weaknesses:

a) Hit ratio fluctuation: Since the cache size cannot cope with certain situations the hit ratio drops steeply and suddenly.
b) Heavy parameterization: The most researched topic in caching is replacement strategy. The previous strategies may become very complicated if they leverage too many parameters such as workload, recency, and relative object popularity [Jin2000a, Jin2000b]. Heavy parameterization is counterproductive because of its long computing time. The real problem may disappear by the time the remedy is computed. Using the out-dated remedy to correct a spurious problem would produce deleterious/undesirable effects.
c) Internet traffic: The extant caching strategies from the literature do not take the Internet traffic ill effects into account. This is dangerous because the Internet traffic patterns can change suddenly and cause system failures [Paxson1995].

2.10. Stifling Buffer Overflow

This is the eighth effective way to harness the Internet RTT. Buffer is a precious memory resource because it enables a system to work smoothly. It is a must in data communication because data need to be held before they can be transferred from one location to another. Client/server interaction over a TCP channel always involves buffering activities at both the system/router and user levels. For example, the request for an information retrieval service from a client to the server usually waits in the server's queue, which is housed in a buffer space. The server may select any of the requests in the queue to serve according to the predefined scheduling strategy. In fact, before a request has reached the logical server, it would have been relayed from one router to another, inevitably being temporarily queued in the forwarding path of different intermediary routers' queue buffers before it reaches its destination. This path is event-driven and this makes it an operational path of the routing stochastic process. Figure 2.19 shows that client interaction over a sizeable network such as the Internet always carries an error probability ρ, which implies retransmissions [LWD2005].

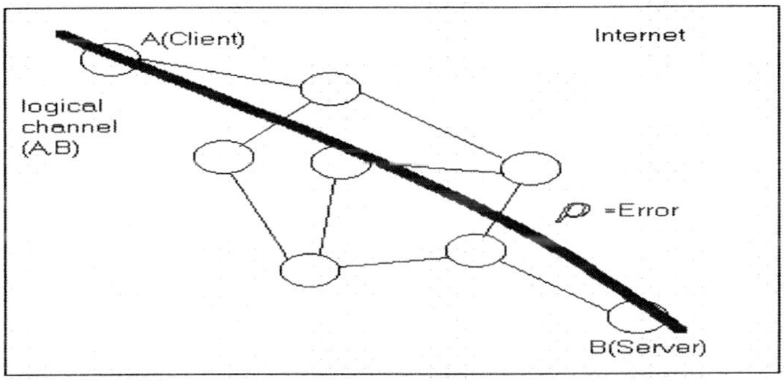

Figure 2.19. Client/server interaction over a logical channel of error probability ρ.

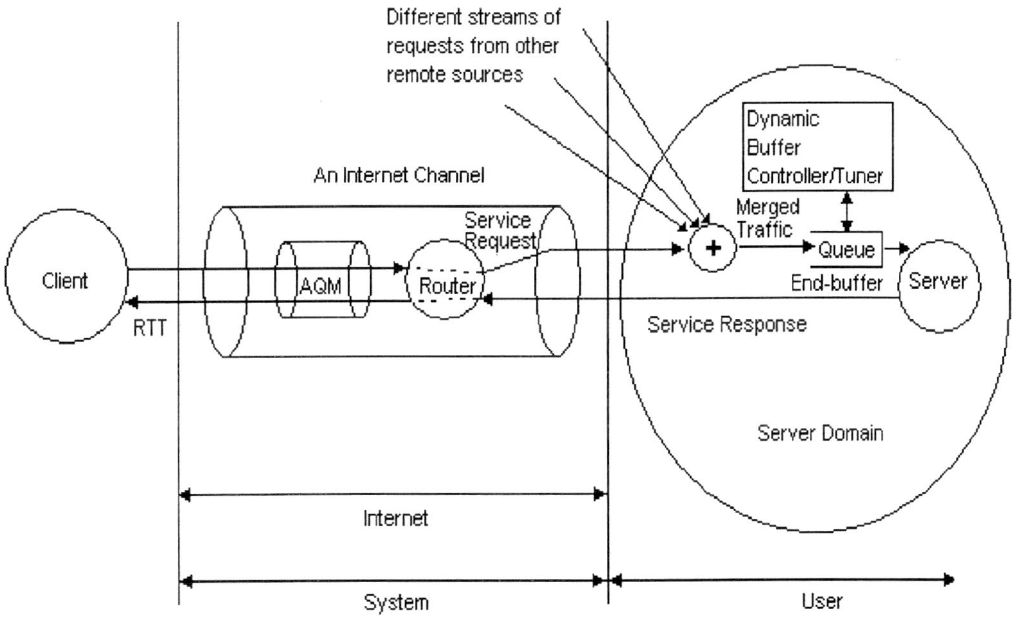

Figure 2.20. End-to-end logical channel between client and server.

Figure 2.20 shows both the system/router and user levels in the transmission operation. The AQM (active queue management) mechanism in the router throttles the sender to slow down transmission to prevent the router from being congested and becoming a bottleneck. If the throttling action fails, the router drops packets in a predefined manner (e.g. random early discard [Floyd1993]). The incoming packets may be discarded in a drop-in-front fashion to quicken retransmissions. The client/server interaction is an asymmetric rendezvous in which one server serves many clients simultaneously. The request streams of various traffic patterns from different clients merge at the server queue buffer (i.e. end-buffer) to create a massive input traffic influx with an unpredictable pattern. This influx can inundate the end-buffer to create widespread retransmissions unless a dynamic buffer controller/tuner exists to temporarily adjust the buffer length on the fly and ensure that buffer length always covers the queue length. This capability is called dynamic buffer size tuning [Wong2002GAC, LWD2005], which is a novel means of eliminating buffer overflow at the user level. As a result, it reduces the overall channel error probability ρ for less retransmissions and thus better service RTT.

In the sphere of pervasive computing, the contribution of dynamic buffer size tuning to better system performance is significant. A pervasive computing system is basically a distributed one with two additional capabilities. It:

a) Supports client mobility: This is achieved by applying the location-aware technologies for clients such as the small-form-factor (SFF) devices (e.g. PDA, mobile phone, etc.) carried by human travellers. The important notion of mobility is that the client in one wireless cell makes a request to a remoter server for service and then switches itself off. After this client has moved to a new wireless cell, the server locates it and returns the service result.
b) Tracks the client's intent: The server can sense the user's intent and renders the service result immediately usable. For example, the client has requested the server to retrieve an English document. Since the server senses that the client is going to France, it returns the retrieved document and prepares two copies: one in English and another in French.

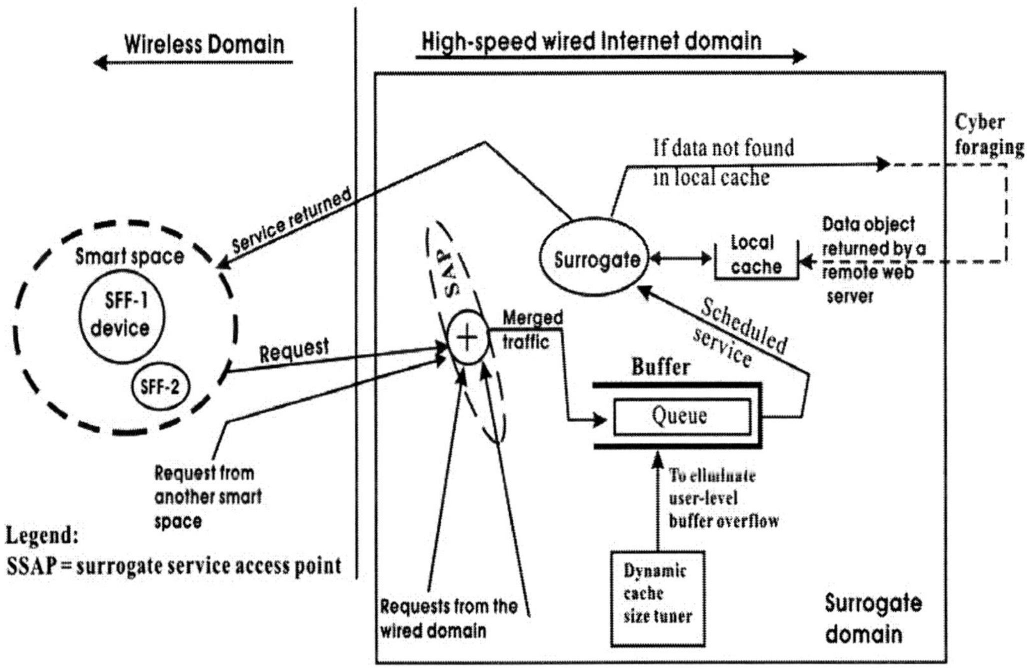

Figure 2.21. Interaction between a SFF device (client) and a surrogate.

The ability of a logical entity to always track the user's intent correctly is still far-fetched, and that is why pervasive computing is very much in the experimental stage. So far, there are only a few such experimental systems, including the Aura by Carnegie-Mellon University and the Oxygen by MIT in the USA. Figure 2.21 shows a pervasive computing environment for information retrieval. It consists of two major components: the wireless smart space and the pervasive computing infrastructure (PCI). The PCI assigns a special node, called the surrogate, to serve a specific smart space. Since the surrogate provides an information retrieval service to the SFF clients, it maintains a cache and a request queue. If the surrogate finds the requested information in the local cache, it returns it right away. Otherwise, it enlists other nodes in the PCI to help find the needed data, through a process called cyber foraging [Garlan2002]. Let's assume a Markovian system view in which the surrogate works as a M/M/1 model and cyber foraging has utilized the distributed parallelism in the PCI and produced a potential speedup of $S_{cyber} = \frac{[1-(\varsigma/n)]}{(1-\varsigma)}$, where ς is the system utilization in the PCI domain [Lewis1996]. If the surrogate does not have dynamic buffer size tuning support, then its buffer overflow would greatly diminish the advantage provided by cyber foraging because those requests lost in the overflows do not have the chance to reap the S_{cyber} speedup benefits.

2.11. SUMMARY

Moore's Law forecast that the network bandwidth would increase much faster than the hardware speed, which has reached the limit of physics – the speed of light. The forecast anticipated that the hardware speed improvement (without parallelism) would cease in mid-2000. After that, any further speedup gain can only be obtained from distributed parallelism, which has the ultimate goal of $RTT_{ac} = RTT_a * N^0$. Achieving this goal, however, cannot depend solely on bandwidth technology because many factors can seriously delay RTT_{ac}. Examples of delays include partial hardware failures in the network, congested processors and communication channels. Other accessory approaches become necessary in order to successfully reap the benefits of the network bandwidth improvement process. This chapter provides a concise description of how various useful methods have been proposed to assist in the process. These methods include the following: scheduling, sharing dependable links, fair bandwidth usage, transmitting multiple copies of the same message, neutralizing traffic effects in a real-time manner, preventing denial of service attacks, caching, and stifling buffer overflow. The rest of this book will concentrate on discussing three related, novel issues, namely, dynamic buffer size control, dynamic cache size control and real-time traffic pattern detection. By addressing these issues successfully, network congestion would be reduced and application timeliness over the Internet would be improved.

2.12. KEY REFERENCES

[AJWong2001] Allan K.Y. Wong and Joseph H.C. Wong, A Convergence Algorithm for Enhancing the Performance of Distributed Applications Running on Sizeable Networks,

The International Journal of Computer Systems, Science and Engineering, 16(4), July 2001, 229-236

[Alex2001] Alex Ma, Skitter, http://wwwdev.caida.org/tools/measurement/skitter/index.xml, 2001

[Amp1] Active Measurements, http://watt.nlanr.net/active//

[Amp1999] Monitoring for the NLANR Active Measurement Program, http://www-iepm.slac.stanford.edu/monitoring/amp/, June 1999

[Anjum1999] F.M. Anjum, L. Tassiulas, Balanced-RED: An Algorithm to Achieve Fairness in the Internet, *Infocom* 1999, March 1999

[Bennet1997] J.C. Bennet and H. Zhang, Hierarchical Packet Fair Queuing Algorithms, *IEEE/ACM Transactions on Networking,* 5(5), October 1997

[Bharat] Bharat and A. Broder, Measuring the Web, http://www.research.digital.com /SRCwhatsnew/sem.html

[Braden1998] Braden et.al, Recommendations on Queue Management and Congestion Avoidance in the Internet, *RFC 2309,* April 1998

[Brakmo1994] L. Brakmo, S. O'Malley and L. Peterson, TCP Vegas: New Techniques for Congestion Detection and Avoidance, *Proc. of the ACM SIGCOMM,* 1994

[CERT] http://www.cert.org/advisories/CA-1996-21.html, CERT Coordination Center, Software Engineering Institute, Carnegie Mellon University

[Chatranon2004] G. Chatranon, M.A. Labrador and S. Banerjee, A Survey of TCP-friendly Router-Based AQM Schemes, *Computer Communications,* v. 27, 2004

[cisco] Strategies to protect against distributed denial of service (DDoS) attacks, http://www.cisco.com/warp/public/707/newsflash.html

[Cottrel1999] L. Cottrel, M. Zekauskas, H. Uijterwaal and T. McGregor, Comparison of Some Internet Active End-to-End Performance Measurement Projects, http://www.slac.stanford.edu/comp/net/wan-mon/iepm-cf.html, 1999

[Cottrel2001] L. Cottrel, Passive vs. Active Monitoring, http://www.slac.stanford.edu/comp /net/wan-mon/passive-vs-active.html, March 2001

[Demers1995] A. Demers, S. Keshav and S. Shenkar, Analaysis and Simulation of a Fair Queuing Algorithm, *ACM Computer Communication Review,* 25(1), January 1995

[Fan2000] Li Fan, Pei Cao, Jussara M. Almeida, Andrei Z. Broder: Summary cache: a scalable wide-area web cache sharing protocol. *IEEE/ACM Transactions on Networking,* 2000, 8(3), 281-293

[Floyd1993] S. Floyd and V. Jacobson, Random Early Detection Gateways for Congestion Avoidance, *IEEE/ACM Transactions on Networking,* 1(4), August 1993, 397-413

[Floyd1995] S. Floyd and V. Jacobson, Link-sharing and resource Management Models for Packet Network, *IEEE/ACM Transactions on Networking,* 3(4), August 1995

[Floyd1999] S. Floyd and K. Fall, Promoting the Use of End-to-End Congestion Control in the Internet, *IEEE/ACM Transactions Networking.* 7(4), 1999

[Garlan2002] D. Garlan, D. P. Siewiorek, A. Smailagic and P. Steenkiste, Project Aura: Toward Distraction-free Pervasive Computing, *IEEE Pervasive Computing,* 1(2), April 2002, 22 – 31

[Gartner1999] F. Gartner, *Fundamentals of Fault-tolerant Distributed Computing in Asynchronous Environments, ACM computing surveys,* 31(1), March 1999, 1-26

[Han1998] S. Han and K.G. Shin, A Primary-Backup Channel Approach to Dependability Real-Time Communication in Multihop Networks, *IEEE Transactions on Computers,* 47(1), January 1998

[Hwang1985] K. Hwang and F.A. Briggs, *Computer Architecture and Parallel Processing,* McGraw Hill, 1985

[Ip2001]May T.W. Ip, Wilfred W.K. Lin, Allan K.Y. Wong, Tharam S. Dillon and Dian Hui Wang, An Adaptive Buffer Management Algorithm for Enhancing Dependability and Performance in Mobile-Object-Based Real-time Computing, *Proc. of the IEEE ISORC'2001,* Magdenburg, Germany, May 2001, 138-144

[Ip2002] Allan K.Y. Wong, May T.W. Ip and Tharam S. Dillon, M^3RT: An Internet End-to-End Performance Measurement Approach for Real-Time Applications with Mobile Agents, *Proc. of the ISPAN''002,* 2002, 119-124

[Jacobson1988] V. Jacobson, Congestion Avoidance and Control, *Proc. of the ACM SIGCOMM'88 Conference,* 1988

[Jacobson1990] V. Jaconson, Berkeley TCP Evolution from 4.3-Tahoe to 4.3-Reno, Proc. of the 18th Internet Engineering Task Force, 1990

[Jain1992] R. Jain, The Art of Computer Systems Performance Analysis, Techniques for Experimental Design, Measurement, Simulation, and Modeling, Wiley, 1992

[Jain1999] R. Jain, A. Durresi and G. Babic, Throughput Fairness Index: An Explanation, ATM Forun/99-0045

[Jensen1985] E. D. Jensen, C. D. Locke, and H. Tokuda, A Time-Driven Scheduling Model for Real-Time Operating Systems, *Proc. of IEEE real-Time Systems Symposium,* 1985

[Jin2000a] S. Jin and A. Bestavros, Popularity-Aware Greedy Dual-Size Web Proxy Caching Algorithms, Proceedings of the Int'l Conf. on Distributed Computing Systems, 2000

[Jin2000b] S. Jin, and A. Bestavros, Temporal Locality in Web Request Streams: Sources, Characteristics, and Caching Implications, *Proc. of the International Conference on Measurement and Modeling of Computer Systems*, 2000

[Jonckheere2002] E. Jonckheere, K. Shah and S. Bohacek, Dynamic Modeling of Internet Traffic for Intrusion Detection, *Proceedings of the 2002 American Control Conference,* Volume 3, 8-10 May 2002, 2436 - 2442

[Karp1975] R.M. Karp, *On the Computational Complexity of Combinatorial Problems, Networks,* 5(1), January 1975

[Karray2002] F. Karray, W. Gueaieb, and S. Al-Sharhan, "The hierarchical expert fining of PID controllers using tools of soft computing," *IEEE Trans. Systems, Man, and Cybernetics,* Part B, vol. 32, no. 1, February 2002, 77-90

[Kim1998] W.J. Kim and B.G. Lee, FRED-fair random early detection algorithm for TCP over ATM networks, *Electronics Letters,* 34(2), January 1998, pp.152-154

[Kim2001] J. Kim and K.G. Shin, Performance Evaluation of Dependable Real-Time Communication with Elastic QoS, *Proc. of the IEEE DSN2001 Conference, 2001*

[Knadlur1994] D.D. Kandlur, K.G. Shin and D. Ferrari, Real-Time Communication in Multi-hop Networks, *IEEE Transactions on Parallel and Distributed Systems,* 5(10), October 1994

[Krishna2003] G.P. Krishna, M.J. Pradeep and C. Siva Ram Murthy, A Segmented Backup Scheme for Dependable Real-Time Communication in Multihop Networks, *IEEE/ACM Transactions on Networks,* 11(1), February 2003

[Krishnamurthy2002] R. Krishnamurthy, S. Yalamanchili, K. Schwan, R. West and M. Rosu, Architecture and Hardware for Scheduling Gigabit Packet Streams, *Proc. of the 10th IEEE Conference on High-Performance Interconnects,* August 2002

[Lakshman1996] T. Lakshman, A. Neidhardt, and T. Ott, The Drop from Front Strategy in TCP over ATM and its Interworking with other Control Features, *Proc. INFOCOM'96,* 1242-1250

[Lewis1996] T. Lewis, The Next 10000_2 Years: Part 1, *IEEE Computer,* April 1996

[Lin2004] Wilfred W. K. Lin, Richard S.L. Wu Allan K. Y. Wong, and Tharam S. Dillon, A Novel Real-Time Traffic Pattern Detector for Internet Applications, Proc. of the Australasian Telecommunication Networks and Applications Conference, Sydney, Australia (ATNAC'04), Dec 2004, 221 227

[Locke1986] C.D. Locke, Best-Effort Decision Making for real-Time Scheduling, Ph.D. Thesis, Department of Computing, Department of Computer Science, Carnegie Mellon University, *CMUCS-86-134,* 1986

[LWD2005] Wilfred W.K. Lin, Allan K.Y. Wong and Tharam S. Dillon, Application of Soft Computing Techniques to Adaptive User Buffer Overflow Control on the Internet, *IEEE Transactions on Systems, Man and Cybernetics,* Part C, 2005

[Mah2001] Bruce A. Mah, http://www.mirrors.wiretapped.net/security/network-mapping/pchar

[Mathis] M. Mathis, J. Mahdavi, S. Floyd and A. Romanov, *TCP Selective Acknowledgement Options, RFC 2018*

[Matt2000] Warren Matthews and Les Cottrell, The PingER Project: Active Internet Performance Monitoring for the HENP Community, *IEEE Communications Magazine,* May 2000, 2-8

[Matt2001] Warren Matthews, Les Cottrell and Davide Salomoni, Passive and Active Monitoring on a High Performance Research Network, Presented at Passive and Active Monitoring (PAM) 2001, Amsterdam, The Netherlands, April 2001

[Medina2000] A Medina, I Matta and J. Byers, On the Orgiin of Pwer Laws in Internet Topologies, *ACM SIGCOMM Computer Communication Review,* 18-28, 2000

[Millis1995] D.L. Mills, Improved Algorithms for Synchronizing Computer Network Clocks, *IEEE/ACM Transactions on Networking,* 3(3), June 1995, 245-254

[Molnár1999] S. Molnár, T.D. Dang and A. Vidács, Heavy-Tailedness, Long-Range Dependence and Self-Similarity in Data Traffic, Proceedings of 7th International Conference on Telecommunication Systems, Modelling and Analysis, March 1999, Nashville, USA, 18-21

[Ott1999] T. J. Ott, T. V. Lakshman, and L. H. Wong, SRED: Stabilized RED, *Proceedings IEEE INFOCOM '99,* New York, March 1999

[Padhye1998] J. Padhye, V. Firoiu, D. Towsley and J. Kurose, Modeling TCP throughput: A Simple and Its Empirical Validation, *Proc. of the ACM SIGCOMM'98,* 1998

[Pan1999] R. Pan, B. Prabhakar and K. Psounis, CHOKe, A Stateless Active Queue Management Scheme for Approximating Fair Bandwidth Allocation. *Proc of INFOCOM,* March 2000

[Paxson1995] V. Paxson, S. Floyd, Wide area traffic: The Failure of Poisson Modeling, *IEEE/ACM Transactions on Networking,* 3(3), 1995

[Paxson1997] V. Paxson, End-to-End Internet Packet Dynamics, ACM SIGCOMM, *Computer Communication Review,* 27(4), October 1997

[Podlipnig2003] S. Podlipnig and L. Böszörményi, A Survey of Web Cache Replacement Strategies, *ACM Computing Surveys,* 35(4), December 2003, 374 – 398

[Ramanathan1992] P. Ramanathan, Delivery of Time-Critical Messages Using a Multiple Copy Approach, *ACM Transactions on Computer Systems,* 10(2), 1992

[RFC768] J. Postel, User Datagram Protocol, *RFC 768,* August 1980

[RFC896] J. Nagle, Congestion Control in IP/TCP Internetworks, *RFC896,* January 1984

[Ryu1996] B.K. Ryu and S.B. Lowen, Point process approaches to the modeling and analysis of self-similar traffic .I. Model construction, Proc. of the 15th Annual Joint Conference of the IEEE Computer Societies - *Networking the Next Generation.* Vol. 3, March 1996, 1468 - 1475

[Shin2000] K.G. Shin, C.C. Cjou and S.K. Kweon, Distributed Route Selection for Establishing Real-Time Channels, *IEEE Transactions on Parallel and Distributed Systems,* 11(3), March 2000

[Stankovic1998] J.A. Stankovic et al, *Deadline Scheduling for Real-Time Systems*, Kluwer Publishers, 1998

[Stankovic1998] J.A. Stankovic, M. Spuri, K. Ramamritham and G.C. Buttazzo, *Deadline Scheduling for Real-Time Systems – EDF and Related Algorithms,* Kluwer, 1998

[Stevens2001] W. Stevens, TCP Slow Start, Congestion Avoidance, fast Transmit, and Fast Recovery, *IETF RFC 2001,* 2001

[Sunil1999] Sunil Kalidindi and Matthew J. Zekauskas, Surveyor: An Infrastructure for Internet Performance Measurements, *INET'99,* San Jose, June 1999

[Taqqu2003] M.S. Taqqu, Fractional Brownian Motion and Long-Range Dependence, in Theory and Applications of Long-Range Dependence, P. Doukhan et al., Eds., Birkhuser 2003, 5-38

[VTune2002] Intel's VTune Performance Analyzer, http://ww.intel.com/support/performancetools/vtune/v5

[Wang2004] J. Wang and B. Ravindran, Time-Utility Function-Driven Switched Ethernet: Packet Scheduling Algorithm, Implementation and Feasibility Analysis, *IEEE Transactions on Parallel and Distributed Systems,* 15(2), February, 2004

[Wang2004] J. Wang, B. Ravindran, Time-Utility Function-Driven Switched Ethernet: Packet Scheduling Algorithm, Implementation, and Feasibility Analysis, *IEEE Transactions on Parallel and Distributed Systems,* 15(2), February 2004

[Wang99] J. Wang, A Survey of Web Caching Schemes for the Internet, *ACM Computer Communication Review,* 29(5), 1999, 36 – 46

[Willinger2003] W. Willinger, V. Paxson, R.H. Hiedi and M.S. Taqqu, Long-Range Dependence and Data Network Traffic, in *Theory and Applications of Long-Range Dependence,* P. Doukhan et al., Eds., Birkhuser 2003, 373-408

[WLin2005] Wilfred W. K. Lin, Allan K. Y. Wong, and Tharam S. Dillon, A Novel R^2-FLC Dynamic Buffer Size Tuner to Support Time-Critical Applications over the Internet by Improving Logical Channel Fault Tolerance, Proc. of the 11th International Symposium on Pacific Rim Dependable Computing (PRDC'2005), Changsha, PRC, August, 2005

[WMW2003] Allan K. Y. Wong, May T. W. Ip, Richard S. L. Wu, A Novel Dynamic Cache Size Adjustment Approach for Better Data Retrieval Performance over the Internet, *Journal of Computer Communication,* September 2003, 26(14), 1709-1720

[Wong1999] Allan K.Y. Wong and Joseph H.C. Wong, A Convergence Algorithm to Help Enhance the Performance of Distributed Systems on Large Networks, *Proc. of the 1999*

International Symposium on Parallel Architectures, Algorithms, and Networks (I-Span'99), Fremantle Australia, June 1999, 302-307

[Wong1999] Allan K.Y. Wong and Tharam S. Dillon, A Fault-Tolerant Data Communication Setup to Improve Reliability and Performance for Internet-Based Distributed Applications, the Proceedings of the 1999 Pacific Rim International Symposium on Dependable Computing (PRDC'99), December 1999, Hong Kong (SAR), P.R. China

[Wong2000] Allan K.Y. Wong and Tharam S. Dillon, A Fault Tolerant Model to Attain Reliability and High Performance for Distributed Computing over the Internet, *Journal of Computer Communications,* vol. 23, 2000

[Wong2001A] A.K.Y. Wong and J.H.C. Wong, A Convergence Algorithm for Enhancing the Performance of Distributed Applications Running on Sizeable Networks, International *Journal of Computer Systems Science and Engineering,* 16(4), July 2001, 229-236

[Wong2001B] Allan K.Y. Wong, Tharam S. Dillon, Wilfred K.W. Lin and May T.W. Ip, M^2RT: A Tool Developed for Predicting the Mean Message Response Time for Internet Channels, *Computer Networks* 36(2001), 557-577

[Wu2003] C.H. Wu, D.C. Su, J. Chang, C.C. Wei, K.J. Lin and J.M. Ho, The Design and Implementation of Intelligent Transportation Web Services, *IEEE International Conference on E-Commerce* (CEC 2003), 24-27 June 2003, pp.49-52

[Wu2004] Richard S.L. Wu, Allan K.Y. Wong and Tharam S. Dillon, RDCT: A Novel Reconfigurable Dynamic Cache Size Tuner to Shorten Information Retrieval Time over the Internet, *International Journal of Computer Systems, Science and Engineering,* 19(6), 2004, pp. 363-372

[Zhang1993] L. Zhang, S. Deering, D. Estrin, S. Shenker and D. Zappala, RSVP: A New Resource Reservation protocol, *IEEE Network,* vol. 7, September 1993

[Zhu2001] K. Zhu, Y. Zhuang and Y. Viniotis, Achieving End-to-End Delay Bounds by EDF Scheduling without Traffic Shaping, *Proc. of IEEE Infocom2001,* April 2001

Chapter 3

REAL-TIME TRAFFIC PATTERN DETECTION AND ITS IMPORTANCE

3.1. INTRODUCTION

Applications running over a large network such as the Internet are naturally object-based. The logical entities that make up an application interact in a client/server relationship by message passing [Lewandowski1998]. In such a relationship over the Internet channel, as shown in figure 3.1, the channel performance is characterized by the service roundtrip time (RTT), which is alternatively known as the response time (W). RTT or W is the interval/delay from the service request initiation by the client to the point when the result is correctly returned.

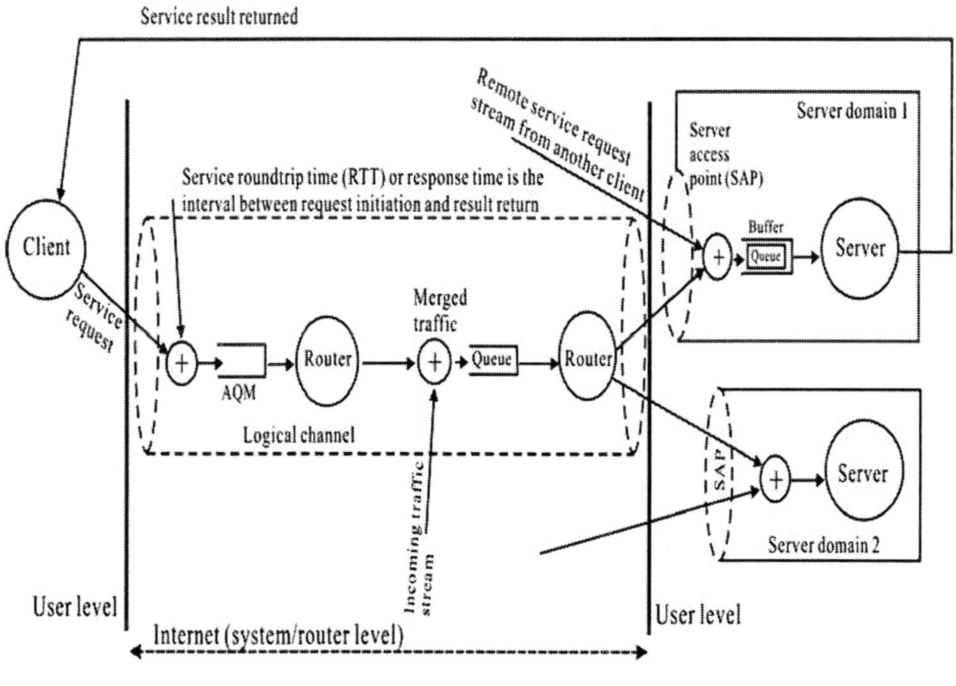

Figure 3.1. Client/server interaction over the Internet.

Figure 3.1 also summarizes the activities inside the logical TCP (Transmission Control Protocol), which include routing the request by one router to another and active queue management (AQM) by each router. Every router receives routing requests from other collaborating routers in the system as well; therefore, the traffic into a router's queue buffer results in a merged and unpredictable pattern at any time. These traffic patterns could be short-range dependence (SRD) (e.g. Markovian) and long-range dependence (LRD) (e.g. heavy-tailed and self-similar) [Molnár1999]. From the user point of view, this client/server interaction is outside the domain of the TCP channel. But in reality, the system and user levels together form the end-to-end (EE) communication path.

AQM (in figure 3.1) is a throttling mechanism used by the server to prevent its local buffer from being congested. The first step is to throttle the sender (i.e. the client) by "choke packets" that ask the sender to voluntarily lower its transmission rate. The second step involves dropping either the incoming packets or some of those in the queue [Lakshman1996, Lakshman1997]. Some of the AQM strategies such as the BLACK [Chatranon2004] even arbitrate fair bandwidth usage between the responsive (to throttling) TCP traffic and the unresponsive UDP (User Datagram Protocol). The UDP is unresponsive because it has no mechanism for detecting congestion and signalling the sender to be throttled. The bandwidth saved by TCP throttling would be usurped by UDP. Gradually, the TCP operations wither due to bandwidth starvation and eventually falter. UDP is widely used in multimedia applications such as video stream transmissions, while TCP is the main support for applications such TELNET and FTP.

The merged traffic is indicated by the $\oplus$ symbol in figure 3.1. The client/server relationship is *asymmetric rendezvous*, which means that one server serves different clients simultaneously. It is inevitable that a popular server would receive many different streams of remote requests. Since these streams would assume different inter-arrival time (IAT) traffic patterns (e.g. SRD and LRD) at any time, the resultant merged traffic pattern would be unpredictable. The traffic pattern can affect the server performance in different ways. For example, it may cause a static size buffer to overflow in server domain 1 in figure 3.1. This can lead to widespread retransmissions and thus long service RTT, which is undesirable for time-critical applications. The buffer overflow problem can be resolved by using the technique of *dynamic buffer size tuning* [GAC2002], as long as the problem is not persistent. The tuning process ensures that the buffer length always covers the queue length on the fly. If a server has no buffering system (e.g. server domain 2), compensation measures may be needed to make the server operation immune to the ill effects of traffic. For example, in the RTPD/MACSC dynamic cache size maintaining system, the real-time traffic detection (RTPD) component enables the MACSC (model for adaptive cache size control) mechanism [Wu2004] to reconfigure with respect to the traffic pattern identified. In this way, the MACSC tuner adjusts the cache size on the fly to maintain the given cache hit ratio consistently even without a buffering system.

The type and volume of traffic on the Internet affect system performance in terms of throughput and stability in the light of delivering the expected outcome accurately. In order to ascertain this, we note that the RTT is a good indicator of channel performance because a lower average RTT means a higher throughput. On the contrary, a long average RTT implies problems such as router bottlenecks inside the logical channel. On this basis, the IEPM (Internet End-to-End Performance Measurement) school of thought arose [Cottrell1999,

Cottrel2001]. The aim is to monitor and gauge the channel behavior through the mean end-to-end RTT. The argument is that this is the only viable solution because it is impractical, if not impossible, to measure and leverage the overwhelming number of Internet parameters. There are two basic IEPM approaches:

a) Macro approach: The IEPM tool should be installed at both hosts/nodes that represent the two ends of the logical channel. The collected RTT samples reveal what happens inside the channel. Macro tools include AMP [Amp1, Amp99], pchar [Jacobson1997, Mah2001], PingER [Ping1999, Matt2000], Skitter [Alex2001], Surveyor [Sunil1999], and M^2RT [Wong01B].
b) Micro approach: The IEPM tool operates as a logical object that can be invoked for service anywhere and any time. The only known example from the literature is the M^3RT. Similar to its macro M^2RT counterpart, the M^3RT is the implementation of the Convergence Algorithm (CA) at the micro level.

The aim of IEPM is to provide some insight into the way the RTT changes over time for a communication channel. With this insight, the user can use correct measures to rectify the related problems. For example, an Internet application may include the M^3RT as part of its construct. Then this application can use it to measure the RTT between itself and all other collaborating object entities. If all these entities provide the same service, the application would choose the one with the shortest RTT. As a result, the whole execution time of the application is reduced. Meanwhile, it was observed that the system could fail under different traffic conditions. This is particularly so when the system is designed with a preconceived mathematical model in mind. For example, traditional systems, which are designed with the Poisson paradigm, can fail under the bombardments by heavy-tailed and self-similar traffic patterns [Paxson1995]. In general, there are two main areas of traffic analysis as follows:

a) Off-line traffic analysis (OTA): This involves statistical tools that are capable of identifying the traffic pattern embedded in a pre-collected trace. Then the user can correlate the detected traffic pattern and system problems in an after-the-fact manner.
b) Real-time (on-line) traffic analysis (RTA): The aim is to identify the traffic pattern embedded in an aggregate X^m in a stochastic process X on the fly. m is the block size (number of data points sampled) of the aggregate. If the RTA capability is integrated into an application, then the latter can use the detected result to reconfigure and ward off the traffic's ill effects on its performance. Systems that make use of the RTA for successful on-line reconfigurations include the RTPD/MACSC and the RTPD/FLC. The FLC (Fuzzy Logic Controller) is a real-time dynamic buffer size tuner that ensures that buffer length always covers the queue length to eliminate any chance of user-level buffer overflow.

In this chapter, we will first introduce the IEPM school of thought, examine the ill effects of traffic and explore two different approaches for traffic analysis, namely off-line traffic analysis and real-time traffic analysis.

3.2. THE IEPM (INTERNET END-TO-END PERFORMANCE MEASUREMENT) SCHOOL OF THOUGHT

Among the first groups of researchers that looked at the IEPM issue was the Stanford University team in the USA [Cottrel1999]. The objective was to statistically measure the mean service RTT (also called message response time) of a logical channel. An excessively long mean RTT is a telltale sign of a channel with problems such as the existence of a bottleneck on the end-to-end (EE) path and many retransmissions (i.e. large ANT (*average number of trails*) to get a transmission success). Subsequently, different IEPM tools such as PingER were proposed. There are two basic types of IEPM tools, categorized by their way of measuring the mean service RTT:

a) *Active*: The host (master) of a logical client sends out probes to all the collaborating hosts. From continuous communications with these probes, the master host can estimate the mean service RTT between itself and these hosts. These mean values would be updated continually.
b) *Passive*: The host of a client or the client itself would estimate the mean service RTT between the client and the logical server, without using any probes.

Traditionally, IEPM tools (e.g. the PingER and M^2RT) are *macro* in nature because the tool must be installed at two nodes that represent the ends of the EE path. Therefore, macro measurements entail human intervention. Contemporarily, an IEPM *micro* tool (e.g. Convergence Algorithm (CA), which is implemented in the M^3RT form) is achieved by converting the M^2RT tool into a logical object that can be invoked for service any time and anywhere by message passing. This tool is micro because it requires no human intervention at all and it is therefore suitable for real-time applications. The M^3RT (micro mean message response time) is the only known IEPM tool that is dedicated to real-time or time-critical applications over the Internet.

3.2.1. The Convergence Algorithm (CA)

The Convergence Algorithm or CA was invented and published by the research team in the Department of Computing, Hong Kong Polytechnic University (HK PolyU) [Wong01B]. The CA is based on the Central Limit Theorem and therefore its accuracy is independent of any waveforms, which include the IAT traffic patterns. The essence of CA can be summarized by the following equations, which were described in Chapter 2:

$$M_i = \frac{M_{i-1} + \sum_{j=1}^{j=F-1} m_j^i}{F} \text{.....(2.6.1)}; M_0 = m_{j=0}^{i=1} \text{....(2.6.2)}; i \geq 1$$

The parameter M_i is the mean of the distribution estimated for the time in which the *F* (*flush limit*) number of data samples is collected. Previous experience shows that F=14 yields the fastest convergence to the estimated mean. The other parameters are as follows: a) M_{i-1} is the feedback of the last estimated mean to the current estimation cycle, b) m_j^i is the jth sample in the ith M_i estimation cycle, $j = 1,2,3,(F-1)$, and c) M_0 is the first data sample when CA had first started. Figure 3.2 shows the M_i predicted by M^3RT over time and the RTT trace of the TCP channel between the HK PolyU and a remote university in Australia. In this case M_i always settles to the value of 480ms in the steady state. With the same trace, the M^3RT produces the same result. M^3RT and M^2RT which are both different implementations of the CA, have the same functionality except that the former is dedicated to real-time Internet applications and the latter is simply a macro measuring tool that requires human intervention.

Previous experience shows that the implementations based on the Convergence Algorithm (e.g. M^2RT and M^3RT) could outperform other existing macro IEPM tools. The differences in performance can be attributed to the following:

a) The feedback loop, namely, M_{i-1} in the M_i (equation (2.6.1).
b) The simplicity of the M_i computation.
c) The fact that the CA is based on the Central Limit Theorem makes its accuracy independent of any types of traffic waveforms.

Figure 3.3 compares the performance between the PingER, which does not have a feedback loop, and the M^2RT CA implementation. The latter outperforms the former in both accuracy and convergence smoothness.

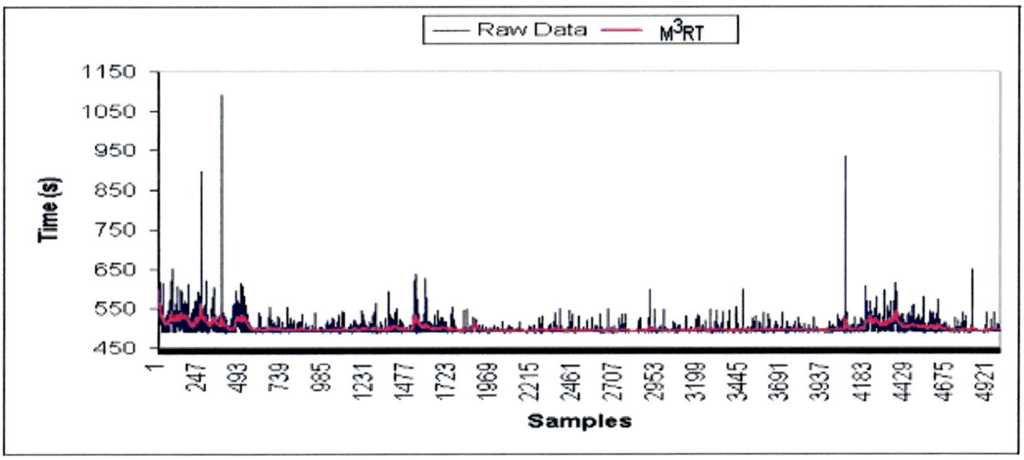

Figure 3.2. M_i predicted by M^3RT for the "HK PolyU – LaTrobe" TCP channel.

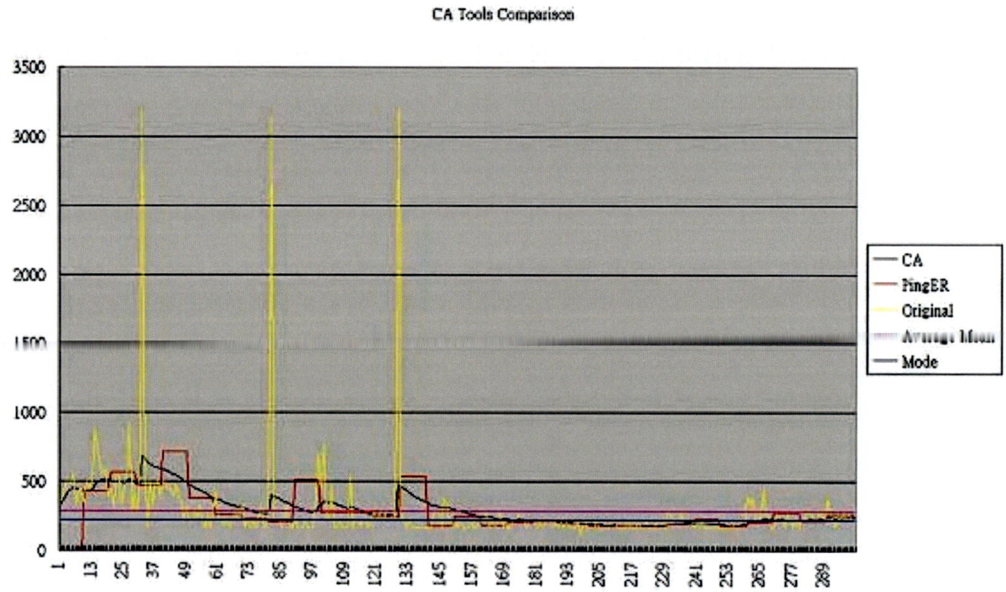

Figure 3.3 Comparing PingER and M[2]RT performance.

3.3. POSSIBLE ILL EFFECTS OF INTERNET TRAFFIC ON SYSTEM STABILITY AND PERFORMANCE

Recent research results indicate that the Internet traffic pattern changes over time, for example, from being Markovian (e.g. Poisson) to fractal (e.g. heavy-tailed and self-similar) or vice versa. Subsequently, different theories have been proposed to explain and characterize the Internet traffic patterns. These theories are built on the concept of stationarity in the *continuous domain* dictated by the exponential mathematical models (i.e. exponential function with the e^{-at} factor). The following terms/statements are useful for understanding Internet traffic analysis:

a) *Stationarity*: A process is stationary if its increments in the time window of interest are Gaussian (i.e. governed by the normal bell curve). That is, two data items separated by lag *k* are independent of each other. This Gaussian property is similar to the Poisson and binomial characteristics for different conditions. The stationarity of a time series is *strict* if for $t_n \, \varepsilon \, Z$ and $k \, \varepsilon \, Z$ the following holds: $F_{x_{t1},x_{t2},\ldots x_{tn}}(x_1,\ldots x_n) = F_{x_{t1+k},x_{t2+k},\ldots\ldots x_{tn+k}}(x_1,\ldots. x_n)$. This relationship is an indication of being memoryless or independent. Considering the *autocovariance* between two *x* variables of *lag k* apart, the stationarity could be "*weakly stationary*", "*second-order stationary*", "*covariance stationary*" or "*wide sense stationary*" since zero covariance still occasionally occurs for dependent variables that have non-zero covariance. This is a matter of whether the test satisfies the given confidence level (e.g. 90%) or not. The $\lim_{m\to\infty} r^m(k) = r(k)$ condition indicates an asymptotic phenomenon, m the aggregate size and $r^m(k)$ the autocorrelation function. The expression $r^{m\to\infty}(k)$ yields $r(k) = \frac{1}{2}[k+1)^{2H} - 2k^{2H} + (k-1)^{2H}$ for exact/strict self-similarity.

b) *Gaussianity*: A distribution is Gaussian provided that its *kurtosis* and *skewness* values equal 3 and 0 (i.e. the $\langle 3,0 \rangle$ pair) respectively. The Gaussian curve is in the continuous domain and therefore the ideal $\langle 3,0 \rangle$ pair seldom exists in real-life measurements because any measurement by "sampling data and then computation" is discrete in nature. This means that an approximation of the Poisson or binomial distribution/process by the Gaussian bell curve can be crude. The approximation possibility correlates the meanings of stationarity (Gaussian) and memoryless (Poisson and binomial).

c) *Discrete stochastic process*: A process is discrete if the data are obtained/measured at different distinct time points. When the measured data are collected into a single file, then it is a *data trace*. It is *stochastic* if it works by operation paths, and each path from beginning to end is event-driven (e.g. tracing a routing path in the Internet).

d) *Heavy-tailedness*: A heavy-tailed distribution F(x) is $1 - F(x) = x^{-\alpha} L(x)$, where L is varying slowly at infinity. The simplest case is the $F(x) = 1 - x^{-\alpha}$ Pareto distribution, where $L(x) \equiv 1$.

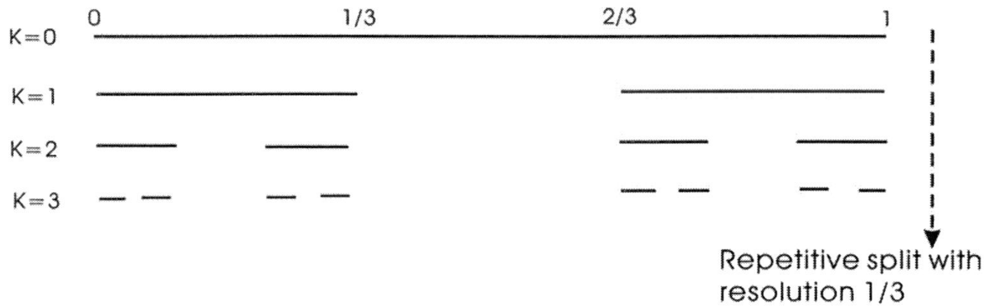

Figure 3.4. The Cantor set.

e) *Self-similarity (self-affinity)*: This means that an object can be geometrically, rotationally and recursively split into similar pieces. A simple view is that at the Kth iteration step the total measure of the object is the "*product of the number of geometrically similar pieces and* O^D". The parameter O is the splitting *resolution/reduction* and D the *similarity dimension* of the object. There should be a linear relationship between the number of similar pieces contained in the object and the measurement precision for a specific interval. For example, in the *Cantor Set* a line segment of interval [0,1] is drawn as the first step (i.e. $K = 0$) as shown in figure 3.4. This line is then manipulated by the subsequent steps: a) divide the line into three equal portions (i.e. *resolution* is $\frac{1}{3}$) and remove the middle portion (i.e. $K = 1$); b) remove the middle portion from the remaining two (i.e. $K = 2$); and c) repeat the last step *ad infinitum*. The Kth iteration produces 2^K similar line segments of length $s = (\frac{1}{3})^K$ each. The *Cantor Set's* (figure 3.5) self-similarity dimension is defined as $D = [\frac{(K\log(2))}{(K\log(3))}] \approx 0.63$. An object is fractal if its D value is non-integer. Different non-converging dimension definitions exist in the field and the *Cantor Set* is only one of them used here as an example. A stochastic process $X(t)$ is H_{ss} (i.e. Gaussian), self-similar and fractal, if its two finite-dimensional distributions $X(at)$ (i.e. frequency or time-scaled) and $a^H X(t)$ (i.e. amplitude-scaled) are identical for $a > 0$. That is, the following holds: $\{X(at_1), X(at_2)...X(at_n)\} \equiv \{a^H X(t_1),...a^H X(at_n)\}$; $\equiv$ means equality and the H value is the scaling *exponent*. The only known Gaussian, exactly self-similar process is the *fractional Brownian motion*, and its independent incremental process is the *fractional Gaussian noise*.

f) *Autocorrelation function (ACF) or correlogram*: This is the plot of the autocorrelation against the lag *k*. It can be written as $r^m(k)$, where *m* is the block size of the spatial aggregate X^m of a stochastic process X as shown in figure 3.5. The lag marks the distance between two variables. The auto-correlation between any two variables *k* apart from the time sequence/series is *derived* from their auto-covariance. The autocorrelation value has different indications: a) a negative value for the sequence, "high, low, high"; b) a positive value for the sequence, "high, high" or "low, low"; and c) zero for independent data points. "High" means a high-value data point and "low" for a low-value data point.

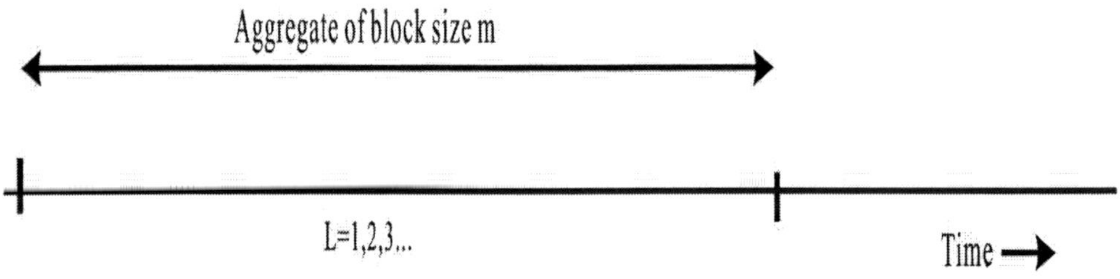

Figure 3.5. A time sequence/series and aggregate X^m of size m and lag $L \geq 1$.

g) *Hurst (H) exponent/value/factor/parameter*: The H range for SRD (short-range dependence) is $0 < H < 0.5$ and $0.5 < H < 1$ for LRD (long-range dependence). The value 0.5 represents white noise and is not used. There is a relationship between the ACF for *second-order stationarity* and the *H* value. Firstly, the ACF or $r^m(k)$ for LRD that includes heavy-tailed and self-similar waveforms is non-summable, as represented by $r^m(k) = \sum_{k=1}^{\infty} r_k^m = \infty$. Secondly, the ACF for SRD that includes Markovian distributions such as Poisson is summable (i.e. $r^m(k) = \sum_{k=1}^{\infty} r_k^m = C$, where C is a finite value). The calculation of H by the R/S (rescaled adjusted statistics) approach will be discussed later.

h) *Decaying variance property (DVP)*: One important LRD feature is the "*asymptotical send-order self-similarity*" defined by $r^m(k) \propto m^{-(2-2H)}$ for $m \to \infty$. It contains the following useful information: i) $Var(X^m) \propto m^{-\beta}$, ii) $\beta = 2 - 2H$ or $H = 1 - (\beta/2)$, and iii) $\log(Var(X^m)) = \log(Var(X)) - \beta \log(m)$ where β is the slope. The β value indicates the dimension of self-similarity cases. If it remains the same throughout the process, then the self-similarity is single/one dimensional (i.e. *monofractal*), otherwise it is multi-dimensional (i.e. *multifractal*). Figure 3.6 and figure 3.7 show how the β values for the LRD and SRD cases are found respectively by DVP. The R^2 (or coefficient of determination) value determines the quality of the linear regression; a higher R^2 value means a better regression. In these two plots, the y-axis "log (Variance)" is for $\log(Var(X^m))$.

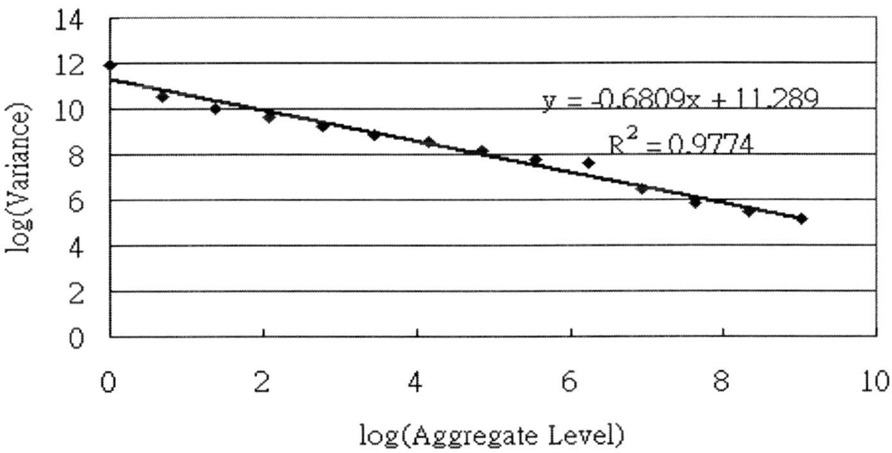

Figure 3.6. Slope = -0.6809(β= 0.6809), R^2= 97.74%.

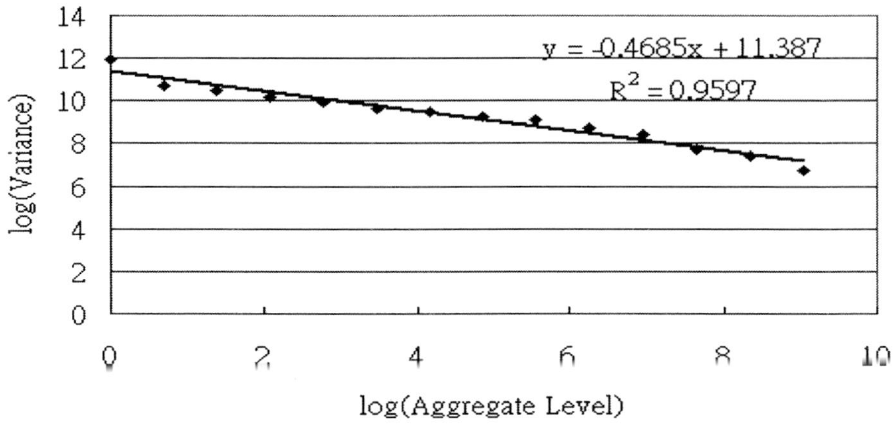

Figure 3.7. Slope = -0.4685(β= 0.4685), R^2= 95.97%.

The following example demonstrates how to apply autocorrelation to a time series to determine whether independence exists.

Example

Thirty-three end-to-end roundtrip time data points were sampled from a TCP interaction. These samples, in milliseconds, are listed in table 3.1. The Kolmogorov-Smirnov (K-S) auto-correlation test approach is used to decide if the autocorrelation value for $i = 2$, $m = 4$ and $\alpha = 0.1$ (i.e. 90% confidence) is indeed independent; i is the starting point of computation, m the block size for a lag, and $\pm Z_{\alpha/2}$ = ± 1.6 as the critical values for rejecting the hypothesis.

Table 3.1. Thirty-three (i.e. $N = 33$) end-to-end TCP roundtrip time samples

0.27	0.21	0.77	0.22	0.54	0.53	0.86	0.39	0.84	0.03	0.74
0.19	0.66	0.39	0.51	0.72	0.84	0.63	0.36	0.27	0.07	0.82
0.45	0.59	0.16	0.04	0.86	0.97	0.33	0.69	0.26	0.59	0.11

The *K-S* test is conducted as follows:

a) M+2 subsequence: For the time sequence of N samples the aggregates of block size m (or lag) are, $R_i, R_{i+m}, R_{i+2m}, \ldots R_{i+(M+1)m}$. The M value is the largest integer to satisfy the condition $[i + (M+1)m] \leq N$.

b) Test statistics: $Z_o = \frac{\rho_{im}}{\sigma_{\rho_{im}}}$, $\rho_{im} = \frac{1}{M+1}[\sum_{k=0}^{M} R_{i+km} R_{i+(k+1)m}] - 0.25$, and

$$\sigma_{\rho_{im}} = \frac{\sqrt{13M+7}}{12(M+1)}.$$

c) Hypothesis (it is independent) rejection: No rejection for $-Z_{\alpha/2} \leq Z_o \leq Z_{\alpha/2}$

The parameter ρ_{im} is the autocorrelation with respect to i and m, and σ_{im} is the Schmidt-Taylor standard deviation estimator. For $\rho_{im} > 0$ the positive correlation implies that successive values at lag *m* will have "high followed by high" and "low followed by low". In contrast, the negative autocorrelation $\rho_{im} < 0$ means "a low value would be followed by a high one", and vice versa. Although it is ideal to have zero autocorrelation for two independent variables, it is difficult to reach this condition exactly by statistics. The use of a confidence level for a hypothesis rejection, for example $\alpha = 0.1$ above, is a more realistic approach. The solution to the problem is as follows:

$i = 2$, $m = 4$ (i.e. every 4 numbers), and $\alpha = 0.1$

$[i + (M+1)m] \leq N$ implies $[2 + (M+1)4] \leq 30$ or $M = 6$

$$\rho_{im} = \frac{1}{M+1}[\sum_{k=0}^{M} R_{i+km} R_{i+(k+1)m}] - 0.25 \text{ implies}$$

$$\rho_{24} = \frac{1}{6+1}[\sum_{k=0}^{6} R_{i+km} R_{i+(k+1)m}] - 0.25 \Rightarrow$$

$$\rho_{24} = \frac{1}{6+1}[0.21 * 0.53 + 0.53 * 0.03 + 0.03 * 0.39 + 0.39 * 0.63 + 0.63 * 0.82 + 0.82 * 0.04 + 0.04 * 0.69] - 0.25 \approx -0.07$$

$$\sigma_{\rho_{im}} = \frac{\sqrt{13M+7}}{12(M+1)} \text{ implies } \sigma_{\rho_{24}} = \frac{\sqrt{13*6+7}}{12(6+1)} \approx 0.110$$

$$\therefore Z_o = \frac{\rho_{im}}{\sigma_{\rho_{im}}} \Rightarrow \frac{\rho_{24}}{\sigma_{\rho_{24}}} = \frac{-0.07}{0.11} = -0.636$$

$$\because \pm Z_{\alpha/2} = \pm 1.6$$

The condition $Z_{\alpha/2} < Z_o$ implies no rejection.

3.3.1. Off-Line Traffic Analysis (OTA)

Since the early 1990s, researchers began to realize that many system failures over the Internet were due to traffic problems. Eventually, some of them understood that systems could fail if they were designed with a preconceived mathematical model in mind (e.g. Poisson) [Paxson1995, Paxson1999] and were inspired to find the correlation between failures and traffic patterns. In the beginning, this was done mainly with pre-collected traffic traces and the analyses were conducted in a statistical manner. These activities represented *aftermath* understanding of the causes of failures. The OTA procedures are summarized in figure 3.8.

There are different OTA tools/methods that can process pre-collected traffic data traces. For example, the following statistical methods can achieve different goals [Molnar1999]:

a) Hurst value computation: R/S (rescaled adjusted statistics) and periodogram
b) Heavy-tailed distribution confirmation: modified QQ-plot, Hill-method, and De Haan's moment
c) Self-similar waveform testing: variance-time plot and Whittle estimator.

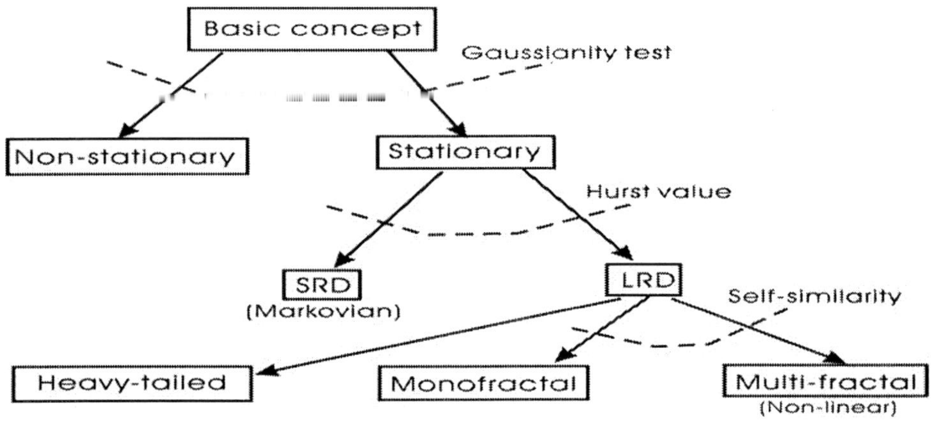

Figure 3.8. The OTA conceptual procedures.

The statistical methods mentioned above involve relatively complicated computation procedures. In their extant forms, they are unsuitable for time-critical applications because of the computation delay. Therefore, they have to be modified for real-time traffic pattern detection (RTPD) as shown by the *enhanced* R/S (E-R/S) version, which will be described later. Karagiannis *et al* [Karagiannis2003] have implemented different extant statistical methods into a package for off-line traffic analysis purposes, and its usage will be demonstrated.

3.3.2. Real-Time Traffic Pattern Detection (RTPD)

The OTA results shed light on what happened historically but do not directly help a system overcome any impending failures. This kind of help is a necessity for a real-time traffic pattern detector (RTPD). It is only recently that the RTPD issue has been addressed [Lin2004], and the conceptual basis of which is shown in figure 3.9.

The aim of the RTPD is to determine the following:

I. To confirm stationarity by using the Gaussianity test.
II. To differentiate short-range dependence (SRD) from long-range dependence (LRD) by computing the Hurst value.
III. To confirm the fractal dimension of a self-similar traffic trace with the self-similarity (S^2) filter.

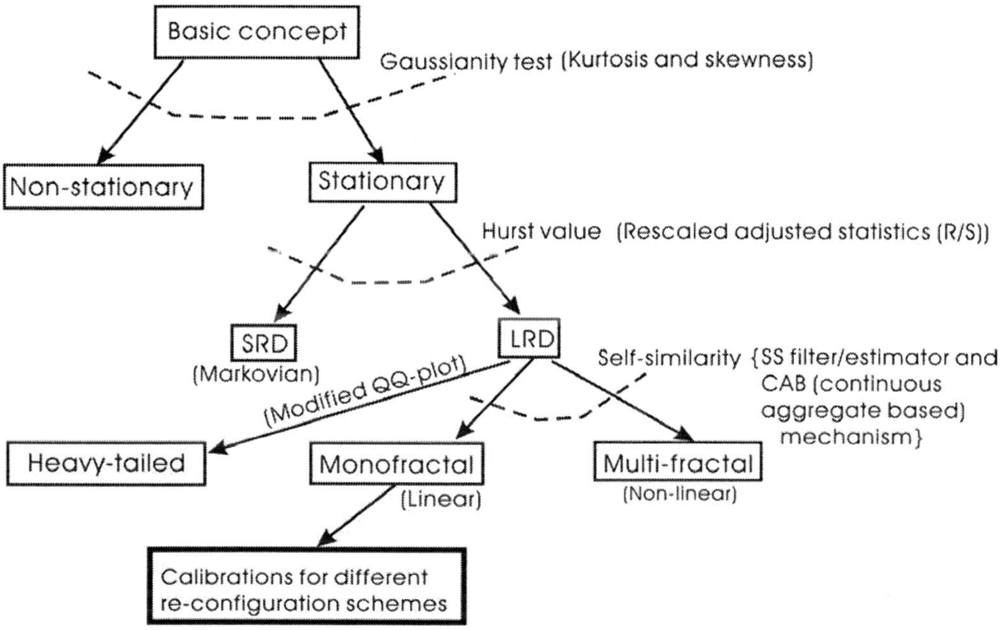

Figure 3.9. The RTPD conceptual procedures.

3.3.2.1. Rescaled Adjusted Statistics (R/S)

The core of the RTPD operation proposed in [Lin2004] is the traditional R/S (*rescaled adjusted statistics*) approach for *non-real-time and stationary* applications. This is the statistical expression, $R/S = \dfrac{\max\{W_i : i=1,2,....,k\} - \min\{W_i : i=1,2,...,k\}}{\sqrt{\operatorname{var}(X)}}$, where k is the aggregate size and W_i is $W_i = \sum_{m=1}^{i}(X_m - \overline{X})$ for $i=1,2,...k$. $\overline{X}$ is the mean computed by $\overline{X} = \frac{1}{k}\sum_{i=1}^{k} X_i$. Yet, the best value for k in this traditional approach has to be found by trial and error. This is the main drawback of the traditional R/S approach because its speed and accuracy depend on k. The R/S ratio is the rescaled range of the discrete process X, $\{X_i : i=1,2,...k\}$. The log-log plot of the $R/S = (k/2)^H$ feature yields the H value (i.e. R/S versus k). The time to compute $\overline{X}$ is unpredictable because of k.

This unpredictability problem is resolved by enhancing the R/S (i.e. *enhanced R/S* or E-R/S) for real-time applications by incorporating the *Convergence Algorithm* (CA). The CA is summarized by the following equations from Chapter 2:

$$M_i = \frac{M_{i-1} + \sum_{j=1}^{j=F-1} m_j^i}{F} \;..........\;(2.1);\; M_0 = m_{j=0}^{i=1} \;..........\;(2.2); i \geq 1$$

The cycle time is the interval for collecting the F (*flush limit*) number of data points physically. It has been previously confirmed that M_i has the fastest convergence for F=14. In the E-R/S case M_i replaces $\overline{X}$ to yield $W_i = \sum_{m=1}^{i}(X_m - M_i)$, which is more suitable for real-time applications. The number of traffic data points (e.g. in the form of inter-arrival time (IAT) or RTT) needed to calculate W_i is now fixed and predictable, in the $9 \leq F \leq 16$ range. The R/S and/or E-R/S implementations are called traffic filters or estimators.

3.3.2.2. The Self Similarity (S^2) Filter

This filter is based on the *decaying variance property* (DVP), which is invoked when the following conditions are satisfied: a) the LRD aggregate X^m of block size *m* in a stochastic process X is not heavy-tailed, and b) X^m is stationary. The core of the S^2 filter operation is summarized by the following equations, where *k* is the *lag* indicator:

$$Var(X^m) = \frac{1}{m^{(2-2H)}} Var(X).....(3.1)$$

$$\lim_{m \to \infty} r^m(l) = r(k)....(3.2)$$

$$\beta = 2 - 2H......(3.3)$$

$$\log(Var(X^m)) = \log(Var(X)) - \beta \log(m)....(3.4)$$

$$H = 1 - (\beta/2).....(3.5)$$

3.3.2.3. On-Line S^2 Operation

The on-line S^2 operation is supported by the "*continuous aggregate based* (CAB)" mechanism [LWD2005] as shown in figure 3.10. First, the CAB evaluates whether an aggregate is stationary on the fly by checking its Gaussian property or "Gaussianity". This is achieved by computing the *kurtosis* and *skewness* values for the current X^m aggregate. A symmetrical normal distribution has perfect Gaussianity indicated by $kurtosis = 3$ and $skewness = 0$. Statistically measured *kurtosis* and *skewness* values are rarely perfect, and a reasonable range from empirical experience (e.g. $(6,3)$) can be used to indicate the presence of a bell curve.

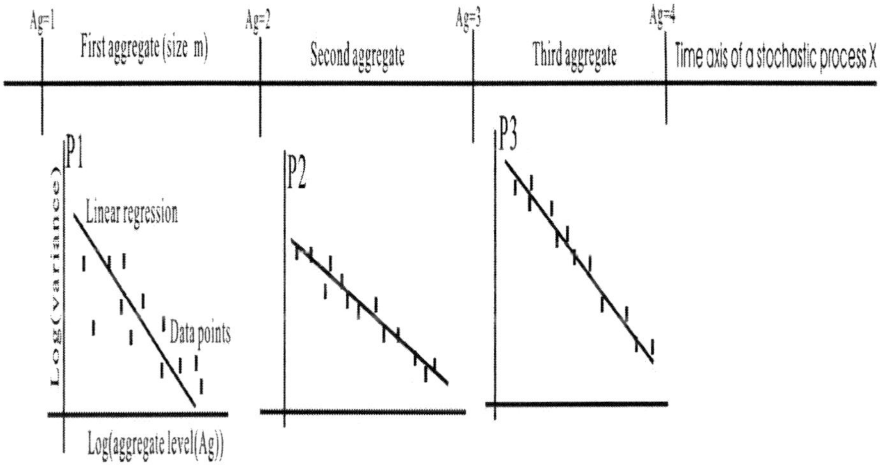

Figure 3.10. The "*continuous aggregate based* (CAB)" approach.

The S^2 *filter* finds β by linear regression. The quality of the regression is reflected by the *coefficient of determination* or R^2, which as a value between 0 and 1. A higher R^2 value implies better quality for the linear regression. By the predefined threshold (e.g. Th_{R^2} equal to 0.85 or 85%) the S^2 *filter* can reject a hypothesis of self-similarity in X^m for $R^2 < Th_{R^2}$. The CAB operation in figure 3.10 works with the aggregates $X^m_{Ag=l}$ in a discrete stochastic process X along the time axis. The assumptions for figure 3.10 are as follows: a) P1, P2, and P3 are the log-log plots for three successive aggregates based on equation (3.4); b) these plots yield different β values, β_1 for P1 with $R^2 = 0.82$, β_2 for P2 with $R^2 = 0.98$, and β_3 for P3 with $R^2 = 0.95$; c) Ag is the aggregate level; and d) $Th_{R^2} = 0.9$. Then, both P2 and P3 confirm self-similar traffic but not P1 (for $R^2 < Th_{R^2}$). If P2 and P3 yield very different β values, their H values by $H = 1 - (\beta/2)$ indicate different similarity dimensions or D.

Table 3.2. S^2 - log(variance) versus log(aggregate level) to find β and H

Time series (rows)	β	$H = (1 - \beta/2)$	R^2 (coefficient of determination)	loading factor ψ	kurtosis	skewness
1	0.6583	0.671	0.956 (95.6%)	0.1 (10%)	0.597045	1.180861
2	0.6809	0.660	0.975 (97.5%)	0.2	-0.56218	0.798282
3	0.6425	0.679	0.977 (97.7%)	0.3	0.40215	1.277175
4	0.6473	0.677	0.972 (97.2%)	0.4	-0.53386	0.861215
5	0.4685	0.766	0.959 (95.9%)	0.5	-0.58417	0.892037
6	0.3762	0.812	0.885 (88.5%) (less than Th_{R^2})	0.6 (rejected)	-1.01033	0.446756
7	0.1978	0.901	0.605 (60.5%)	0.7 (rejected)	-1.16043	0.388599

Skewness measures the symmetry of a bell-shape distribution. It is represented by the $\frac{\sum_{i=1}^{m}(x_i-\bar{x})^3}{(m-1)sd^3}$ expression, where $\bar{x}$ and sd are the measured mean and standard deviation of the distribution respectively. A positive value indicates that the bell curve skews right; that is, the right tail is heavier than the left. Kurtosis is the $\frac{\sum_{i=1}^{m}(x_i-\bar{x})^4}{(m-1)sd^4}$ expression, and its value decides whether the bell curve is peaked (for positive value) or flat (or negative value) as compared to the normal Gaussian distribution with $kurtosis = 3$ and $skewness = 0$. The loading factor ψ in table 3.2 (produced by the CAB mechanism in figure 3.10) indicates the intensity and complexity of the time series where the X^m aggregate came from. In this case, the R^2 threshold chosen for rejecting X^m as self-similar is 90% (i.e. $Th_{R^2} = 0.9$). In table 3.2 the fractal dimensions for row 1 to row 4 are approximately the same as indicated by the β values. The noticeable change from $H = 0.677$ in row 4 to $H = 0.766$ in row 5 indicates a change in the fractal dimension. A high R^2 value of 95.9% or 0.959 indicates high-quality regression. The increase in the H value in row 6 with a lower R^2 value (i.e. 0.885) means: a) the self-similar nature of the aggregate is questionable; and b) there are possible bursts of fractal breakdowns inside the aggregate [Nikiforov1993, Shereshevsky2003]. Fractal breakdown occurs when a self-similar process has encountered a chaotic and unstable condition. Theoretically, a fractal breakdown can be confirmed by computing the Holder exponent (HE) [Daoudi1998]. For real-time applications, however, the Holder exponent for any data point in a time series should be calculated in an instantaneous manner. At this moment, however, instantaneous HE calculation is an open issue with very little experience published in the literature. In Chapter 7, the importance of real-time HE calculation will be discussed.

3.3.3. Uncovering the Composite Nature of Internet Traffic

The nature of the Internet traffic is composite, changing from SRD to LRD and vice versa anytime. An OTA exercise conducted with a large trace may not reveal the composite nature of the embedded traffic. But, if it is divided into appropriate sections, or aggregates to be collected on-line, then the analysis of each section would reveal its true nature. A sizeable time series is a distribution that normally embeds different degrees of local fractality at different data points or sections. Here, we call these data points or sections the "atomic elements" because the characteristic of the whole distribution being scrutinized is a trace of the behavior of these elements over time. Therefore, if a large chunk of a distribution is arbitrarily taken as an aggregate, then the net effect is lumping different atomic elements together for analysis. The analytic result would be composite because it reflects the combined effect of different embedded atomic elements. Therefore, OTA of a large trace is basically a *lump* analysis.

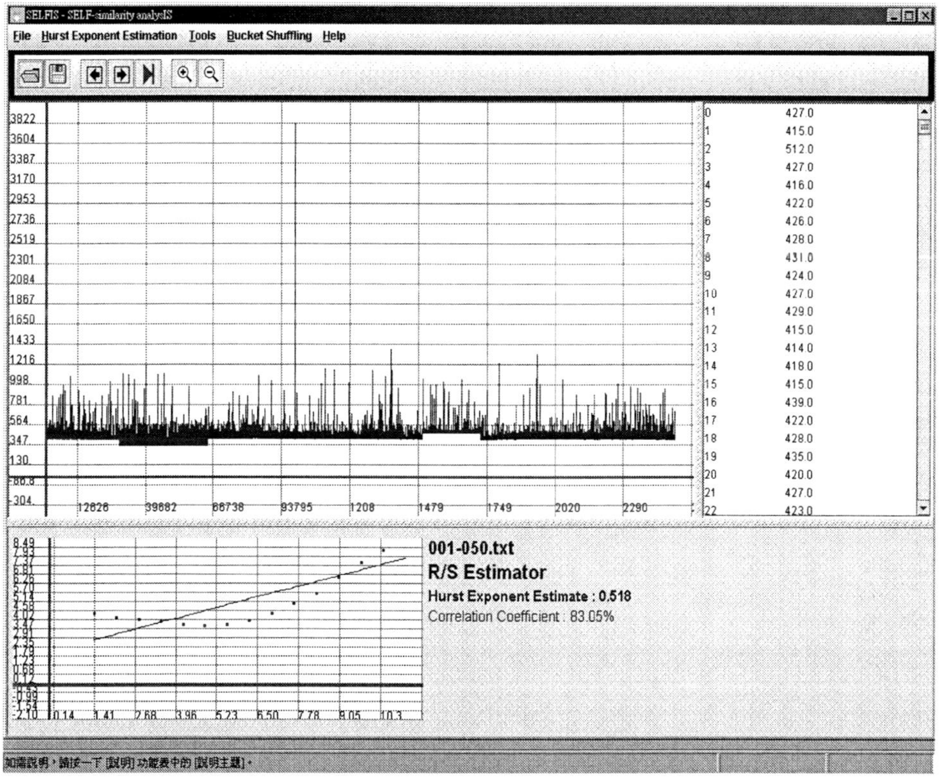

Figure 3.11. Trace analysis (001-050.txt) with the Karagiannis tool package.

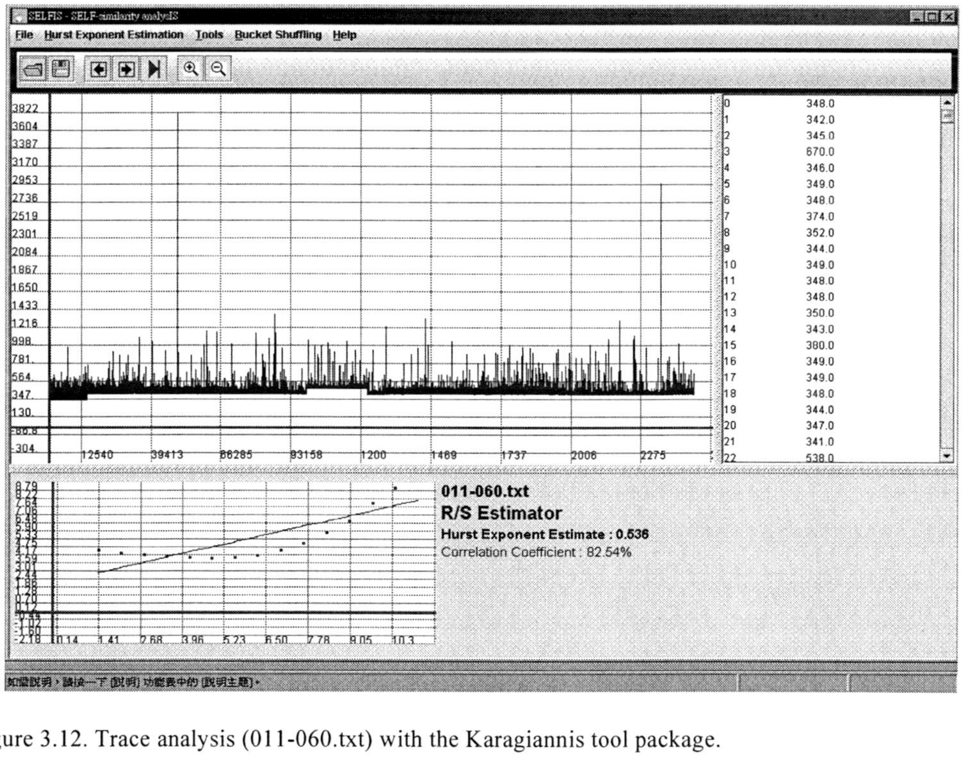

Figure 3.12. Trace analysis (011-060.txt) with the Karagiannis tool package.

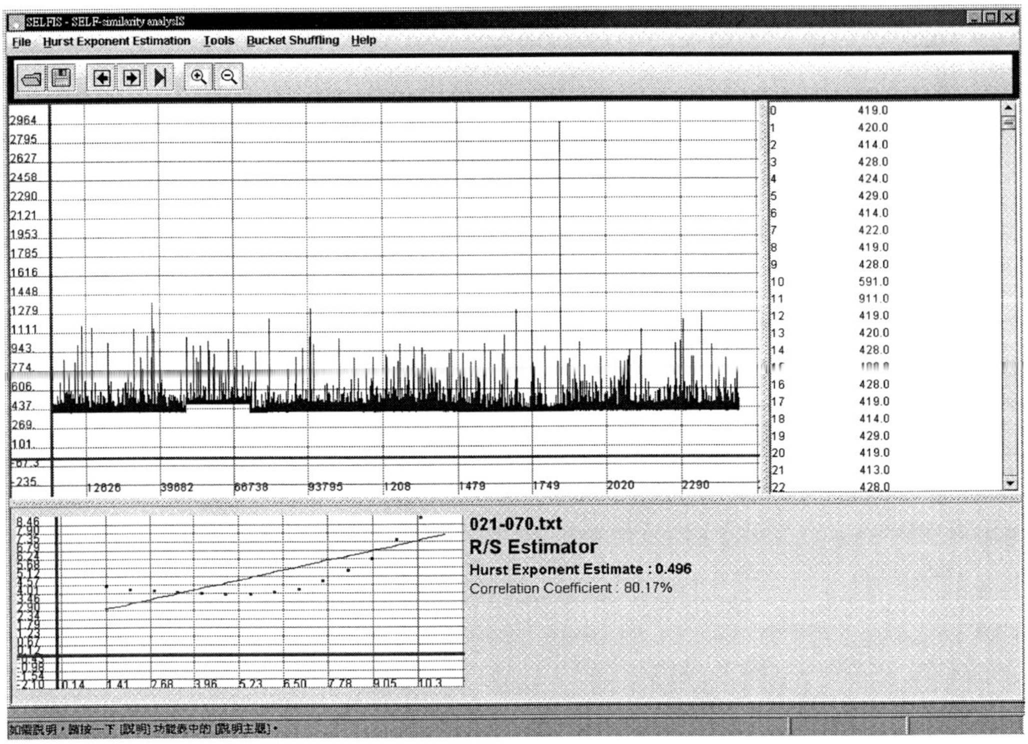

Figure 3.13. Trace analysis (021-070.txt) with the Karagiannis tool package.

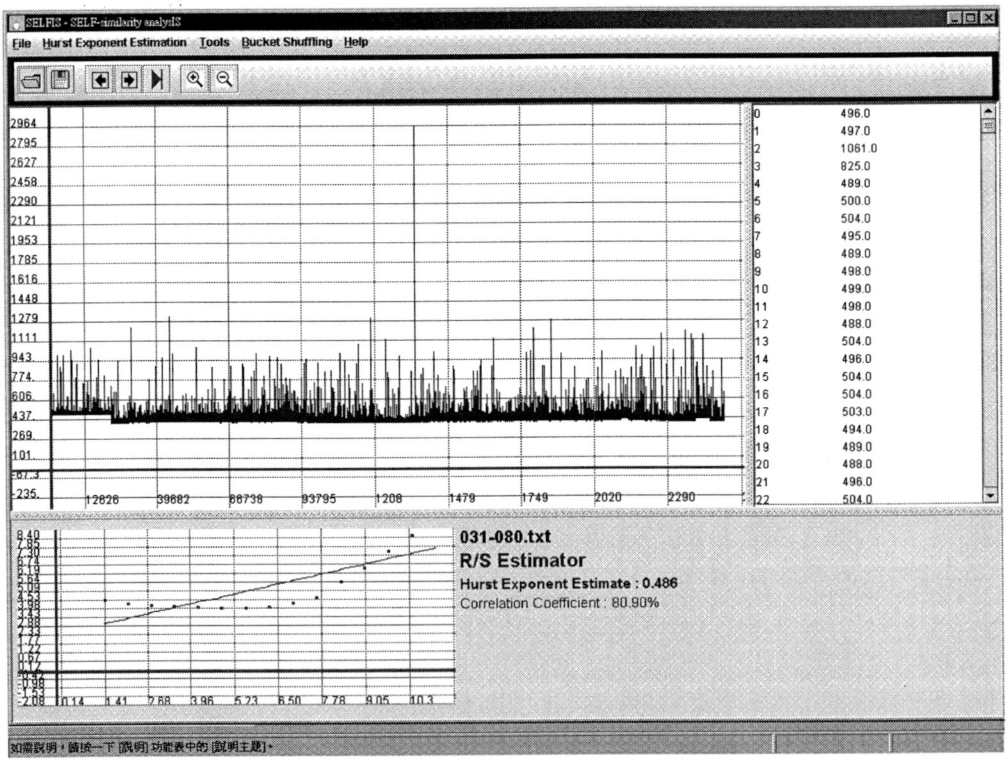

Figure 3.14. Trace analysis (031-080.txt) with the Karagiannis tool package.

In this section, the Karagiannis tool [Karagiannis2003], which can be used to analyze real-life RTT traces, is introduced. The plots (e.g. figure 3.11) are based on those traces collected for the TCP channel interconnecting the Hong Kong Polytechnic University and LaTrobe University in Melbourne, Australia. Before a plot is made, the stationary nature of the data section should be confirmed. The confirmation is supported by the CAB mechanism. The Hurst value is then computed to differentiate the SRD and LRD properties by invoking either the R/S estimator or the periodogram filter.

The data sections, 001-050.txt and 011-060.txt (figure 3.11 and 3.12) exhibit the LRD characteristics for $H \geq 0.5$. The other two sections from the same trace, 021-070.txt and 031-080.txt (figure 3.13 and figure 3.14), on the contrary exhibit the SRD trend.

3.3.4. Summary

The Internet follows the power laws and its traffic pattern can change suddenly from short-range dependence (SRD) to long-range dependence (LRD) and vice versa. The SRD traffic includes Markovian patterns such as Poisson and the LRD traffic includes heavy-tailed and self-similar patterns. It has been observed that different Internet traffic patterns produce various ill effects on system performance. To maintain system stability and performance, it is essential to neutralize these ill effects in a real-time manner. Although there are many techniques for off-line Internet traffic analysis, the only published technique for real-time applications is the real-time traffic pattern detector (RTPD) approach. This chapter shows how the Hurst (H) value can be used to differentiate SRD (for $0 < H < 0.5$) and LRD (for $0.5 < H < 1$) patterns in a dynamic manner. The novel self-similarity (S^2) filter that detects and identifies self-similar traffic on the fly is also introduced. Finally, the Karagiannis tool is used to demonstrate how the H values for the different stationary sections of a pre-collected data trace can be found. The stationarity confirmation process is supported by the CAB mechanism.

3.4. Key References

[Alex2001] Alex Ma, Skitter, http://wwwdev.caida.org/tools/measurement/skitter/index.xml, 2001

[Amp1] Active Measurements, http://watt.nlanr.net/active//

[Amp99] Monitoring for the NLANR Active Measurement Program, http://www-iepm.slac.stanford.edu/monitoring/amp/, June 1999

[Chatranon2004] G. Chatranon, M.A. Labrador and S. Banerjee, A Survey of TCP-friendly Router-Based AQM Schemes, *Computer Communications,* v. 27, 2004

[Cottrel1999] L. Cottrel, M. Zekauskas, H. Uijterwaal and T. McGregor, Comparison of Some Internet Active End-to-End Performance Measurement Projects, http://www.slac.stanford.edu/comp/net/wan-mon/iepm-cf.html, 1999 [Cottrel2001] L. Cottrel, Passive vs. Active Monitoring, http://www.slac.stanford.edu/comp/net/wan-mon/passive-vs-active.html, March 2001

[Daoudi1998] K. Daoudi, J. Vehel and Y. Meyer, Construction of Continuous Functions with Prescribed Local Regularity, *Journal of Constructive Approximation,* 14(3), 349-385, 1998

[GAC2002] Allan K.Y. Wong, Wilfred W.K. Lin, May T.W. Ip and Tharam S. Dillon, Genetic Algorithm and PID Control Together for Dynamic Anticipative Marginal Buffer Management: An Effective Approach to Enhance Dependability and Performance for Distributed Mobile Object-Based Real-time Computing over the Internet, *Journal of Parallel and Distributed Computing (JPDC),* vol.62, Sept. 2002, 1433-1453

[Jacobson1997] V. Jacobson, Pathchar – A Tool to Infer Characteristics of Internet Paths, *Network Research Group Lawrence Berkeley National Laboratory*, Berkeley, CA, MSRI, April 21, 1997

[Karagiannis2003] T. Karagiannis, M. Faloutsos, M. Molle, A User-friendly Self-similarity Analysis Tool, *ACM SIGCOMM Computer Communication Review,* 33(3), July 2003, 81-93 (http://www.cs.ucr.edu/~tkarag/Selfis/Selfis.html)

[Lakshman1996] T. Lakshman, A. Neidhardt and T. Ott, The Drop from Front Strategy in TCP over ATM and Its Internetworking with other Control Features, *INFOCOMM* 1996

[Lakshman1997] T. Lakshman U. Madlow, The Performance of TCP/IP for Networks with High Bandwidth-Delay Products and Random Loss, *IEEE/ACM Transactions on Networking,* 5(3), June 1997, 336-350

[Lin2004] Wilfred W. K. Lin, Richard S.L. Wu, Tharam S. Dillon and Allan K. Y. Wong, A Novel Real-Time Traffic Pattern Detector for Internet Applications, *Proceedings of the 2004 Australian Telecommunication Networks and Applications Conference (ATNAC),* Sydney, Australia, December 2004, 224-227

[LWD2005] Wilfred W. K. Lin, Allan K. Y. Wong, and Tharam S. Dillon, A Novel R2-FLC Dynamic Buffer Size Tuner to Support Time-Critical Applications over the Internet by Improving Logical Channel Fault Tolerance, *Proc. of the 11th International Symposium on Pacific Rim Dependable Computing (PRDC'2005)* Changsha, PRC

[Mah2001] Bruce A. Mah, http://www.mirrors.wiretapped.net/security/network-mapping/pchar

[Matt2000] Warren Matthews and Les Cottrell, The PingER Project: Active Internet Performance Monitoring for the HENP Community, *IEEE Communications Magazine,* May 2000, 2-8

[Matt2001] Warren Matthews, Les Cottrell and Davide Salomoni, Passive and Active Monitoring on a High Performance Research Network, Presented at Passive and Active Monitoring (PAM) 2001, Amsterdam, The Netherlands, April 2001

[Molnár1999] S. Molnár, T.D. Dang and A. Vidács, Heavy-Tailedness, Long-Range Dependence and Self-Similarity in Data Traffic, Proceedings of 7th International Conference on Telecommunication Systems, Modelling and Analysis, March 1999, Nashville, USA, 18-21

[Nikiforov1993] I.V. Nikiforov and M. Basseville, Detection of Abrupt Changes: Theory and Application, Prentice Hall, 1993

[Paxson1995] V. Paxson and S. Floyd, Wide-Area Traffic: The Failure of Poisson Modeling. *IEEE/ACM Transactions on Networking,* 3(3), June 1995, 226-244.

[Paxson1999] V. Paxson, End-to-end Internet Packet Dynamics, *IEEE/ACM Transactions on Networking,* 7(3), June 1999, 277 -292

[Ping1999] The PingER Project, http://www-iepm.slac.stanford.edu/pinger/, 1999

[Shereshevsky2003] M. Shereshevsky2003, J. Crowell, B. Cukic, V. Handikota and Y. Liu, Software Aging and Multfractality of Memory Resources, *Proc. of the 2003 IEEE International Conference on Dependable Systems and Networks* (DSN'03), 2003

[Sunil1999] Sunil Kalidindi and Matthew J. Zekauskas, Surveyor: An Infrastructure for Internet Performance Measurements, *INET'99,* San Jose, June 1999

[Wong01B] Allan K.Y. Wong, Tharam S. Dillon, Wilfred K.W. Lin and May T.W. Ip, M^2RT: A Tool Developed for Predicting the Mean Message Response Time for Internet Channels, *Computer Networks.* 36(2001), 557-577

[Wu2004] Richard S.L. Wu, Allan K.Y. Wong and Tharam S. Dillon, RDCT: A Novel Reconfigurable Dynamic Cache Size Tuner to Shorten Information Retrieval Time over the Internet, *International Journal of Computer Systems, Science and Engineering,* 19(6), 2004, -372

Chapter 4

DYNAMIC BUFFER MANAGEMENT

4.1. BACKGROUND

Applications running on the Internet are basically object-based, and the constituent objects collaborate in an end-to-end client/server relationship. This relationship is an asymmetric rendezvous because the server can serve many clients at the same time. Figure 4.0 shows the two levels of the end-to-end path (i.e. EE-path) in a client/server interaction. The system/router level involves all the activities inside the TCP (Transmission Control Protocol) channel, and the user-level includes only the client and the server that make use of the channel for communication. In general, it is difficult to harness the roundtrip time (RTT) of an EE-path in a time-critical application because of the sheer size and heterogeneity of the Internet. Practically, it is impossible to monitor every one of the overwhelming number of network parameters in order to control the RTT. If the EE-path error probability for retransmissions is ρ, the *average number of trials* (ANT) for a successful transmission is $\sum_{j=1}^{\infty} j[\rho^{j-1}(1-\rho)] \approx \lim_{j\to\infty} 1/(1-\rho)$. The ρ value encapsulates all the possible faults and errors along the EE-path, one of which is the chance of user-level buffer overflow at the receiver/server end. Those methods devised to prevent network congestion at the system level are known as active queue management (AQM) [Braden1998] approaches. The only known method from the literature that can eliminate user-level buffer overflow is *dynamic buffer size tuning* (DBST), and this is explained in this chapter.

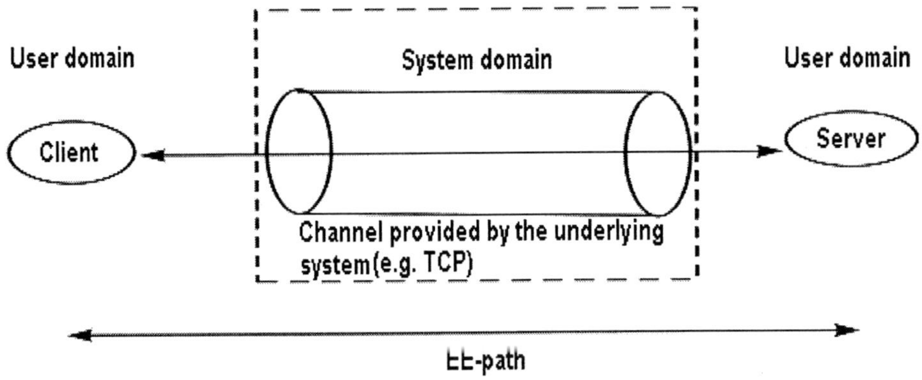

Figure 4.0. The EE path.

4.2. The PD ("P+D") Controller

The first dynamic buffer size controller that can be identified from the literature is the "P+D" or PD model [Wong1999]. For this controller, which works with different given thresholds, the proportional (P) control is the ratio of "queue length over buffer length (QOB)" to predict the chance of overflow. The rate or derivative (D) control, which decides how fast the buffer would become full, is the rate of change in the queue length (i.e. dQ/dt). The PD control algorithm is depicted in figure 4.1a. The parameters are as follows: L_{now} for current buffer length, $L_{minimum}$ for the minimum buffer size estimated from the past performance, and B_a as the prescribed constant or "*seed*" for the particular implementation.

If {(dQ/dt > prescribed_positive_threshold) OR [(dQ/dt is_positive) AND $(QOB_i >$ *prescribed_positive_threshold)]} Then* $L_{now} = L_{now} + B_a$; $L_{now} \geq L_{minimum}$
Else If {(dQ/dt < prescribed_negative_threshold) OR [(dQ/dt is_ negative) AND $(QOB_i <$ *prescribed_negative_threshold)]} Then* $L_{now} = L_{now} - B_a$; $L_{now} \geq L_{minimum}$

Figure 4.1a. The basic PD control model.

The PD controller worked well in simulations that were set up to verify the model with different chosen data sets, which supposedly mimicked the different real-life Internet traffic conditions. Yet, it produced frequent buffer overflows in real deployments over the Internet. Subsequent analyses [Ip2001] indicated that the overflows were due to the unrealistic expectation of using a set of fixed thresholds and a static B_a seed to cater for the whole spectrum of buffer dynamics. The desire to resolve this problem led to the proposal of the PID controller or PIDC, which is basically the PD controller augmented by integral (I) control. The set-up for the PD simulations, which mimics the real-life deployment configuration, is shown in figure 4.1b. The server at the user level serves different clients simultaneously and the requests for service from the clients can be grouped into different streams. The number of streams conceptually grows with the popularity of the server. The streams merge (indicated by the ⊕ symbol) at the logical *service access point* (SAP) of the server domain before entering the server's queue buffer. The merged traffic can assume any traffic pattern because the patterns of the request streams vary and change over time, for example, from short-range dependence (e.g. Markovian such as Poisson) to long-range dependence (e.g. self-similar or heavy-tailed) and vice versa. A sudden burst of incoming requests easily causes the queue to overflow the buffer unless the length of the latter adaptively covers the queue length at anytime. Therefore, the basic requirement of dynamic buffer size tuning is to make sure that the buffer length always covers the queue length on the fly. The dynamic buffer tuner uses the current buffer and queue lengths to compute the real-time buffer length adjustment as depicted in figure 4.1b. Since this setup represents solid experience in verifying and validating the usability of a dynamic buffer tuner, it is the basis for experiments with other tuners, which will be described later.

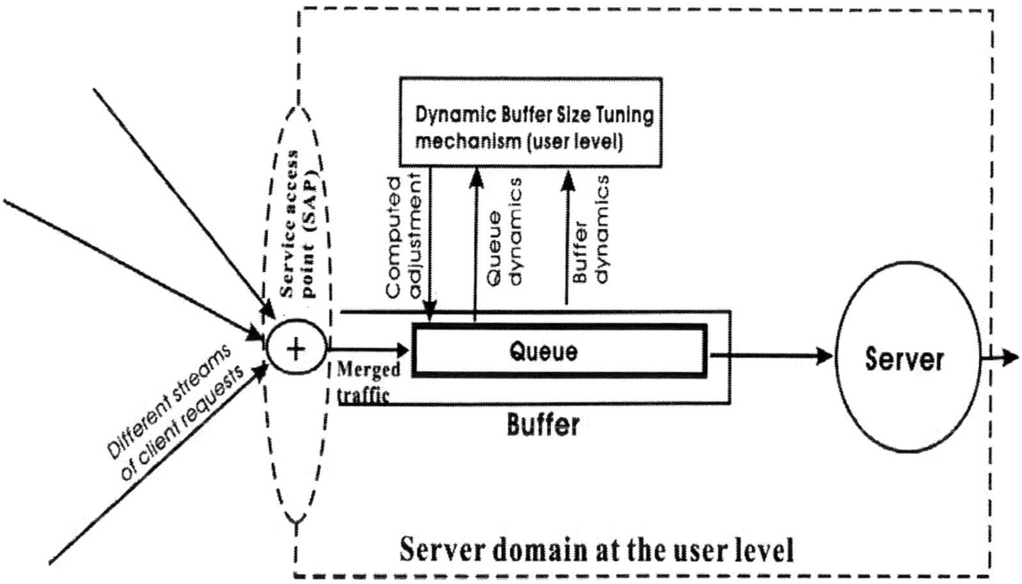

Figure 4.1b. The PD controller set up.

4.3. The PID Controller (PIDC)

Buffer size tuning, similar to industrial control processes, may involve P, I and D control elements [Karray2002]. In the PIDC the P and D parameters are the same as the PD Controller. The integral control is the history of changes in the queue length. The P, I and D control elements in the PIDC should be construed on a conceptual basis [Ip2001]. They are different from the traditional meanings in process control theory because the PIDC does not explicitly consider the feedback system gain. The PIDC is formed by adding integral control to the previous PD tuner, which was the first of its kind [Wong1999]. Although the PD tuner worked well in simulations with selected datasets, it failed in real situations over the Internet. The main cause of failure is the "*hard-coded*" nature of the PD control parameters. Since these parameters do not register new knowledge, the controller does not have enough power

deployment cases known so far. However, it was observed in a few cases that the queue length can get dangerously close to the buffer length, threatening overflow.

4.4. Safety Margin and a Novel Objective Function for Dynamic Buffer Tuning

The desire to eliminate the PIDC shortcomings led to the introduction of the safety margin Δ concept. The three intelligent tuners, GAC, FLC and NNC, adaptively maintain Δ on the fly about the chosen reference (i.e. "0") of the $\{0,\Delta\}^2$ objective function. The difference between the controlled buffer length and the current queue length should stay inside the user-specified tolerance band of $\pm\Delta$ about the reference point. This reference point is the "queue length over buffer length" ratio chosen by the user, QOB_R.

Next is the definition of the objective function $\{0,\Delta\}^2$, which is utilized in the remainder of the text in this chapter for dynamic buffer size tuning. This objective function is a far more effective method for ensuring that we have a constant safety margin Δ between the buffer length and the current queue length. This margin, which is maintained on the fly, deals with any sudden surges in the number of entries into the reception buffer. In fact, the $\{0,\Delta\}^2$ objective function is used in all our research for the Genetic Algorithm Controller (GAC), the Neural Network Controller (NNC) and the Fuzzy Logic Controller (FLC). The use of this safety margin in an objective function is an important departure from previous approaches to buffer tuning.

4.4.1. The Genetic Algorithm Controller (GAC)

Genetic algorithms are a form of evolutionary computing [Michalewicz1996] that mimics natural evolution in the reproduction process, including chromosome crossover and mutation of genes. From the perspective of conventional or algorithmic PID, control genes are the threshold values. The goal of the GAC is to eradicate the shortcomings of the algorithmic PIDC by adjusting the set of thresholds. The safety margin concept Δ and the $\{0,\Delta\}^2$ objective function were first introduced in the GAC proposal and development [Wong2002GAC]. Conceptually, the GAC is the "PIDC plus GA plus the $\{0,\Delta\}^2$ objective function" combination.

Since, in the buffer length tuning process, the GA treats the PIDC parameters as genes, every parameter set is a chromosome in the GA context. The buffer size estimated by the refined PIDC is fed to the objective function $\{0,\Delta\}^2$ to check its fitness. In effect, $\{0,\Delta\}^2$ is the fitness function. The aim is to ensure that the difference between the controlled buffer length and the current queue length stays within the $\pm\Delta$ tolerance band about QOB_R. If there is an indication that the $\pm\Delta$ criterion may not be satisfied, the GA immediately reproduces new chromosomes by mutation and crossover. It then selects the fittest chromosome to replace the existing set of PIDC parameters as a refinement process. By doing so, the GA tries to prevent the QOB deviating from QOB_R by more than $\pm\Delta$. The operation of the GAC, which is a GA-augmented PIDC, is shown in figure 4.2.

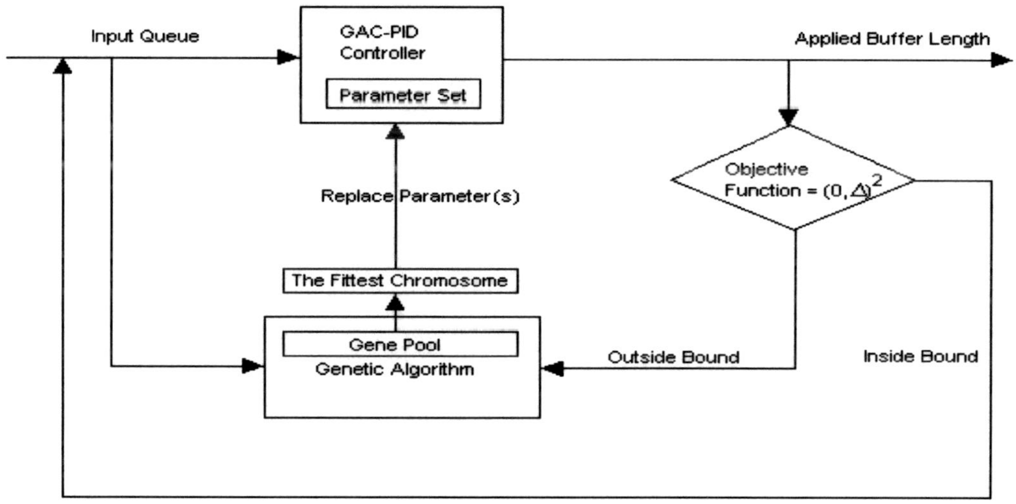

Figure 4.2 The GAC model for marginal buffer control.

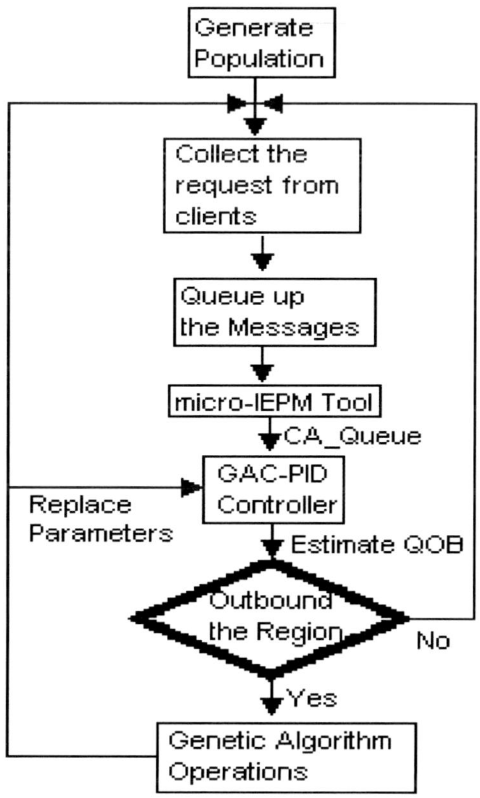

Figure 4.3 The GA logic flowchart.

It was observed in different tests that oscillations might occur right after replacements with new chromosomes, and this leads to subsequent system instability and occasional buffer overflow. A solution to alleviate such vicious oscillations is to give the GAC enough time to adjust to the new parameters. This grace period is called the *adaptation time window* (ATW). The subsequent deeper analysis shows that the ATW helps but cannot eliminate the chance of buffer overflow at all. The analysis of this phenomenon revealed that this is caused by the very nature of the GA not to guarantee the global-optimal solution of the *hyperplane* [Mitchel1999]. In the GAC, the PIDC and the GA mechanism work in parallel with the same data input. The chromosome is made up of two different sets of thresholds, namely, QOBL (Lower) and QOBU (Upper). The GA logic is illustrated in the flowchart shown in figure 4.3.

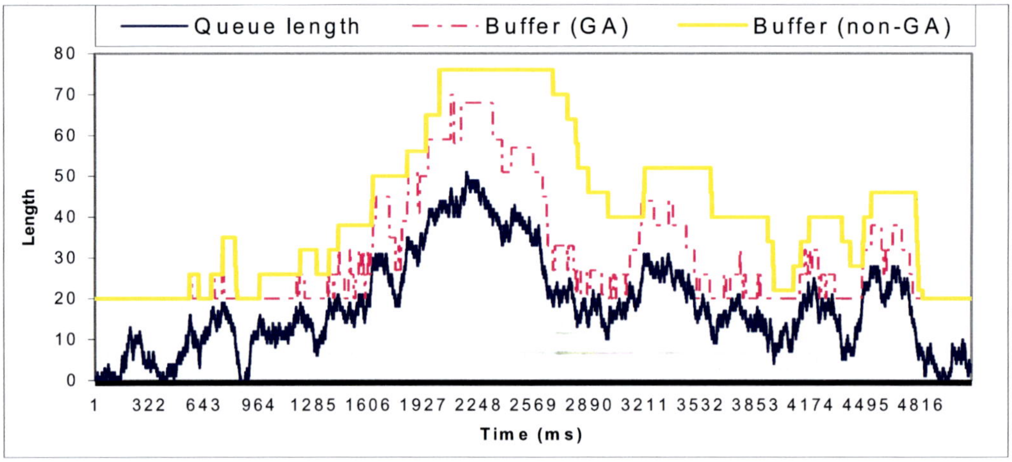

Figure 4.4. The GAC yields a more responsive result than the PIDC.

Table 4.1. A record of buffer overflow after GAC chromosome replacement

Time	Queue length	Buffer (GA)	Buffer (non-GA)	RLQI (GA)	RLQD (GA)	RLQI (non-GA)	RLQD (non-GA)	Action
588	0	20	20	0.716605	0.574195	0.716605	0.574195	
1174	1	20	20	0.716605	0.574195	0.716605	0.574195	
1379	0	20	20	0.716605	0.574195	0.716605	0.574195	
546589	18	20	26	0.856595	0.583624	0.716605	0.574195	
547178	19	20	26	0.856595	0.583624	0.716605	0.574195	
547781	20	20	26	0.856595	0.583624	0.716605	0.574195	REPLACE
547941	19	20	26	0.823966	0.539837	0.716605	0.574195	
548374	20	20	26	0.823966	0.539837	0.716605	0.574195	INSIDE_ ADAPTATION _PERIOD
548980	21	20	26	0.823966	0.539837	0.716605	0.574195	INSIDE_ ADAPTATION _PERIOD
549391	20	26	32	0.823966	0.539837	0.716605	0.574195	
549509	19	26	32	0.823966	0.539837	0.716605	0.574195	
549587	20	26	32	0.823966	0.539837	0.716605	0.574195	

Figure 4.4 shows that for the given queue-length data trace the GAC eliminates the shortcomings of the PIDC (non-GA) by yielding more responsive buffer overflow control. For the same data trace, however, it also produced an overflow as shown in table 4.1. The overflow occurred at the time point of 548980 after chromosome replacement at the time point 547781.

4.5. THE FUZZY LOGIC CONTROLLER (FLC)

Although the GAC produces occasional buffer overflow, it eliminated the PIDC shortcomings completely and confirmed that the $\{0,\Delta\}^2$ objective function is a sound and powerful concept. The FLC proposal represents the quest for a better intelligent model that can: a) work with the PIDC as a component minus its shortcomings; b) use the $\{0,\Delta\}^2$ objective function as the operational basis; and c) produce no overflow at all. In this sense, the FLC should be more powerful and accurate than the GAC. The FLC conceptual framework is the "PIDC plus fuzzy logic plus the $\{0,\Delta\}^2$ objective function" combination. The fuzzy logic divides the PIDC control domain into many smaller fuzzy control regions (e.g. table 4.2) and supports each of them with a predefined fuzzy rule or a "*don't care*" state. The "*don't care*" state requires no action/computation and in this way it offsets the FLC computation complexity and reduces its control cycle time [Lin2005a]. Therefore, the FLC is a *fuzzy region based* (FRB) approach [Berkan1997, Zadeh1994]. The control domain, which now consists of many fuzzy regions, is known as the *fuzzy knowledge base*. The adaptive adjustment of the buffer length, by addition or subtraction, depends on the current fuzzy region of operation. In effect, the original algorithmic PIDC has only two fuzzy regions if compared to the FLC approach. The "*don't care*" is marked by X in the FLC[4x6] design shown in table 4.2.

Table 4.2 A FLC [4x6] design example

QOB			dQ/dt					
			NL	NM	NS	PS	PM	PL
	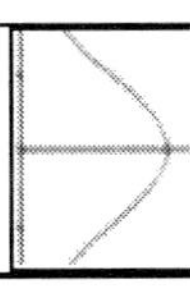	ML	-	-	-	-	-	-
0.7		L	-	-	X	X	+	+
0.8		G	-	-	X	X	+	+
0.9		MG	+	+	+	+	+	+

The "*dot*" in table 4.2 marks the QOB_R, which in this case is equal to 0.8 (80%). The FLC experimental result presented in this section is based on this design, and this implies Δ to be 0.2 or 20%. The linguistic variables (representations), which are used for denoting the fuzzy regions of the FLC design in table 4.2, are defined as follows:

a) For the ratio of Queue Length Over Buffer Length (QOB)

- ML - *M*uch *L*ess than optimal point

- L - *L*ess than optimal point
- G - *G*reater than optimal point
- MG - *M*uch *G*reater than optimal point

b) For the rate of change of Queue length (dQ/dt)

- NL - *N*egative *L*arge than optimal point
- NM - *N*egative *M*edium than optimal point
- NS - *N*egative *S*mall than optimal point
- PS - *P*ositive *S*mall than optimal point
- PM - *P*ositive *M*edium than optimal point
- PL - *P*ositive *L*arge than optimal point

The control action to be taken by the FLC depends on the two input parameters, namely, QOB (i.e. proportional or P control) and dQ/dt (i.e. derivative or D control). The three possible FLC decisions/actions are: a) *Addition or* "+", b) *Subtraction or*"-" and *don't care or* "*X*". The FLC decisions are indicated in table 4.2, with each cell corresponding to the particular action. The *X* state prevents unnecessary oscillation in the buffer length control process. The *quantum* for *addition (*buffer elongation*)* or *subtraction (*buffer shortening*)* is still computed by the refined PIDC mechanism, which is a component of the FLC. Refinement here means that the operation of the PIDC algorithm depends on the fuzzy region in which the controller is currently operating. The FLC Java prototype for the FLC[4x6] design shown by table 4.2 has the following fuzzy rules, which moderate the integral control represented by RICM (*Refined Integral Control Mechanism* [Lin2002FLC]):

Rule 1: If (QOB is ML) AND (dQ/dt is NL) Then Action is "-"(Subtraction) AND $L_{new} = L_{old}$ - RICM
Rule 2: If (QOB is ML) AND (dQ/dt is NM) Then Action is "-"(Subtraction) AND $L_{new} = L_{old}$ - RICM
Rule 3: If (QOB is ML) AND (dQ/dt is NS) Then Action is "-"(Subtraction) AND $L_{new} = L_{old}$ - RICM
Rule 4: If (QOB is ML) AND (dQ/dt is PS) Then Action is "-"(Subtraction) AND $L_{new} = L_{old}$ - RICM
Rule 5: If (QOB is ML) AND (dQ/dt is PM) Then Action is "-"(Subtraction) AND $L_{new} = L_{old}$ - RICM
Rule 6: If (QOB is ML) AND (dQ/dt is PL) Then Action is "-"(Subtraction) AND $L_{new} = L_{old}$ - RICM
Rule 7: If (QOB is L) AND (dQ/dt is NL) Then Action is "-"(Subtraction) AND $L_{new} = L_{old}$ - RICM
Rule 8: If (QOB is L) AND (dQ/dt is NM) Then Action is "-"(Subtraction) AND $L_{new} = L_{old}$ - RICM
Rule 9: If (QOB is L) AND (dQ/dt is NS) Then Action is "X"(Don't care) AND $L_{new} = L_{old}$
Rule 10: If (QOB is L) AND (dQ/dt is PS) Then Action is "X"(Don't care) AND $L_{new} = L_{old}$
Rule 11: If (QOB is L) AND (dQ/dt is PM) Then Action is "+"(Addition) AND $L_{new} = L_{old}$ + RICM
Rule 12: If (QOB is L) AND (dQ/dt is PL) Then Action is "+" (Addition) AND $L_{new} = L_{old}$ + RICM
Rule 13: If (QOB is G) AND (dQ/dt is NL) Then Action is "-"(Subtraction) AND $L_{new} = L_{old}$ - RICM
Rule 14: If (QOB is G) AND (dQ/dt is NM) Then Action is "-"(Subtraction) AND $L_{new} = L_{old}$ - RICM
Rule 15: If (QOB is G) AND (dQ/dt is NS) Then Action is "X"(Don't care) AND $L_{new} = L_{old}$
Rule 16: If (QOB is G) AND (dQ/dt is PS) Then Action is "X"(Don't care) AND $L_{new} = L_{old}$
Rule 17: If (QOB is G) AND (dQ/dt is PM) Then Action is "+"(Addition) AND $L_{new} = L_{old}$ + RICM
Rule 18: If (QOB is G) AND (dQ/dt is PL) Then Action is "+"(Addition) AND $L_{new} = L_{old}$ + RICM
Rule 19: If (QOB is MG) AND (dQ/dt is NL) Then Action is "+"(Addition) AND $L_{new} = L_{old}$ + RICM
Rule 20: If (QOB is MG) AND (dQ/dt is NM) Then Action is "+"(Addition) AND $L_{new} = L_{old}$ + RICM
Rule 21: If (QOB is MG) AND (dQ/dt is NS) Then Action is "+"(Addition) AND $L_{new} = L_{old}$+ RICM
Rule 22: If (QOB is MG) AND (dQ/dt is PS) Then Action is "+"(Addition) AND $L_{new} = L_{old}$+ RICM

Rule 23: If (QOB is MG) AND (dQ/dt is PM) Then Action is "+"(Addition) AND $L_{new} = L_{old}$ + RICM
Rule 24: If (QOB is MG) AND (dQ/dt is PL) Then Action is "+"(Addition) AND $L_{new} = L_{old}$ + RICM

Let us consider Rule 1 as an example. We note that inputs QOB are Much Less than the Optimal Point and dQ/dt is Negative Large than Optimal Point. This corresponds to the FLC[1,1] entry in the design shown by table 4.2. The buffer tuning action is "old" buffer length minus the integral control output (called the RICM or refined integral control measure).

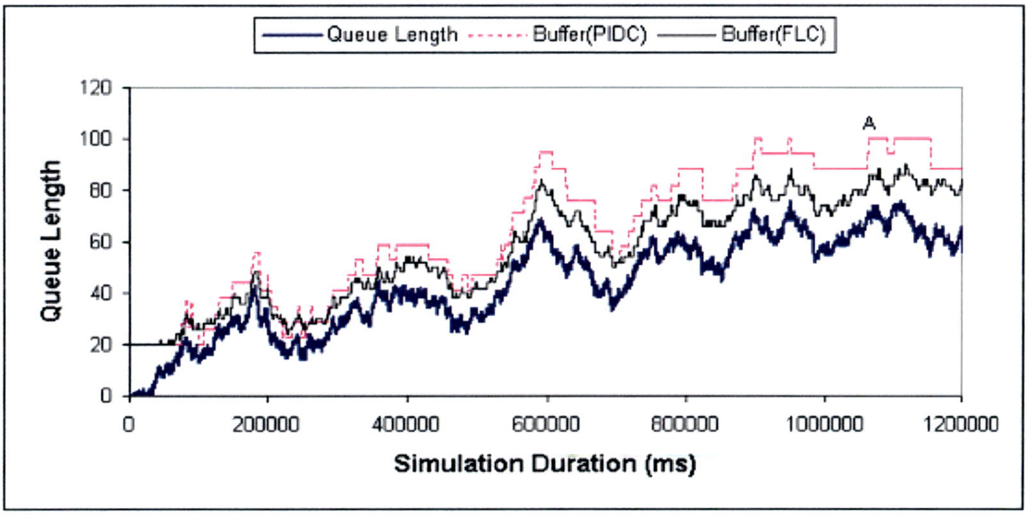

Figure 4.5. A case of performance comparison between the PIDC and the FLC ($QOB_R = 0.8, \Delta = 0.2$).

The FLC always yields a more responsive buffer tuning operation than the PIDC minus the latter's shortcomings. Figure 4.5 is one case in which the FLC consistently maintains the safety margin Δ for the $\{0, \Delta\}^2$ objective function. Point A in figure 4.5 indicates that the FLC has eliminated the PIDC shortcoming of staying at the high buffer length value (i.e. unused buffer space still being locked by the controller). All the experimental results indicated that the FLC preserves the merit of the $\{0, \Delta\}^2$ objective function. It is faster than the GAC and does not produce any occasional buffer overflows [Lin2005b], as experienced with the GAC.

4.5.1. Optimal FLC Design

There are basically two approaches to determine whether an optimal FLC design is possible. The first approach is to represent the FLC in its mathematical form and use mathematical manipulation such as theorem proving to confirm the possibility. The second approach is empirical and utilizes sensitivity analysis, which means that the following occurs: a) experiments for different FLC designs are carried out; and b) the correlation between the FLC structural complexity and the chosen performance index, such as the mean QOB deviation from the given QOB_R reference, is found. The second approach is chosen for addressing the issue because the different FLC designs have to be tested against different Internet traffic patterns

The accumulated FLC experimental data indicated that it was possible to have an optimal FLC design. Figure 4.6, which is plotted with the mean deviations from QOB_R by the different FLC designs tested in different experiments, revealed approximately where the optimal region is. This region may vary with respect to different traffic patterns. In this plot the mean deviation from the QOB_R reference stabilizes around 0.02 (or 2%) after the FLC[4x6] design. More experiments confirmed that more complex FLC designs do not yield less deviation after this point. The possibility of having optimal FLC designs made it worthwhile to explore the correlation among the following in the future work: the mean deviation from QOB, the FLC design complexity (i.e. the matrix size), and the metrics being leveraged (e.g. traffic pattern). If this correlation could be formally established, then proper intelligence could be incorporated to let the FLC auto-tune its configuration in a dynamic and timely manner (i.e. the matrix size and the matrix entries) for cost and effectiveness. A simpler FLC design is always desirable because it yields shorter execution and better RTT timeliness to enhance the chance of success for time-critical applications.

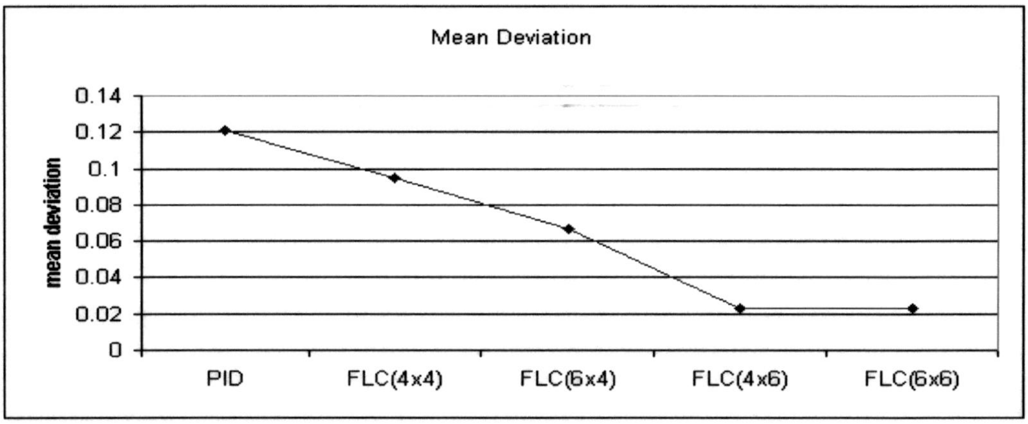

Figure 4.6. Optimal FLC design is possible (mean deviation stabilizes around 0.02).

4.5.2. The Adaptive/Reconfigurable Fuzzy Logic Controller

The A-FLC (adaptive/reconfigurable FLC) model uses a static adjustment size to tune the "*don't-care region's range-threshold*". This is basically the combination: "*don't-care region's range-threshold auto-tuning capability + FLC*" [Lin2004a]. The PIDC component in the FLC uses two static thresholds to achieve its control purpose, namely, *Th1* and *Th2*. The PIDC working alone conceptually should have four control regions, defined by different $\pm$ *Th1* and $\pm$ *Th2* combinations. The FLC fuzzy logic divides these thresholds into the finer membership functions, with *range-thresholds* among them. In the original FLC, the range-thresholds are static and decide in which fuzzy control region the dynamic buffer tuner should operate at the time. The static nature of the range-thresholds introduces an intrinsic delay for the corrective action by a fuzzy control. For example, if the dQ/dt value increases but less than the range-threshold of the current "*don't care*" region, there will be no control action. By the time any control action is triggered (range-threshold exceeded) there would be significant overshoot or undershoot already. The overshoot/undershoot accumulations make the FLC control process oscillate.

The A-FLC differs by preventing any significant overshoot/undershoot proactively in a timely manner. The prevention is achieved by adapting the range-threshold of the current "*don't care*" fuzzy region on-line. At anytime, if the increase (or decrease) of dQ/dt is more than (or less than) the given "*gradient threshold* (GT)", the range-threshold is adjusted by the "*given percentage* (GP)" in a timely manner. Even though the GT and GP are fixed values, the experimental results showed that the A-FLC had much better performance than the original FLC by yielding less mean deviation from the QOB_R reference. Figure 4.7 shows how the "*don't care*" range-threshold of a growing dQ/dt value is "*squeezed*" to enlarge the range-threshold on the right side (now larger than *Ra*). This enlargement, in effect, urges the A-FLC to take immediate action instead of waiting passively for the "dQ/dt *predefined range-threshold*" condition to hold. The dynamic "*squeezing*" action based on the GT and GP parameters quicken the A-FLC response. In the R^2-*FLC* (Reconfigurable Real-time Fuzzy Logic Controller) model GP is *adjusted again* in a dynamic manner with respect to the traffic pattern identified by the RTPD capability.

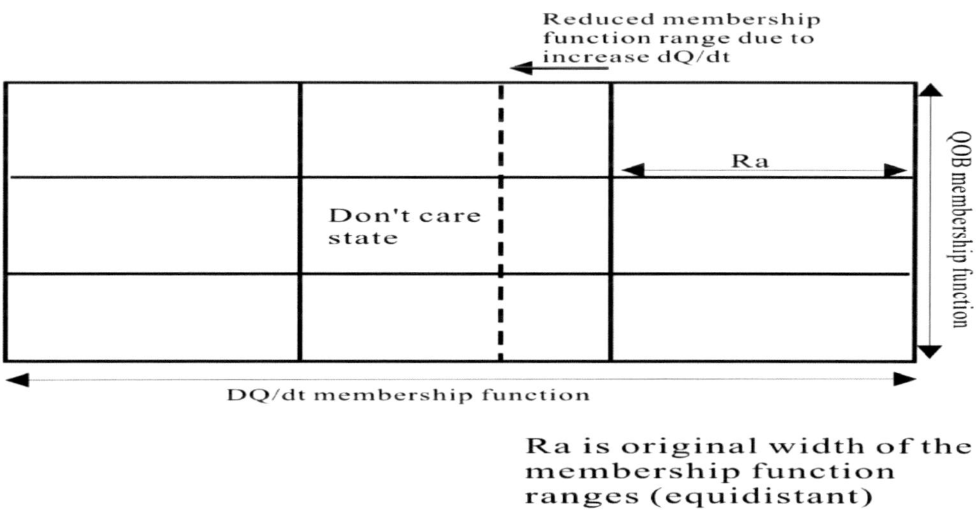

Figure 4.7. A-FLC adjustment of the range threshold of the *don't care* state on the fly.

4.5.2.1. Experimental Results

Different experiments were conducted over the Internet to verify the A-FLC prototype implemented in Java. The preliminary results indicated that it is indeed more efficient and less oscillatory than its FLC predecessor. Different QOB_R and Δ values were tried in the experiments, and the results presented here are based on: $\Delta = 0.2$ (or 20%), and

$QOB_R = 0.8$ (or 80%). The QOB_R value is the reference point chosen for the $\{0,\Delta\}^2$ objective function (i.e. corresponding to the "0" position in $\{0,\Delta\}^2$). Similar to its predecessor the A-FLC never failed to upkeep the Δ safety/tolerance margin in the experiments. Figure 4.8 shows the MD of the A-FLC control. The MD is measured by the M^3RT component in the A-FLC. If the A-FLC operation stops the last MD value together with the given safety margins, *Th1* (for QOB or P control) and *Th2* (for dQ/dt or D control) become a new point, namely, *[MD,(Th1,Th2)]* in the *MD-vs-Thresholds* graph. In this way, the graph records the past experience for the future determination of sounder *Th1* and *Th2* initializations for the A-FLC to run again. Figure 4.9 shows the A-FLC deviation situations with the same set of data as for figure 4.8 but with the capability to auto-tune the range threshold for "dynamic threshold" operations is absent. The absence makes the deviations more prominent. Figure 4.10 shows figure 4.8 and figure 4.9 in a comparative manner to make the difference in the deviations conspicuous. Figures 4.11, 4.12 and 4.13 are plots for another experiment. The results from this set concurred with the observations for the previous one. In fact, all the experiments indicated that auto-tuning of the range thresholds for the "*don't care*" fuzzy regions are important for yielding smoother, more responsive buffer overflow control. For the experimental results presented in this book the GT and GP values are respectively 0.003 radians and 5%. The readers can refer to the key references for more details.

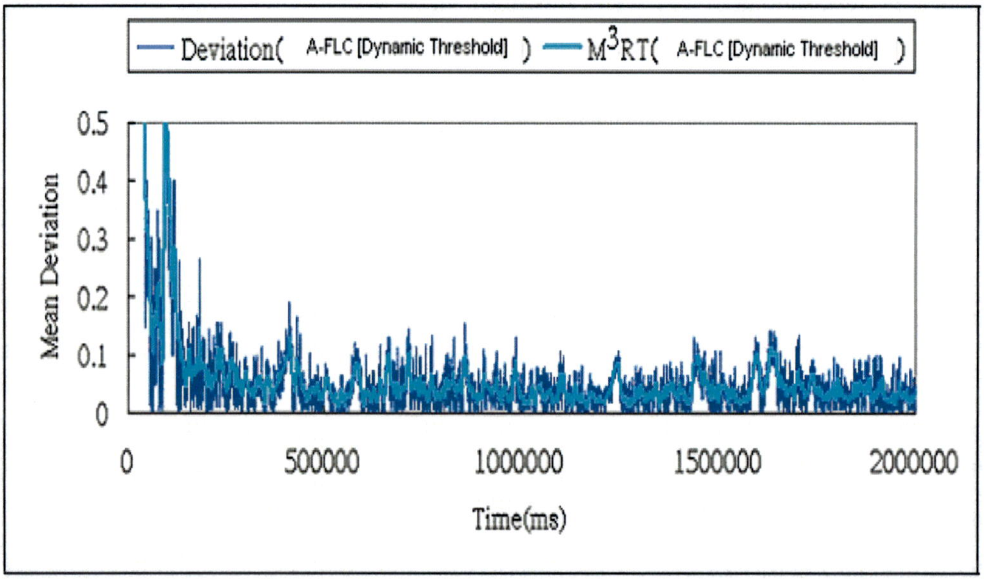

Figure 4.8. MD value by the M^3RT over time for A-FLC with "dynamic threshold".

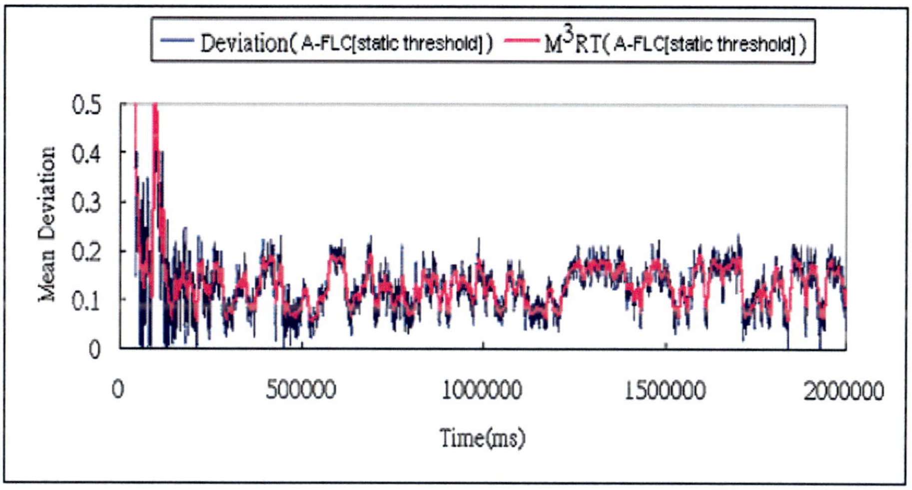

Figure 4.9. MD value by the M^3RT over time for A-FLC "static threshold".

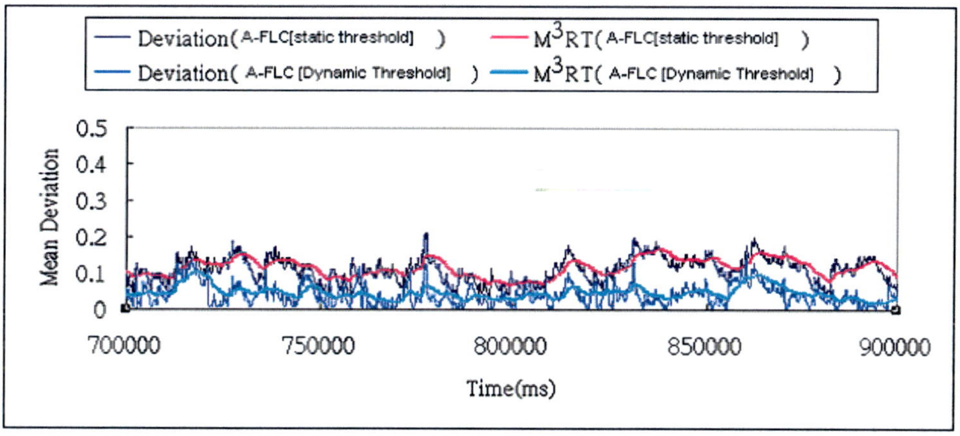

Figure 4.10. Comparing the A-FLC[static threshold] and the A-FLC[dynamic threshold].

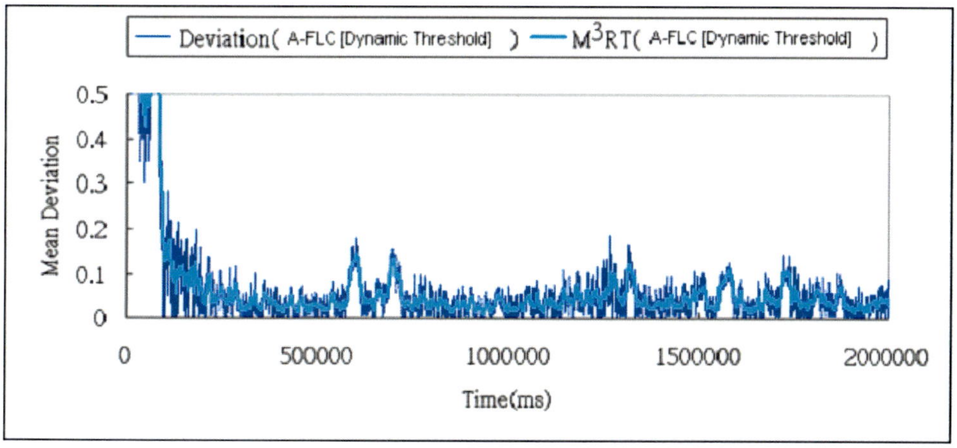

Figure 4.11. MD value by the M^3RT over time for A-FLC dynamic threshold.

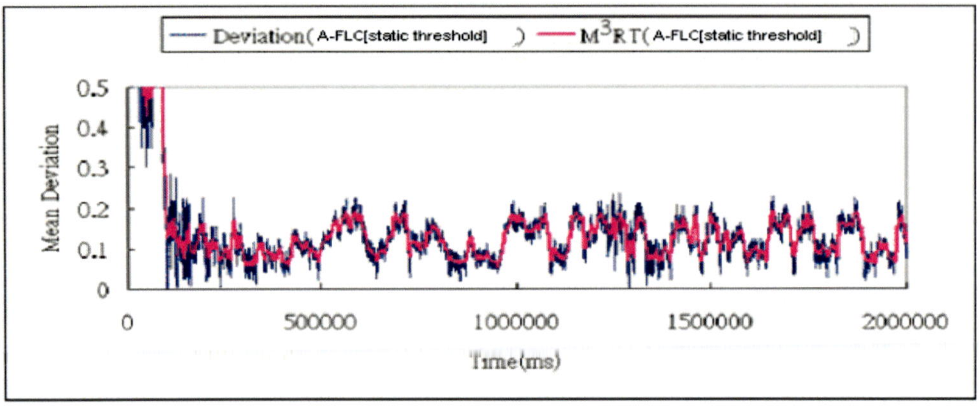

Figure 4.12. MD value by the M^3RT over time for A-FLC static threshold.

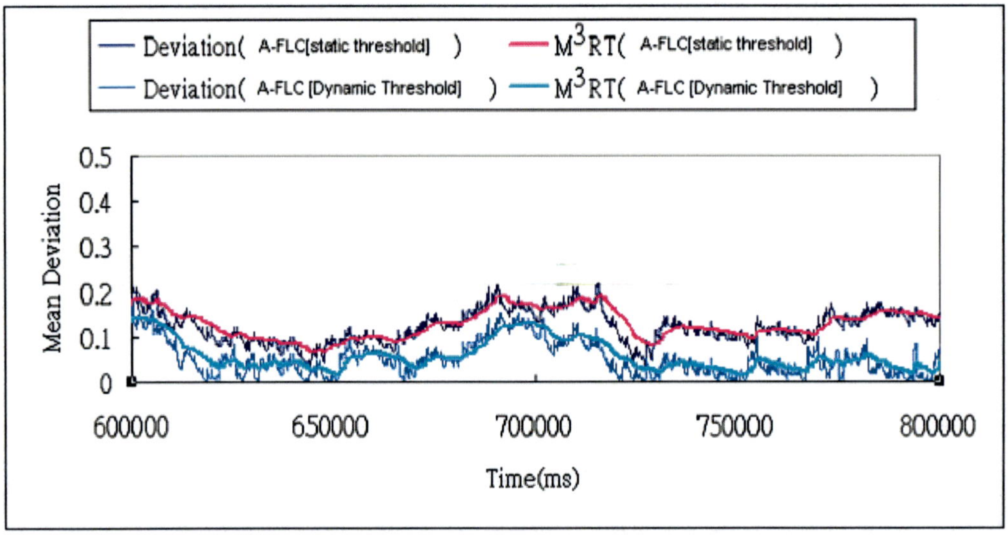

Figure 4.13. Comparing A-FLC [static threshold] and the A-FLC [dynamic threshold].

4.6. The Neural Network Controller (NNC)

Although the FLC preserves the PIDC merits minus its shortcomings, its convergence towards QOB_R can be oscillatory. The desire to attain a smoother QOB_R convergence for the $\{0,\Delta\}^2$ objective function led to the NNC proposal, which was also inspired by the success of applying the neural network (NN) techniques in AQM (Active Queue Management) algorithms (e.g. [Aweya1998]). After some detailed preliminary investigation it was concluded that the NN approach should be based on the feedforward network with backpropagation (BP). The argument is that the BP approach is simpler and the NN controller can be trained efficiently with Δ as the teacher signal. Therefore, the NNC was proposed as a feed-forward BP perceptron [Lin2001NNC] with supervised training [Rumelhart1986], as shown in figure 4.14.

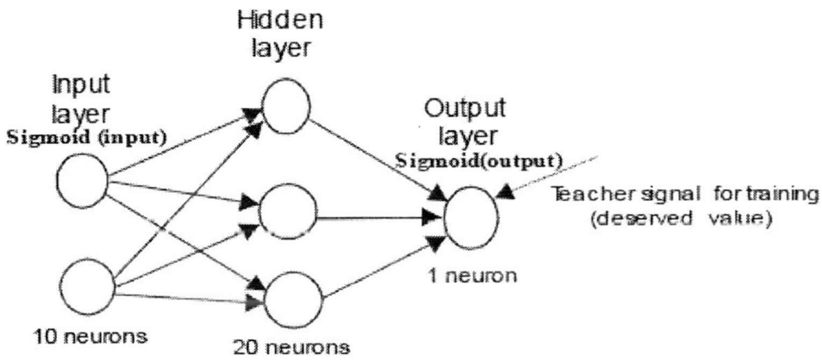

Figure 4.14. Backpropagation NNC control model.

The NNC prototype's configuration consists of: a) a single input layer of 10 neurons; b) a single hidden layer of 20 neurons; and c) a single neuron in the output layer. The training with Δ is based on the Sigmoid function represented by $f(x) = 1.0/(1.0 + e^{-x})$. The activation values (energy) for the neurons in the hidden and output layers are computed respectively as follows:

a) Sigmoid($\sum$ InputActivation * weight (input-hidden))
b) Sigmoid($\sum$ OutputActivation * weight(hidden-output))

The NNC has an input vector Q_{vector} of ten variables as follows:

a) *Nine queue-length samples*: They are sampled at equal time distances within the chosen renewal window or period of W. If we divide W equally into nine portions then each sample is denoted by Q_{tX}, where X is 1,2,...9.
b) *10th element*: This is the queue length estimated by the M^3RT at the t9. That is, at the time point t9, which is the end point of the current W cycle, two samples are included, namely, $Queue_{CA\_estimate}$ and the queue length at that point. This means that M^3RT must run in parallel with the NNC as a logical entity.

The inclusion of $Queue_{CA\_estimate}$ (output from the M^3RT) is the basis for the argument that the NNC has the capability to proactively maintain the safety margin Δ. The rationale is that the main function of M^3RT is to predict the trend of the queue length distribution and therefore the instantaneous value of $Queue_{CA\_estimate}$ at t9 should reflect the next move of the queue length accurately. The output from the NNC is the predicted buffer length required to ensure that the queue is completely covered so that the safety margin Δ criterion will be met in the next W. The computation approach for the NNC is given by equations (4.1) and (4.2). The predicted buffer length $L(W+1)$ for the W+1 cycle is a function ($\int_{NN}(..)$ *is the symbolic representation*) of the variables vector Q_{vector} (W) and $Queue_{CA\_estimate}$ ($t9_W$).

$$L(W+1) = \int_{NN} [Q_{vector}(W), Queue_{CA\_estimate}(t9_w)] \ldots\ldots(4.1)$$

$$Q_{vector} = \{Q_{t1_W}, Q_{t2_W}, Q_{t3_W}, Q_{t4_W}, Q_{t5_W}, Q_{t6_W}, Q_{t7_W}, Q_{t8_W}, Q_{t9_W}\} \ldots..(4.2)$$

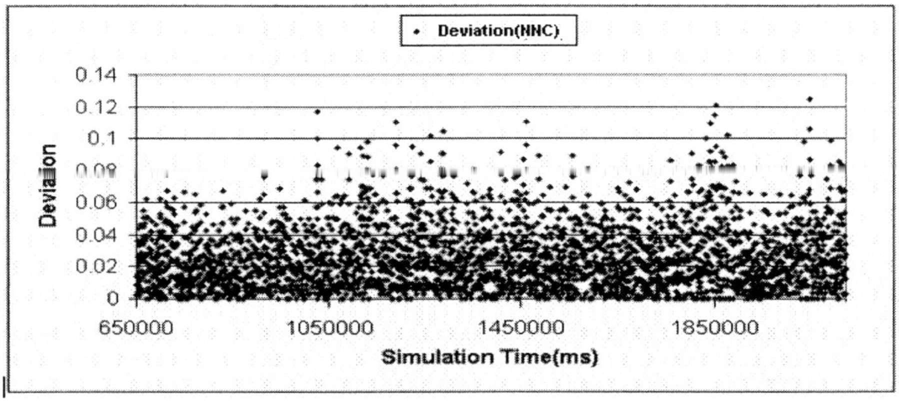

Figure 4.15. Deviation by NNC from objective function with QOB=0.8 (test case 1).

The NNC operation is divided into two phases, namely, *training* and *prediction*. The first is the training process for the BP approach to learn to respond properly by yielding the desired value with respect to the teacher signal; in this case, the teacher is the given Δ. Before training starts the weights of the NN arcs are randomized. The error, which is the difference between the predicted output and the desired value (DV) defined by the $(QOB_R - \Delta) \le DV \le (QOB_R + \Delta)$ range, should gradually decay as the learning process progresses. The training is considered to be completed if the controlled output is consistently within the DV range. The simulation performance by the NNC and that by the "NNC+M^3RT", namely, the NNC supported by the M^3RT in the form of $Queue_{CA\_estimate}$ or Q_{10} element in the Q_{vector}, are depicted in figures 4.15 and 4.16. M^3RT is synonymous with CA (*Convergence Algorithm*) for the former is the validated micro version of the CA *macro* Java implementation called the M^2RT.

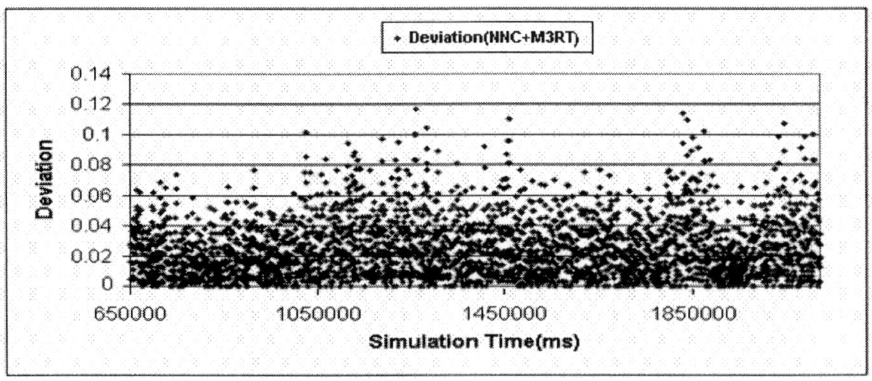

Figure 4.16. Deviation by (NNC+ M^3RT) from objective function, QOB=0.8 – test case 2.

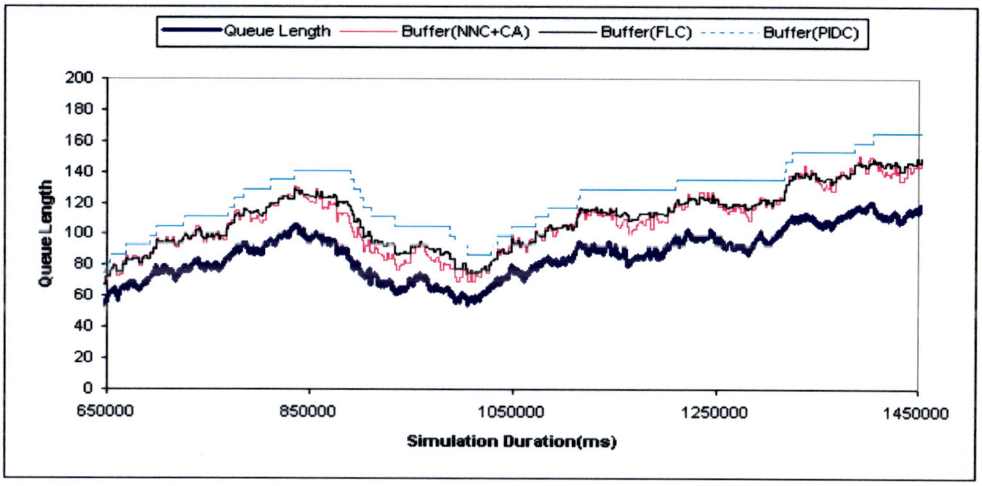

Figure 4.17. Comparing the PIDC, FLC and NNC ($QOB_R = 0.8$).

The average of the deviation of the NNC output is measured by the following equation: $\left[\sum_{i=1}^{k} | \Delta - QOB_i |\right] \Big/ k$. Table 4.3 ($\Delta = 0.2$, sample size k = 7200) shows three cases out of the many simulations, which confirm that the "NNC+M^3RT" consistently has at least 5 percent or less of deviation from the QOB_R than the NNC working alone. Without the M^3RT incorporation, the deviation can be as large as 25% in some cases, and our analysis indicates that this phenomenon is due to the fact that the knowledge from the last training of the NNC is not enough to deal with unexpected new situations. With the M^3RT presence, the largest deviation by the "NNC+ M^3RT" is around only 15%. This is the result of the integral effect provided by the M^3RT convergence process. Figure 4.17 compares the smoothness of convergence towards QOB_R by the PIDC, FLC and NNC (supported by CA/ M^3RT). The NNC and the FLC eliminate the PIDC shortcomings and consistently maintain the safety margin Δ. The maintenance by the NNC is much smoother than the FLC.

Table 4.3. Comparing three cases of deviations between NNC and "NNC+ M^3RT"

Controller	Case 1	Case 2	Case 3
NNC	0.02386	0.01853	0.02245
NNC+ M^3RT	0.02260	0.01655	0.02115
Performance improvement: $\frac{NNC - "NNC + M^3RT"}{NNC} * 100\%$	5.28%	10.7%	5.8%

4.6.1. Sensitivity Analysis of the Hidden Layer

The NNC stability can be analyzed by measuring the mean deviation (MD) from the chosen QOB_R reference in terms of "*the number of neurons in the NNC hidden layer versus different traffic patterns*". Figure 4.18 is one example.

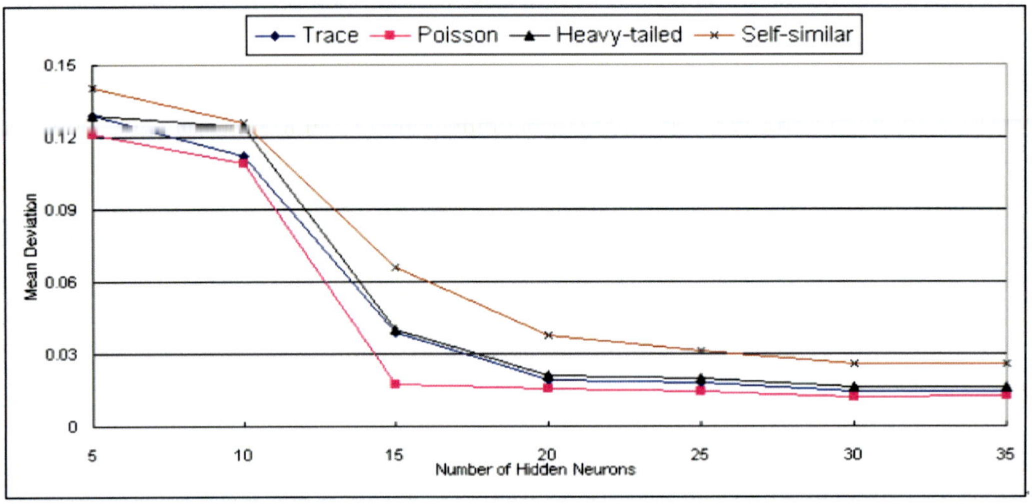

Figure 4.18. Mean deviation errors for using different numbers of neurons in the NNC hidden layer versus different possible Internet traffic patterns.

In this example, the empirical data shows that for maximum control effect the NNC hidden layer should have 20 neurons, which is the breakpoint. Using more neurons does not produce better performance by yielding a lower MD. For the Poisson trace, the mean deviation error settles down for 15 hidden neurons in the hidden layer, but for other traffic patterns at least 20 neurons are needed. All the experimental results from this stage indicate that it is safer to use 20 neurons for the hidden layer for Internet applications because Internet traffic pattern, which includes all the patterns in figure 4.18, switches quickly without warning.

4.6.2. Real-Time NNC Pruning

The aim of real-time pruning is to optimize the NNC configuration in an on-line manner to adaptively lower its control cycle time. In fact, the average NNC execution time is roughly four times that of the FLC tuner. After a thorough literature search, it was found that the existing pruning techniques are for off-line applications. In the off-line process, the neural network (NN) is first run to obtain some data for analysis and then optimized manually before it is run for the next round. This is basically a trial and error process [Gallant1992, Hagan1996]. The off-line approach is not suitable for real-time application because the NN should be able to adapt its configuration on the fly to suit the current operational conditions. With respect to the on-line and timeliness requirements, the *Hessian-based pruning* (HBP) is one effective technique proposed [Lin2004]. The HBP optimizes the NNC configuration at run-time in an adaptive, dynamic and cyclical manner. The "NNC plus HBP" combination is the new O-NNC (Optimized NNC) controller. In action, the HBP is a renewal process, and the optimization in every renewal cycle has two phases of operations, as shown in figure 4.19:

a) *First phase*: The *Learner* computes the weights of all the arcs in its neural network. After that, all the insignificant arcs are marked by the principle of *dynamic sensitivity analysis*.
b) *Second phase*: After the *Learner* becomes the *Chief* all the marked arcs are virtually pruned (excluded) from its computation to shorten the control cycle time. Virtual pruning means that the physical skeletal NNC configuration is intact and provides the *bare basis* for every pruning operation.

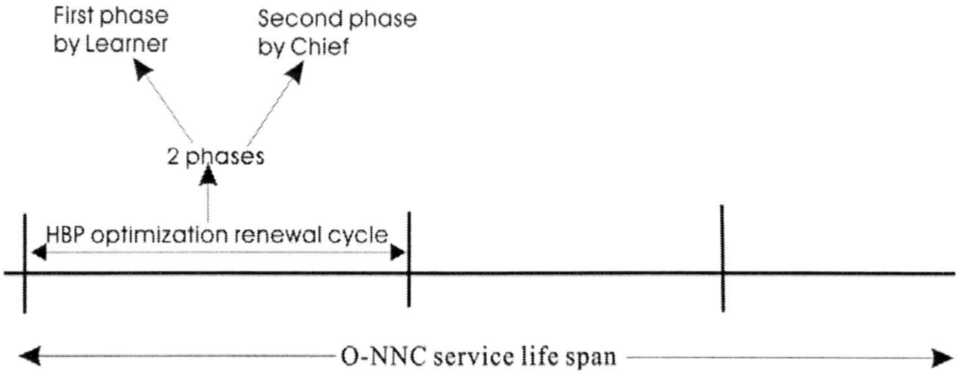

Figure 4.19. The HBP is as a renewal process.

The choice of HBP over other techniques is dictated by the fact that the NNC optimization process is real-time and its simplicity is the key to success. Other techniques from the literature normally require complex mathematical manipulations. Besides, the published experience for the feed-forward neural network pruning is exclusively off-line. This makes them unsuitable for the on-line NNC application. The HBP operation is based on *dynamic sensitivity analysis*. The rationale for this is to mark and skip a neural network connection if the error/tolerance of the neural computation is insensitive to its presence. For the NNC the error/tolerance is the $\pm\Delta$ band about the QOB_R reference. The core of the HBP technique is this concept: "*if a neural network converges toward a target function so will its derivatives* [Gallant1992]". In fact, the main difference among all the identified *performance-learning* laws from the literature [Hagan1996] is how they leverage the different parameters (e.g. weights and biases).

The HBP adopts the Taylor Series [Finney1994] (equation (4.3)) as the vehicle to differentiate the relative importance of the different neural network (NN) parameters. The meanings of the parameters in equation (4.3) are: F() – the function; w – the NN connection weight; Δw – the change in w; $\nabla F(w)$ – the gradient matrix (4.4); and $\nabla^2 F(w)$ – the *Hessian* matrix (4.5). The symbols in the equations mean the following: T for transpose, O for higher order term, n for the nth term, and $\partial / \partial w_1$ for partial differentiation. Thus, the expansion about w of $F(w+\Delta w)$ is given by equation (4.3).

$$F(w+\Delta w) = F(w) + \nabla F(w)^T \Delta w + \frac{1}{2}\Delta w^T \nabla^2 F(w) \Delta w + O(\|\Delta w\|^3) + \textit{more terms} \ldots \quad (4.3)$$

$$\nabla F(w): \begin{bmatrix} \frac{\partial}{\partial w_1} F(w) & \frac{\partial}{\partial w_2} F(w) \ldots & \frac{\partial}{\partial w_n} F(w) \end{bmatrix}^T \ldots\ldots\ldots\ldots (4.4)$$

$$\nabla^2 F(w): \begin{bmatrix} \frac{\partial^2}{\partial w_1^2} F(w) & \frac{\partial^2}{\partial w_1 w_2} F(w) & \ldots & \frac{\partial^2}{\partial w_1 \partial w_n} F(w) \\ \frac{\partial^2}{\partial w_2 \partial w_1} F(w) & \frac{\partial^2}{\partial w_2^2} F(w) & \ldots & \frac{\partial^2}{\partial w_2 \partial w_n} F(w) \\ \ldots & \ldots & \ldots & \ldots \\ \frac{\partial^2}{\partial w_n \partial w_1} F(w) & \frac{\partial^2}{\partial w_n \partial w_2} F(w) & \ldots & \frac{\partial^2}{\partial w_n^2} F(w) \end{bmatrix} \ldots\ldots\ldots (4.5)$$

The preliminary O-NNC results confirmed that the HBP performs as expected. The findings from the preliminary HBP experiments also concurred with similar experience published previously [Oh1998]. That is, the weighing factors (*synaptic weights* or *learning rates*) affect the convergence speed. Many different experiments were carried out to study the effect of different learning rates, and one set of results is presented in figure 4.20 for demonstration purposes. It shows how the correlation between the learning rate and the *mean square error* (MSR) varies. A learning rate is the magnitude of change when a connection weight is adjusted in training. For example, the desired output is $w_{i,j}^m(k+1) = w_{i,j}^m(k) - \alpha \partial F(x) / \partial w_{i,j}^m$, with $w_{i,j}^m(k)$ as current weight and α as the learning rate. The MSR, defined as, $MSR = \boldsymbol{E}[(\textit{target output} - \textit{actual output})^2]$, measures the control accuracy, with $\boldsymbol{E}$ as the averaging operator. The MSR should decrease when the convergence gets closer to the QOB_R reference. The experimental results, however, indicated that bigger learning rates may yield oscillatory convergence, as shown by the rates 23 and 24 in figure 4.20. In contrast, the smaller rates 21 and 22 produce much smoother control. Under the equation (4.3), the learning/training process should converge to the QOB_R reference, which is mathematically known as the *target global minimum surface*. The convergence makes the gradient vector $\nabla F(w)$ insignificant and eliminates the "$\nabla F(w)^T \Delta w$" term from equation (4.3). This implies not only that the larger ordinal terms in equation (4.3) can be ignored, but also a simplified form (equation (4.6)) is possible for the equation. Further simplification of equation (4.6) based on $\Delta F = F(w+\Delta w) - F(w)$ yields equation (4.7).

$$F(w+\Delta w) = F(w) + \frac{1}{2}\Delta w^T \nabla^2 F(w) \Delta w \quad (4.6)$$

$$\Delta F = \frac{1}{2}\Delta w^T \nabla^2 F(w) \Delta w \quad (4.7)$$

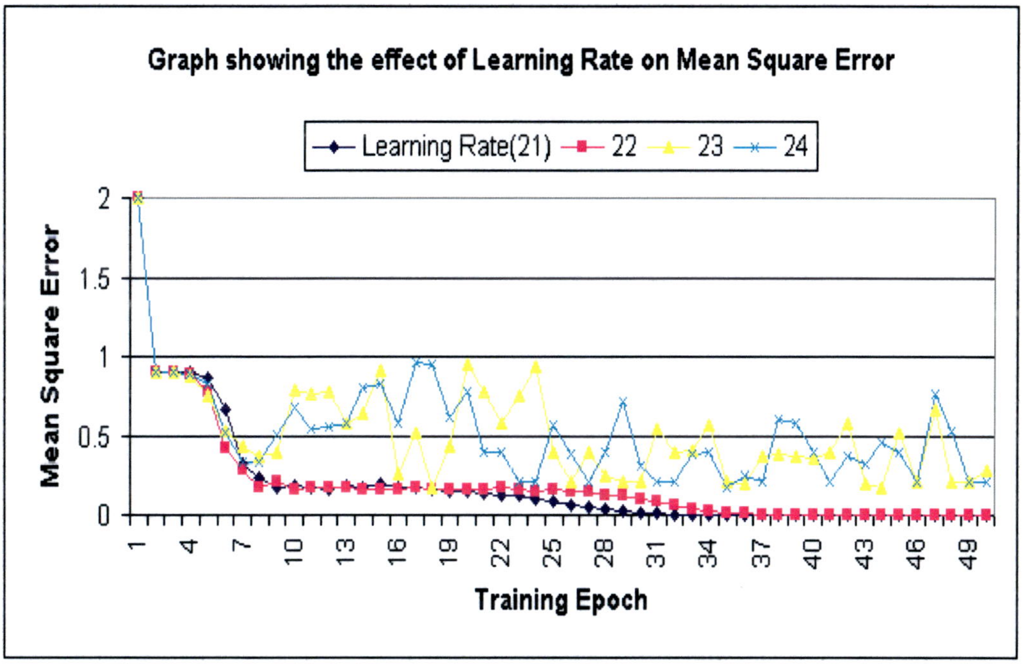

Figure 4.20. The graph showing the effect of learning rate on mean square error.

The HBP optimization cycle has two phases. The first phase is applied only to the *Learner* and the second to the current *Chief* role. The details involved are as follows (first three points belong to the first phase and the fourth point to the second phase):

a) Use Taylor series (equation (4.3)) to identify the significant neural network parameters.
b) Choose appropriate learning rates for the significant parameters to avoid convergence oscillations, as illustrated in figure 4.20.
c) Mark the synaptic weights that have insignificant impact on the Taylor series.
d) After the *Learner* has become the *Chief*, it excludes all the marked connections in its neural computation. The exclusion, represented by equation (4.8) is, in effect, virtual pruning of the insignificant connections. It is a logical, virtual process because the skeletal NNC neural network configuration remains intact except for excluding the marked connections in the subsequent O-NNC control. The pruning decision is based on the *Lagrangian* index S (to be explained later).

Since the optimization starts anew every time the *Learner* has completed training, which means new weights for the neural network connections, the optimized outcome should be unique. This makes the HBP optimization process dynamic and adaptive.

$$w_i+\Delta_{wi}=0 \tag{4.8}$$

$$S=\frac{1}{2}\Delta w^T\nabla^2 F(w)\Delta w-\lambda(U_i^T\Delta w+w_i) \tag{4.9}$$

If *Δw* in equation (4.7) is replaced by equation (4.8), then the *Lagrangian* equation (4.9) is formed. Now, equation (4.3) has become a typical *constrained optimization* problem [Bertsekas1982]. The symbols: U_i^T and λ in equation (4.10) are the unit vector and the Lagrange multiplier respectively. The optimum change in the weight vector w_i (equation (4.8)) is shown in equation (4.10). Every entry in w_i associates with a unique Lagrangian index S_i (equation (4.11)). In the first phase of the HBP optimisation process the S_i values are sorted so that the corresponding less significant w_i (neural network connection) can be excluded from the $Chief's$ neural computation, starting from the lowest S_i. The pruning stops if the exclusion of the current S_i affects the accuracy of the convergence process. Only after the virtual pruning process has been completed does the *Learner* become the *Chief* [Lin2004].

$$\Delta_{wi} = -\frac{w_i}{[\nabla^2 F(w)^{-1}]_{i,i}} \nabla^2 F(w)^{-1} U_i \tag{4.10}$$

$$S_i = \frac{w_i^2}{2[\nabla^2 F(w)^{-1}]_{i,i}} \tag{4.11}$$

4.6.2.1. Experimental Results

Different experiments with different waveforms (e.g. SRD and LRD) were conducted to verify the efficacy and correctness of the HBP technique and the O-NNC. The set up for the experiments is similar to figure 4.1b. The preliminary results confirmed that HBP technique shortens the O-NNC control cycle time consistently. The skeletal configuration of the O-NNC in the experiments is the same as the NNC prototype with 10 input neurons, 20 neurons for the hidden layer, and one output neuron. This configuration is fully connected, with 200 connections between the input layer and the hidden layer, as well as 20 connections between the hidden layer and the output layer. The O-NNC result in figure 4.21 is produced by a configuration that has a hidden layer of 187 arcs instead of the 220 full connections because 33 of them are pruned by the dynamic HBP. Different experimental results indicated that the O-NNC has the capability to yield the same level of buffer overflow elimination efficacy as the un-optimized NNC, but with shorter convergence time to reach QOB_R. Figure 4.22 shows that O-NNC always ensures that the QOB value is within the tolerance band of $|2\Delta|$ (QOB_R=0.8). It compares the QOB deviation profiles of the three controllers. As illustrated by table 4.4, the O-NNC, however, has a larger mean deviation (MD) than the un-optimized NNC, $MD = \left[\sum_{i=1}^{k} |\Delta - QOB_i|\right] / k$.

The PID controller (PIDC) is algorithmic in nature. It is therefore also referred to as the Algorithmic PID (A-PID) controller [Ip2001]. The PIDC makes use of the Convergence Algorithm (CA), which is implemented at the *micro level.* At this level the CA exists as an independent logical object that runs in parallel with the PIDC main body. In this form, the CA is called the M^3RT entity that can be invoked for service anytime and anywhere by message passing.

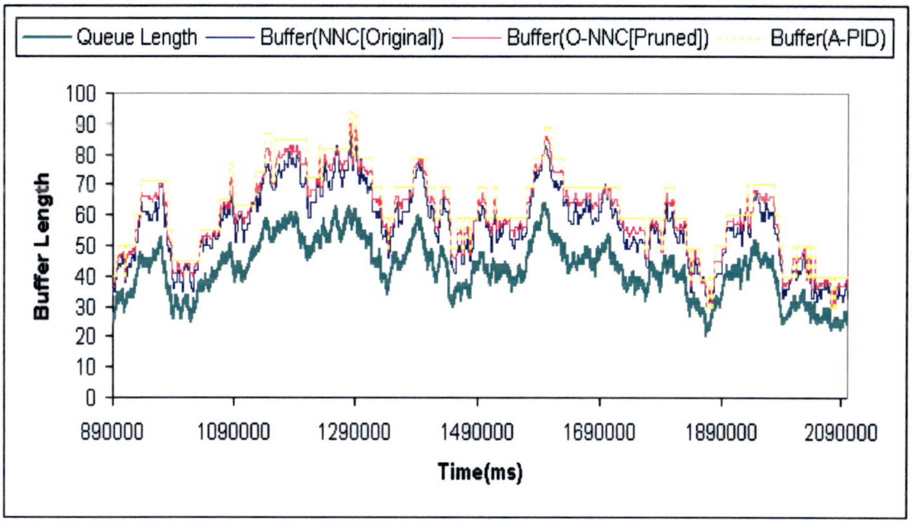

Figure 4.21. A set of experimental results to compare NNC, O-NNC and A-PID.

Table 4.4. Mean deviations for figure 6.2.1.2

Controller/tuner	Mean Deviation
NNC (Original)	0.0536
O-NNC (Pruned)	0.0916
A-PID	0.1279

Table 4.5. Comparing the average number of clock cycles per tuner cycle

Controller/tuner	The measured average number of clock cycles per tuner control cycle
NNC (Original and un-optimized)]	10800
O-NNC (Pruned/optimized)	9250 ($9250/10800 \approx 0.857$; 85.7%)

The average control cycle time or CCT for the O-NNC is only 9250 clock pulses compared to the 10800 for the NNC (table 4.5). The CCT in clock pulses are measured with the *Intel's VTune Performance Analyzer* [VTune2002], and they can be converted easily into the *physical control cycle time* for any platform by $P\_CCT = CCT * 1/Hz$, where *Hz* is the platform's operating speed in Hertz. Figure 4.22 also compares the three controllers O-NNC, NNC and A-PID in terms of the convergence smoothness. Figure 4.23 provides more convergence stability details for figure 4.22 in terms of the individual deviations over time from the QOB_R reference of the $\{0, \Delta\}^2$. The performance of the NNC (original) and the O-NNC (pruned) is better than A-PID by having a smaller deviation error.

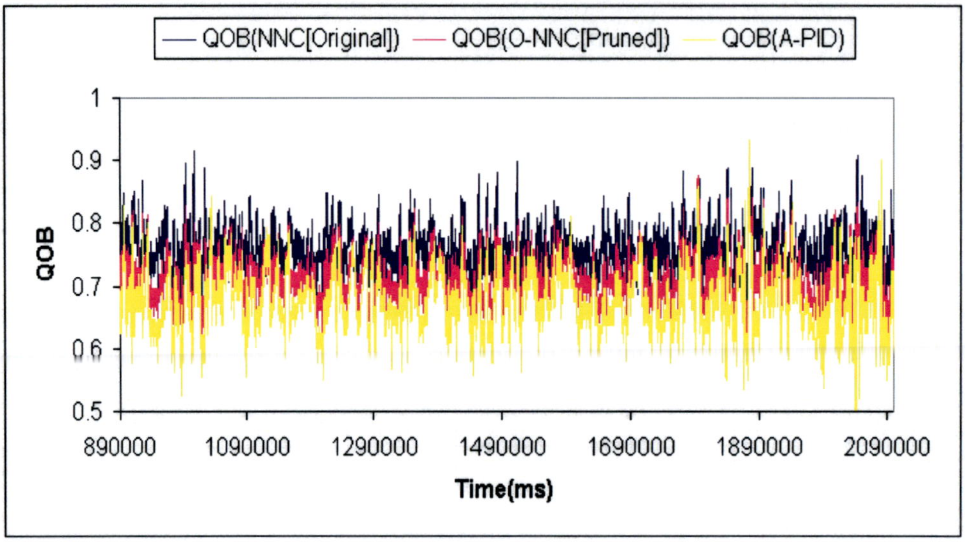

Figure 4.22. Indication of the HBP convergence stability.

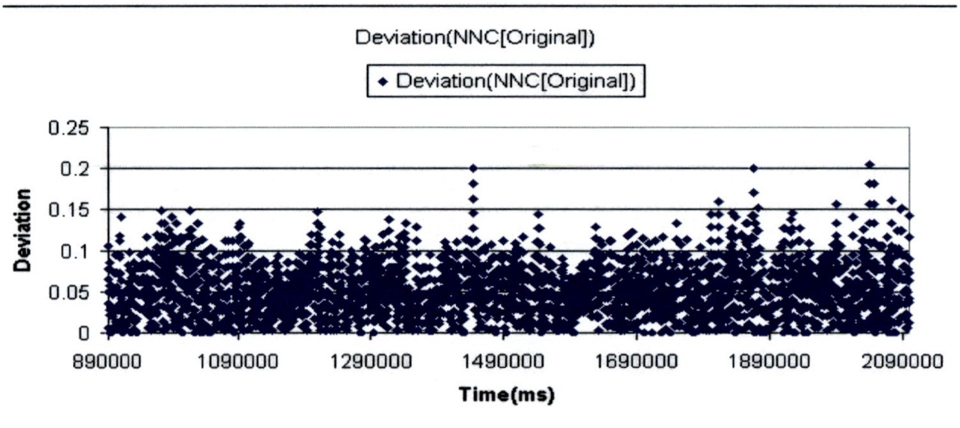

Figure 4.23a. Deviation profile of the original NNC.

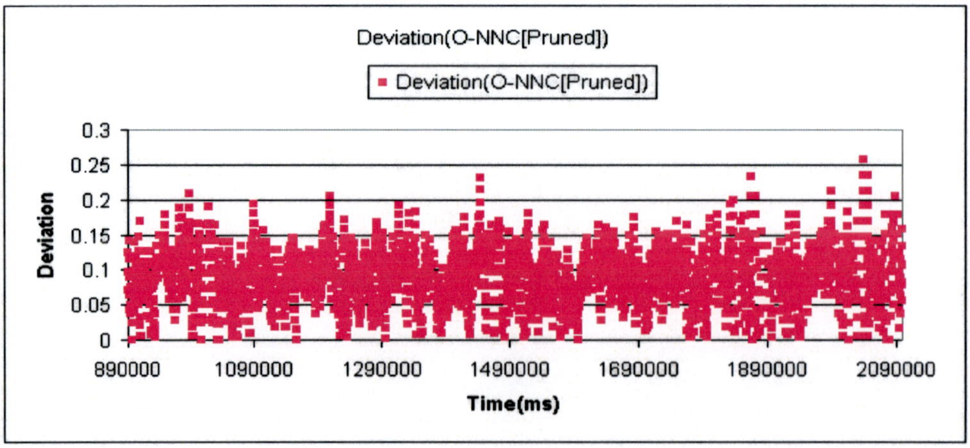

Figure 4.23b. Deviation profile of the O-NNC.

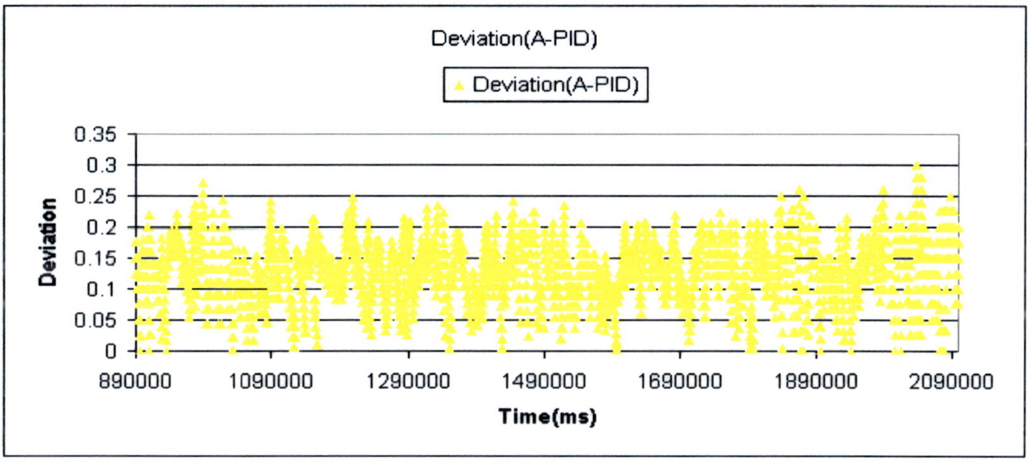

Figure 4.23c. Deviation by the A-PID controller.

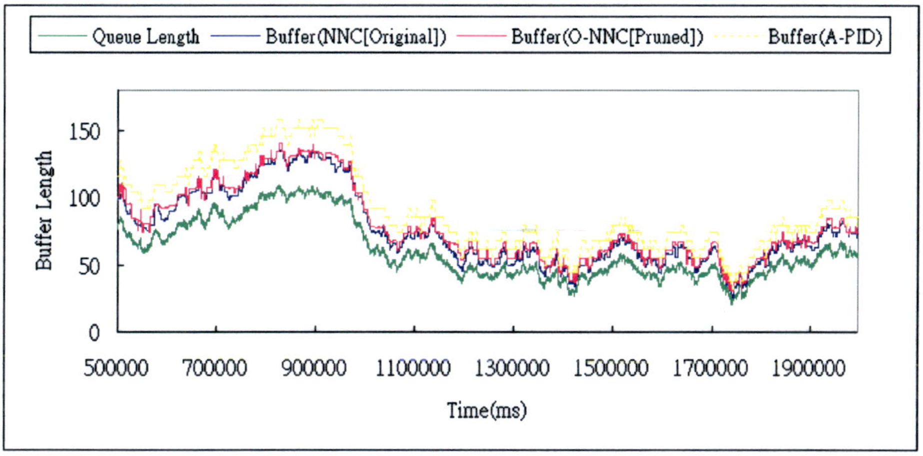

Figure 4.24. Another comparison of three controllers.

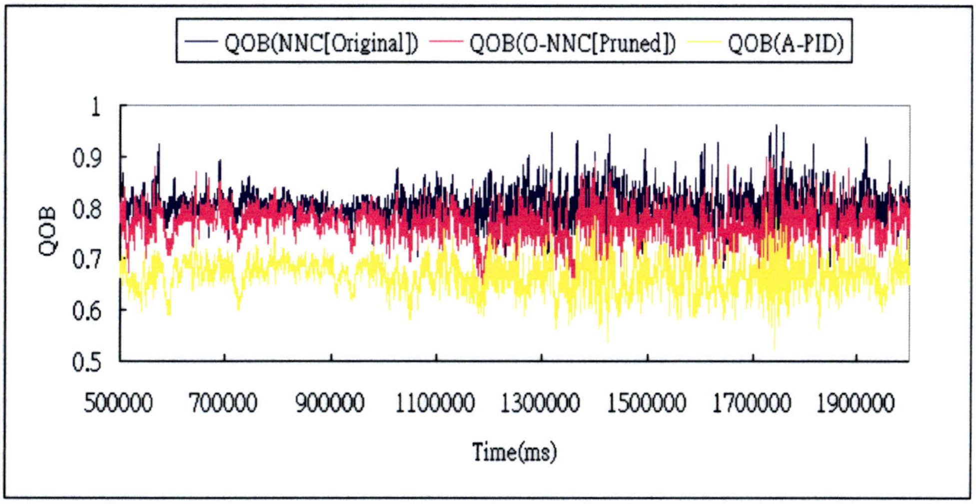

Figure 4.25. The QOB profiles of the three controllers.

Figure 4.24 is another comparison of the three controllers in terms of their efficacy in the dynamic buffer adjustment/tuning process. Figure 4.25 compares the QOB profiles of the three controllers, and figure 4.26 to figure 4.28 show the deviations of the individual controllers. Different experimental results concluded that both the NNC and the O-NNC perform as efficiently as the A-PID but without its shortcomings. Despite its consistency in converging accurately to the QOB_R reference of the $\{0,\Delta\}^2$ objective function, the O-NNC dynamic tuning process is more oscillatory than the un-optimized NNC. The oscillation is an undesirable side effect of the dynamic HBP optimization cycles. Further detailed study of this problem is required so that the oscillation can be smoothed.

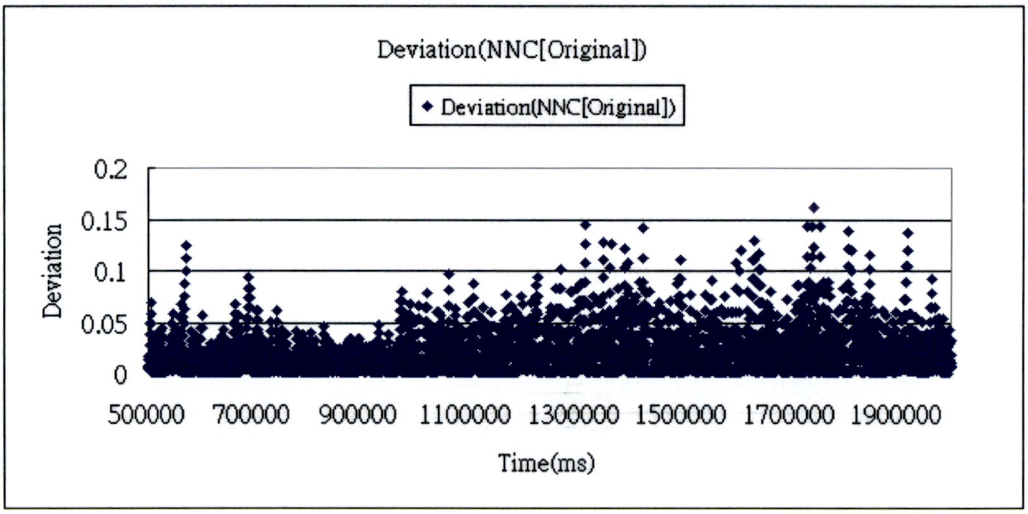

Figure 4.26. The deviation profile by the original NNC.

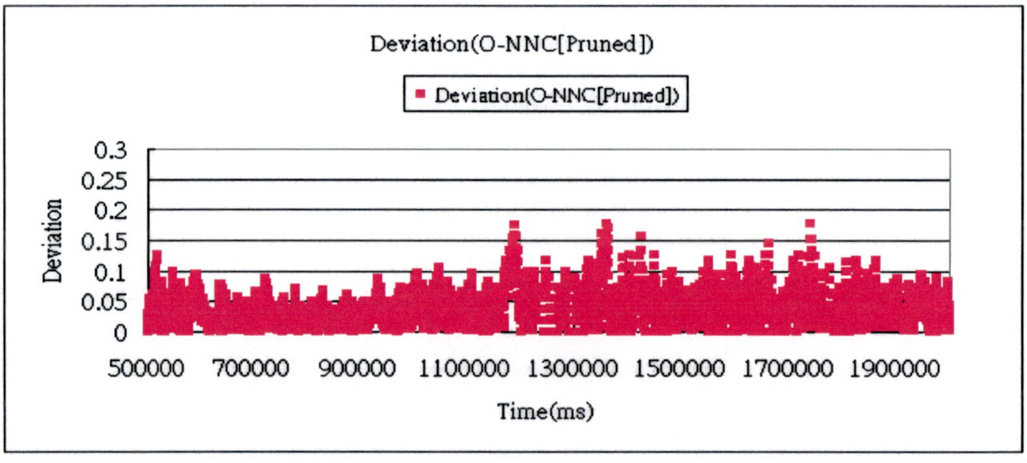

Figure 4.27. The deviation profile by the O-NNC.

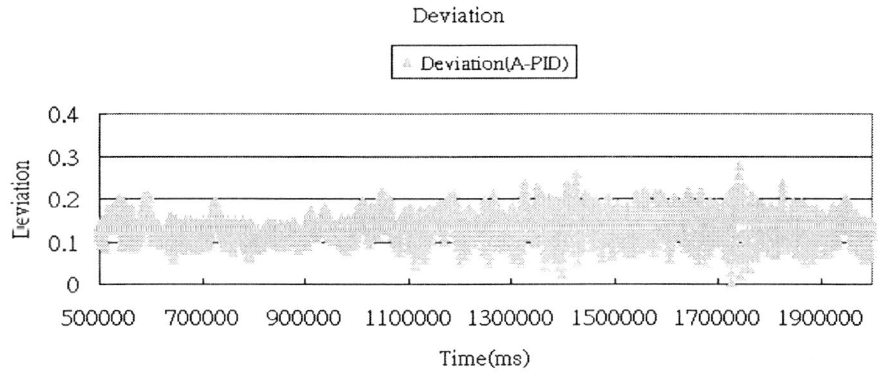

Figure 4.28. The deviation profile by the A-PID.

4.7. SUMMARY

In this chapter, five dynamic buffer tuners, PD, PIDC, GAC, FLC and NNC are introduced. They represent a distinctive school of thought in which the buffer length should cover the queue length at all times. The computation of the necessary buffer length adjustment to achieve the purpose is conducted on the fly. The development of the tuners has been an evolutionary process. The PD model was the first of its kind proposed for dynamic buffer tuning but the possibility of it producing buffer overflow led to the PIDC proposal. PD and PIDC are algorithmic, and the two shortcomings of the PIDC triggered the thought of using soft-computing techniques for their elimination. In the process, the concept of objective function namely $\{0,\Delta\}^2$ was introduced. The aim is to ensure that the difference between the buffer length and the queue length at anytime is within the safety margin or tolerance of Δ.

The PIDC, FLC and NNC are suitable for real-time application because their control cycle times are short. As a result, they do not lead to significant computation delays and possible deleterious effects. The dynamic buffer tuners for user-level (or server-level) applications are important for the success of time-critical applications over the Internet because the active queue management (AQM) mechanism at the system/router level cannot eliminate user-level buffer overflow. The absence of any user-level dynamic buffer tuning means that the effort and resources afforded at the system level to prevent network congestion could be wasted. In addition to the wastage, the consequences could be serious because the server is deprived of the chance to rectify unfavorable conditions earlier and proactively.

The accuracy and stability of the PIDC, GAC, FLC and NNC are, however, sensitive to the pattern changes in the Internet traffic. To eliminate the ill effects of the Internet traffic, the dynamic buffer tuning process can make use of the real-time traffic pattern detection (RTPD) capability. That is, it reconfigures and fine-tunes its control mechanism to ward off the traffic ill effects introduced by dynamic traffic pattern changes. Chapter 3 introduced the RTPD technique, and the case studies in Chapter 6 demonstrate how RTPD can be utilized to support on-line system reconfigurations.

4.8. Key References

[Braden1998] B. Braden et al., Recommendation on Queue Management and Congestion Avoidance in the Internet, *RFC2309,* April 1998

[IP2001] May T.W. Ip, Wilfred W.K. Lin, Allan K.Y. Wong, Tharam S. Dillon and Dian Hui Wang, An Adaptive Buffer Management Algorithm for Enhancing Dependability and Performance in Mobile-Object-Based Real-time Computing, *IEEE ISORC'2001 Conference,* Magdenburg, Germany, May 2001, 138-144

[Lin2004] Wilfred W.K. Lin, Allan K.Y. Wong and Tharam S. Dillon, HBP: An Optimization Technique to Shorten the Control Cycle Time of the Neural Network Controller (NNC) that Provides Dynamic Buffer Tuning to Eliminate Overflow at the User Level, *International Journal of Computer Systems, Science and Engineering,* 2004, 19(2), 75-84

[Lin2004a] W. K. Lin, Allan K. Y. Wong, and Tharam S. Dillon, A Novel Adaptive Fuzzy Logic Controller (A-FLC) to Reduce Retransmission and Service Roundtrip Time for Logical TCP Channels over the Internet, *Proc. of the EU2004 Conference,* August 2004, Japan, 942-951

[Lin2005a] W. K. Lin, Allan K. Y. Wong, and Tharam S. Dillon, Application of Soft Computing Techniques to Adaptive User Buffer Overflow Control on the Internet, *IEEE Transactions of Systems, Man and Cybernetics, Part C*

[Lin2005b] Wilfred W.K. Lin, Allan K.Y. Wong and Richard S.L. Wu, Applying Fuzzy Logic and Genetic Algorithms to Enhance the Efficacy of the PID Controller in Buffer Overflow Elimination for Better Channel Response Timeliness over the Internet, *Journal of Concurrency and Computation: Practice and Experience,* 2005

[Wong1999] Allan K.Y. Wong and Tharam S. Dillon, A Fault-Tolerant Data Communication Setup to Improve Reliability and Performance for Internet-Based Distributed Applications, the Proceedings of the 1999 Pacific Rim International Symposium on Dependable Computing (PRDC'99), December 1999, Hong Kong (SAR), P.R. China, 268-275

[Wong2002GAC] Allan K.Y. Wong, Wilfred W.K. Lin, May T.W. Ip and Tharam S. Dillon, Genetic Algorithm and PID Control Together for Dynamic Anticipative Marginal Buffer Management: An Effective Approach to Enhance Dependability and Performance for Distributed Mobile Object-Based Real-time Computing over the Internet, *Journal of Parallel and Distributed Computing (JPDC),* vol.62, Sept. 2002, 1433-1453

Chapter 5

DYNAMIC CACHE SIZE TUNING

5.1. INTRODUCTION

In section 1.4 of this book we noted many situations that require timely and rapid responses on the Internet. The quality of a service response is characterized by the length of the service roundtrip time (RTT). This is the time interval from the request initiation to the reception of the service result. The size, complexity and heterogeneity of the Internet make it difficult for applications running on it to effectively meet the required deadlines. In this book, two approaches for producing a more rapid service response are outlined, namely (a) dynamic buffer size tuning (DBST), and (b) dynamic cache size tuning (DCST). DBST was discussed in the last chapter, and this chapter focuses on DCST.

Information retrieval over the Internet is a client/server relationship [Mahanti2000] as shown in figure 5.1, with the "first leg" being between the client or requestor and the proxy server, and the "second leg" between the proxy server and the data source (remote web server). It is generally recognized that caching is a technique that can be employed to reduce the service roundtrip time because, if the object can be found in the proxy's local cache, then the "second leg" delay can be obviated (to be explained later in this section). The extra advantage of this is that, by finding the data in the cache, less data need to be transferred remotely across the network. As a result, it frees backbone bandwidth for public sharing for higher network throughput [Aggarwal1999]. Therefore, the overall average service roundtrip time (RTT) for information retrieval is made up of the average RTT_{leg1} for the first leg and the average RTT_{leg2} for the second. If the data object to be retrieved is not in the proxy's cache, then the latter enlists the DNS (*Domain Name Server*) to help locate it in one of the remote data sources (web servers). That is, the second leg goes through the DNS and accumulates a much longer time delay. The advantage of the proxy having a local cache is shown by the speedup calculation given by equation (5.0). In this equation, the average RTT for the first leg is RTT_{leg1} and for the second leg is RTT_{leg2}. If the proxy cache hit ratio ψ is 60% or 0.6 (i.e. miss ratio is $((1-\psi)$ or 40%), $RTT_{leg1}=1$, and $RTT_{leg2}=10$, then $S_{cache} = (1+10)/(1+[1-0.6]*10) = 11/5 = 2.2$ is the speedup.

$$S_{cache} = \frac{(RTT_{leg1} + RTT_{leg2})}{(RTT_{leg1} + [1-\psi] * RTT_{leg2})} \quad (5.0)$$

The S_{cache} speedup provided by caching is essential for sharing WWW information and data efficiently. Empirical evaluation [Bjarat1998, Duska1997] indicates that the web page size increases by 15% monthly, but the Internet backbone bandwidth improves by only 60% yearly. If this continues, the Internet backbone bandwidth will not be able to sustain the large number of web pages to be transferred across the Internet. The result would be massive network congestion, making the Internet lose its appeal. The congestion problem is real because of the following reasons: a) WWW is relatively inexpensive and faster than other communication means; and b) WWW provides a wide range of popular and useful information such as daily news, entertainment programs, weather reports, transportation schedules, financial news, and e-shopping.

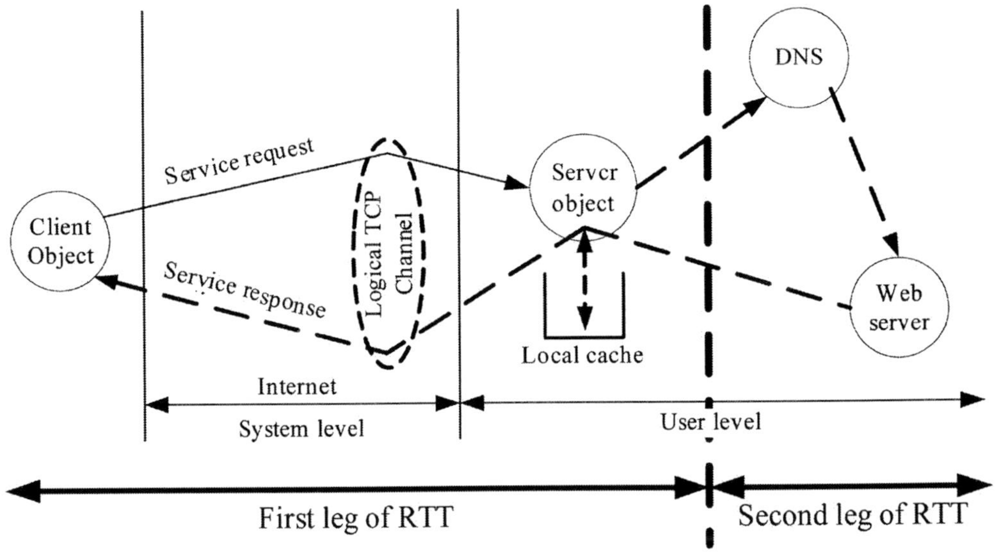

Figure 5.1. The relationship between the client and the proxy server.

The S_{cache} speedup has inspired different areas of research in caching. All the strategies and algorithms from the literature are aimed at producing a high S_{cache} value but not necessarily maintaining it. These approaches use a fixed/static cache size and leverage different parameters. Too many parameters being leveraged at the same time, however, could be counterproductive because heavy parameterization means long execution time [Aggarwal1999, Jin2000a]. A long execution time means that by the time the caching remedy is computed, the actual problem has already disappeared. The remedy ends up correcting a spurious problem leading to undesirable or deleterious consequences. Maintaining a given hit ratio requires dynamic cache size tuning, and the novel MACSC dynamic cache tuner presented in this chapter is designed for this purpose. It has fast execution and thus little chance of producing deleterious effects because of its light parameterization. It leverages the relative data object popularity profile as the sole parameter.

The hit ratio is the probability of finding the required data locally in the proxy's cache. Conversely, the miss ratio is one minus the hit ratio. The hit ratio fluctuates with the clients' shift of preference for certain data items. It is advantageous to have a high proxy cache hit ratio because RTT_2, which involves the DNS, is usually very much longer than RTT_1. The DNS helps the proxy locate the required data objects in the right remote data source.

5.2. Related Work

The S_{cache} speedup benefits have motivated other relevant areas of active caching research. The aims of these areas include [Wang1999]: a) fast information retrieval; b) system robustness for fail-soft operations; c) caching operation transparency; d) system scalability; e) caching adaptivity in response to changing user demands and network environment; and f) stable collaborative caching by avoiding naïve cache routing that introduces Internet perturbations. A summary of various strategies is as follows:

a) *Replacement strategies*: Enhancing a proxy server's S_{cache} by efficaciously pushing out the aged data in a fixed-size cache to make room for the new "hot" ones [Arlitt1999, Abrams1996] is the aim of replacement strategies. There are basically two approaches: LRU (least recently used – recency based) and LFU (least frequently used – frequency based). The recency concept associates with *temporal locality*, which states that the chance η of accessing a data object is inversely proportional to the elapsed time t since its last access (i.e. $\eta \propto 1/t$) [Jin2000a]. The frequency of access of a data object indicates its relative popularity. The log-log plot of access frequencies versus the corresponding ranked data objects is the Zipf-like behavior [Bjarat1998, Zipf]. For the same set of data objects, the Zipf-like behavior from the proxy point of view is different from that of the web server (data source). The difference is due to the fact that more hot data in the cache means less remote access to these objects in the data source (i.e. they are relatively cold). A replacement strategy leverages the chosen parameters to compute the cost/index that determines which cold data objects should be evicted first from the cache.
b) *Filtration of one-timers*: Removal of the rarely accessed "one-timer" objects is necessary to make the hot data objects in the proxy cache more concentrated for a higher hit ratio.
c) *Collaborative caching*: The creation of a hierarchy of different caching systems working together is a concept that enhances the chance of lowering RTT_{leg2} [Chankhunthod1996, Wu2000a]. These systems can work in a confined environment or in a distributed manner such as the CARP (*Cache Array Routing Protocol* [Valloppillil1998]). The problem with hierarchy caching is that the higher level caches would incur long queuing time and easily become the operational bottlenecks. If it is distributed, naïve routing from one cache system to another based on dynamic network statistics can cause serious oscillations in the whole system [Aggarwal1999].

d) *Prefetching*: Proactively putting potential hot data objects into the proxy cache is the aim, but so far this approach has yielded only limited benefits [Kroeger1997].
e) *Cache data coherency*: Empirically, a bigger cache usually yields a higher hit ratio, but it is a source of data incoherence because the stale data in the proxy cache is not flushed frequently enough [Dingle1996].
f) *Dynamic data*: Although this is one of the least explored areas, it is a significant one. Dynamic data are basically non-cacheable unless first manipulated (e.g. data generated dynamically by the server) by special techniques such as active cache and server accelerator [Wang1999].
g) *Web traffic*: This involves two components: a) clients' data objects access patterns as determined by preferences at the time [Barford1999], and b) the information retrieval inter-arrival times (IAT) that intrinsically follow the power laws [Medina2000]. In fact, clients usually shift their preferences towards certain data objects as time goes by. The IAT distribution can switch between LRD (*long range dependence* such as self-similar) and SRD (*short range dependence* such as Markovian), which can cause caching system instability [Wu2004, Wu2005].
h) *Adaptive caching*: The strategies in this area fulfill different *adaptivity* requirements [Wang1999]. From the literature, two main streams can be identified: adaptive replacement and dynamic cache size tuning. The adaptive replacement stream, which is still very rudimentary, addresses the following: 1) adaptive replacement strategies that can activate/deactivate some parameters in a timely manner to achieve a more efficient replacement process [Kelly1999]; and 2) selective application of different replacement strategies in a dynamic manner so that specific conditions such as workload and traffic pattern can be dealt with. The known algorithms for the two approaches mentioned above, however, work with a fixed-size cache. Therefore, they do not have the capability to maintain a given hit ratio under all circumstances.

The dynamic cache size tuning approach not only yields a high hit ratio but also maintains it consistently on the fly. The adjustment process will automatically compensate for any changes that reduce the hit ratio. These changes include swift shift of user preference for certain data objects over time and the ill effects caused by different traffic patterns on the caching system's stability [Wu2004]. The novel MACSC strategy performs dynamic cache size tuning over the Internet. It is a simple strategy, in that it leverages only a single parameter to carry out the tuning process, namely, the *relative object popularity*. The MACSC power and accuracy are independent of the web traffic because it utilizes results statistically computed on the fly by the IEPM (Internet End-to-End Performance Measurement [Cottrell1999]) support, namely, the Convergence Algorithm (CA), which is based on the *Central Limit Theorem*, [Wong2001a, Wong2001b, Wong2002a] to adaptively adjust the cache size.

5.3. THE MACSC FRAMEWORK

The MACSC (*Model for Adaptive Cache Size Control*) is a novel and original framework because it is the only known approach that addresses the issue of dynamic cache size tuning

[Wong2003a]. It maintains the given cache hit ratio adaptively by tuning the cache size according to the current popularity ratio spontaneously computed on the fly. The hit ratio maintenance not only shortens the client/server roundtrip time (RTT) consistently but also reduces the need for long-haul data transfer. As a result, more backbone network bandwidth is freed for public sharing, leading to better network throughput. The MACSC rationale is "*reasonable memory usage to maintain the given cache hit ratio*". The cache size has to be increased/decreased in a timely manner to accommodate enough hot data objects to satisfy the given hit ratio, without depleting the system memory resources.

The MACSC tunes the cache size by leveraging the *relative object popularity* (ROP) of data objects as the sole parameter. The framework is based on the Zipf-like behavior that is intrinsic to large traces of cached data objects [Breslau99, Zipf]. MACSC transforms the Zipf-like curve of the data objects into the bell curve conceptually. This bell curve is called the popularity distribution, which provides the basis for the popularity ratio computation to determine the size of the cache adjustment. It was observed, however, that data traces may deviate from the Zipf-like behavior. To make the MACSC model work, it is necessary to compensate for such deviations.

5.3.1. Popularity Ratio

The MACSC framework leverages the *relative object popularity* of data objects as the sole parameter to achieve dynamic cache size tuning. This is a relatively recent parameter leveraging concept for caching operations. For example, *relative object popularity* is leveraged as an additional parameter in the "*Popularity-Aware Greedy Dual-Size Web Proxy Caching Algorithms*" [Jin2000a]. However, leveraging this parameter alone to attain a higher cache hit ratio was never tried before the MACSC proposal. Using *relative object popularity* only as an additional parameter easily offsets its benefits because of heavy parameterization that prolongs the execution time of the replacement algorithm. The MACSC framework is derived directly from the Zipf-like behavior intrinsic to any caching systems [Bjarat1998, Zipf]. This behavior is represented by the log-log plot in figure 5.2a, which shows that the chance for the rth popular object in the *sorted/ranked list* (x-axis) to be accessed is proportional to $(1/r)^{-\beta}$ (i.e. y(r)), for $0 < \beta \leq 1$.

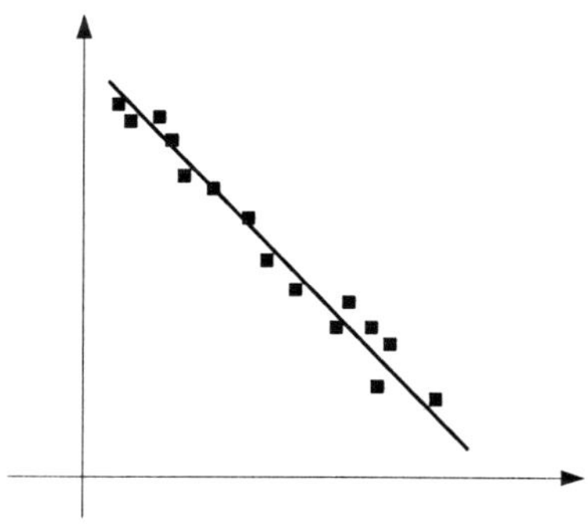

Figure 5.2a. Zipf-like distribution (log-log).

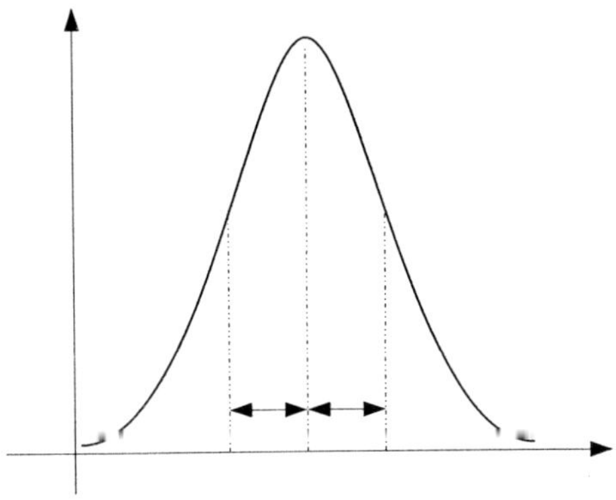

Figure 5.2b. Bell-shape distribution.

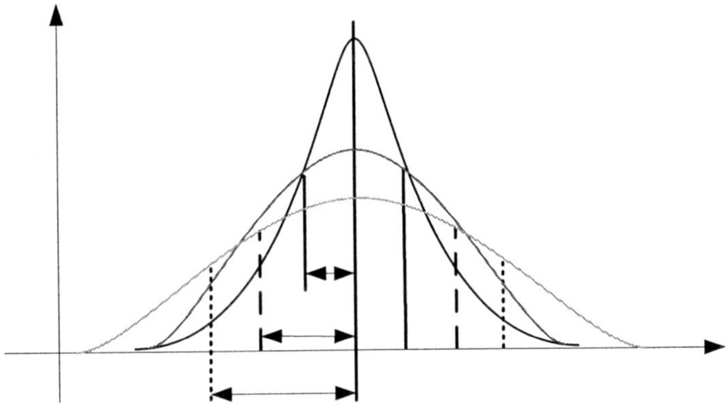

Figure 5.2c. Popularity Distribution (PD) changes over time and reflects the change in user preference.

The original plot of the raw scattered data shown in figure 5.2a can be approximated by the linear regression: $y(r) = f_{highest} - \beta(r-1)$, where β is a curve fitting parameter, r the ranked position of the object, and $f_{highest}$ the highest access frequency for the "*ranked-first*" object in the set. This regression is then mapped into the bell curve in figure 5.2b, which is known as the *popularity distribution* (PD) in the MACSC context. The PD represents the current profile of the relative popularity of the objects. The central region of this curve includes the more popular objects, and $f_{highest}$ is therefore considered as "*mean of the PD distribution*" for the MACSC operation [Wong2003a]. The changing shape of the PD over time is due to changes in the user preference towards specific data objects. The change is immediately reflected by the current standard deviation (SD). For example, the three curves, A, B and C in figure 5.2c, mimic the different PD shapes of three different time points. The running MACSC tuner traces all the PD changes by their current SD values continually and uses these changes to compute and decide how to adjust the cache size adaptively. This tuning process maintains the prescribed minimum hit ratio consistently, and the *adjusted cache size* (ACS) is based on one of the following two equations:

$$ACS_{SR}^{j} = CacheSize_{j-1} * \left(\frac{SD_j}{SD_{j-1}} \right) \quad (5.1)$$

$$ACS_{VR}^{j} = CacheSize_{j-1} * \left(\frac{SD_j}{SD_{j-1}} \right)^2 \quad (5.2)$$

The popularity ratios for equation (5.1) and equation (5.2) are the *standard deviation ratio* (SR) and the *variance ratio* (VR) respectively. SD_j is the measured standard deviation at j^{th} cycle. The basic concept embedded in equation (5.1) is that the current cache size should change with respect to the (SD_j/SD_{j-1}) ratio (i.e. the SR). The main point is to adjust the cache size by using standard deviations of two consecutive tuning cycles (i.e. $(j-1)^{th}$ and j^{th} cycles). The correct implementation of equation (5.1), however, depends on the accurate estimation of the initial cache size before the MACSC starts to run. Any initialization error will propagate throughout the whole dynamic cache size tuning process. To tackle this error propagation problem, the implementation of the concept by equation (5.1) is changed to the form shown by equation (5.3). The ∇ symbol is the number of standard deviations that represents the prescribed hit ratio to be maintained (e.g. $\nabla = 1$ for 68.3% and $\nabla = 2$ for 95%). It is actually part of the numerator as well of the denominator (but cancelled out) in the (SD_j/SD_{j-1}) expression. The $OS_{average}$ value in equation (5.3) is the mean object size that MACSC deals with. Before MACSC runs (i.e. at time $t=0$ and $j=1$) the cache size is initialized by $ACS_{SR_{t=0}}^{j=1} = 2 * \nabla * SD_{t=0}^{j=1} * OS_{average}$. The $SD_{t=0}^{j=1}$ value is the standard deviation computed from the past performance data. Equation (5.3) clearly indicates that for $j > 1$ the cache size tuning process does not depend on $SD_{t=0}^{j=1}$ but the current SD_j value of the jth cycle.

For implementation purposes, equation (5.2) should be changed to the form in equation (5.4). The MACSC cache size initialization is considered as the 1th cycle or $j=1$. The initial cache $ACS_{VR_{t=0}}^{j=1} = 2 * \nabla * \left(SD_{t=0}^{j=1}\right)^2 * OS_{average}$ becomes the "*seed value*" of $CacheSizeSeed_{j-1}$ for $j \geq 1$. In the subsequent dynamic cache tuning cycles, this seed value is replaced by $2 * \nabla * SD_j * OS_{average}$ and the factor "2" means one ∇ on both sides of the mean. This scheme stops the propagation of the initialization error due to inaccurate $ACS_{VR_{t=0}}^{j=1}$ estimation. The VR based tuning process is, hence, tied to the latest computed SD_j value for $j > 1$. The focus of the MACSC so far is mainly on how equation (5.1) or its alternative (5.3) can effectively support small caching systems for $j=1,2,...n$. These inexpensive systems have limited memory but are quite numerous in the field.

$$ACS_{SR}^{j} = 2 * \nabla * SD_j * OS_{average} \quad (5.3)$$

$$ACS_{VR}^{j} = 2 * \nabla * (SD_j)^2 * OS_{average} \quad (5.4)$$

5.3.2. Deviation Behavior Compensation

The popularity ratios of the MACSC framework conceptually come from the popularity distribution shown in figure 5.2b. Firstly, it has been empirically found that large caching systems exhibit Zipf-like behavior [Breslau1999, Zipf]. For every system, this behavior is unique and is characterized by a log-log linear regression of a specific β value in the $0 < \beta \leq 1$ range, where r marks the rth most popular object ranked in descending order (figure 5.3). For a trace of an insufficient number of requests the β value may be outside the $0 < \beta \leq 1$ range. In figure 5.3, the β value of the BU-Web-client is equal to 0.9817. However, the β value of the NASA-HTTP-client in figure 5.4 is equal to 1.1. It is because the number of requests contained in the NASA-HTTP-client trace is not large enough to put β inside the $0 < \beta \leq 1$ range. The deviation outside the range is the *deviation behavior* in the MACSC context. This phenomenon is rectified in two steps. The first is to assess the quality of the log-log linear regression that produces β (i.e. $y(r) = -\beta * r + C$). The quality is reflected by the *coefficient of determination* or R^2 ; a higher R^2 value is needed for better quality. The second step is to choose an appropriate threshold Th_{R^2} and reject the linear regression for $Th_{R^2} > R^2$. Rejection means continuing to use the last popularity ratio until the $R^2 > Th_{R^2}$ condition has been satisfied.

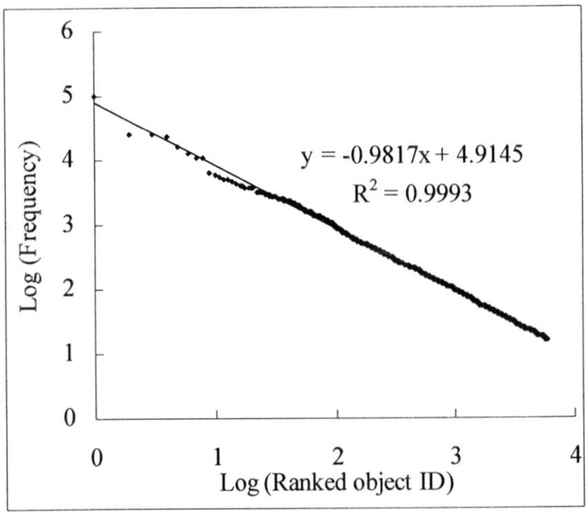

Figure 5.3. The log-log plot of BU-Web-client (169 days).

There are actually two different popularity distributions (PD), namely *bell(r)* and *bell(x)*. *Bell(r)* is the theoretical or conceptual popularity distribution and *bell(x)* is its "*anti-log*" version for implementation purposes. Figure 5.2c, in effect, depicts the changes of the PD shape over time due to shift of user preferences for particular data objects. The y-axis of the PD records the access frequencies (or probabilities) for the corresponding objects on the x-axis. The PD variability (spread) is characterized by the standard deviation (SD) that measures the popularity deviations of different data objects from the "*mean value*": $y(1)=f_{highest}$. The object with the highest access frequency in the Zipf-like correlation has virtually become the "*mean value*" of the PD by mapping. Once the SD of the current PD is statistically computed from the live data points sampled (e.g. SD_A for curve A in figure 5.2c), the *popularity ratio* (PR) (as shown in equation (5.1) or (5.2)) can be estimated for tuning the cache size adaptively to maintain the given cache hit ratio.

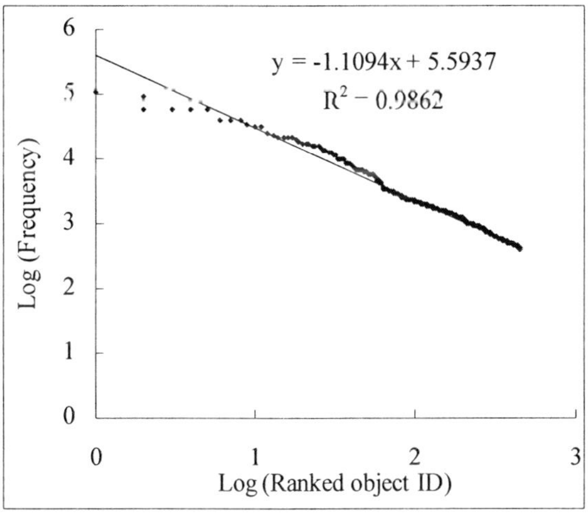

Figure 5.4. The log-log plot of NASA-HTTP-client (31 days).

It is necessary to empirically verify that *bell(x)* indeed produces the same effect as *bell(r)* for PR computation. In the MACSC context, this verification is called the "*kurtosis and skewness* (KS)" test. In the KS test, the skewness is computed by equation (5.5) and kurtosis is computed by the equation (5.6), where $\bar{x}$ and SD are the statistically measured mean and standard deviation respectively for the aggregate of m data points sampled. Skewness measures the symmetry of a bell curve. A positive value indicates that the bell curve embedded in the aggregate skews right (i.e. right tail is heavier than the left). Kurtosis measures whether the bell curve is peaked (positive value) or flat (negative value). For the normal distribution (i.e. Gaussian), kurtosis is equal to 3 and skewness is equal to 0.

$$skewness = \frac{\sum_{i=1}^{m}(x_i - \bar{x})^3}{(m-1)SD^3} \tag{5.5}$$

$$kurtosis = \frac{\sum_{i=1}^{m}(x_i - \bar{x})^4}{(m-1)SD^4} \tag{5.6}$$

The KS tests indicated that all the traces of data object accesses in our experiments were basically bell curves with reasonable kurtosis and skewness values. The KS tests also showed that even when the β values of some linear regressions were not in the $0 < \beta \le 1$ range, the linear regression is still conceptually valid for producing *bell(x)*. This forms the basis for calculating the popularity ratios for dynamic cache size tuning. The kurtosis and skewness validity depends on the predefined thresholds. The KS test will be demonstrated later.

5.4. Three Solutions to Implement the MACSC Framework

The MACSC framework maintains the given hit ratio adaptively by tuning the cache size according to the spontaneous popularity ratio. It is conceptually based on the transformation of the Zipf-like curve into the popularity distribution from which the popularity ratio is calculated. In fact, different statistical methods were employed and compared for such calculations. When these methods are combined with the original MACSC framework, they form different solutions for implementation purposes: MACSC(PE), MACSC((M^3RT), and MACSC(F-PE).

5.4.1. The MACSC(PE) Solution

The MACSC(PE) was the first implemented solution for the MACSC framework and adopts the *point-estimate* (PE) approach to estimate the SD_j value. This approach is represented by the statistical equation (5.4.1) which is based on the *Central Limit Theorem.* The parameters, $\bar{x}$ and s_x are the measured mean and standard deviation of n data points in the current aggregate/sample. Statistically, s_x and $\bar{x}$ are the estimators to predict the minimum sample size N that satisfies the given E and k tolerances. Although the VR-based tuner (equation (5.4.2)) is more effective in maintaining the given hit ratio, it consumes too much memory. This makes the VR-based tuner impractical for small caching systems with limited memory resources [Wu2003].

$$E\lambda = k\delta_{\bar{x}} = k\left(\delta_x \middle/ \sqrt{N}\right) \qquad (5.4.1)$$

$$N = \left(k\delta_x \middle/ E\lambda\right)^2 \qquad (5.4.2)$$

$$N = \left(ks_x \middle/ E\bar{x}\right)^2 \qquad (5.4.3)$$

The PE approach, represented by equation (5.4.1), is also called the $\sqrt{N} - equation$ scheme, which involves the following parameters:

a) *Fractional error tolerance* (E): This is the percentage error between λ, which is the ideal or population mean value and m, which is the mean for a series of *sample means* $\bar{x}$. Each $\bar{x}$ is computed from a sample of n data points or more on the fly; sample size $n \geq 10$. The computation of m is based on the *Central Limit Theorem.*

b) *SD tolerance* (*k*): This refers to the number of standard deviations (SD) that m is away from the *true mean* λ but is still tolerated (same tolerance connotation as E).

c) *Predicted standard deviation* ($\delta_{\bar{x}}$): It is estimated form the same series of sample means $\bar{x}$ of sample size $n \geq 10$. By the *Central Limit Theorem* $\delta_{\bar{x}} = \delta_x / \sqrt{n}$ holds, where δ_x is the population's (or true) SD.

d) *Minimum N value*: From $E\lambda = k\delta_{\bar{x}} = k\left(\delta_x / \sqrt{N}\right)$ relationship the *minimum sample size N* needed to estimate λ and δ_x for the given *k* and *E* values can be computed. In practice λ and δ_x should be substituted by $\bar{x}$ and s_x, and these substitutions convert equation (5.4.2) into equation (5.4.3). s_x is the standard deviation for the sample of data points or aggregate with mean $\bar{x}$. The N estimation is repetitive. In the first trial, a data sample of size n is used, and in every repetition a new sample of size n is added. That is, the number of samples used in the current repetition is $n = n + R * n$, where R indicates the repetition for $R = 0,1,\ldots$ The repetition stops when the $n \geq N$ criterion is satisfied. In every repetition, the PE computes $\bar{x}$ statistically from the n data points first and then computes $s_x = \sqrt{\frac{\sum_{i=1}^{N}(x_i - \bar{x})^2}{N-1}}$, where x_i marks the ith data item in the sample.

The following example demonstrates how the $\sqrt{N} - equation$ satisfies the $n \geq N$ criterion:

a) It is assumed that the initial 60 data samples (i.e. sample size is $n = 60$) have yielded 15 and 9 for $\bar{x}$ and s_x respectively.

b) The given SD tolerance is 2 (i.e. $k = 2$ or 95.4%), and the fractional tolerance *E* is therefore equal to 4.6% (*E*=0.046); both *E* and *k* connote the same error.

c) The *N* value then should be $N = (\frac{2*9}{0.046*15})^2 \approx 680$.

The value of $N \approx 680$ indicates that the initial sample size $n = 60$ is incorrect. To rectify the problem, one of the following compensation methods can be used:

a) The first is to collect (680 – 60) or 620 more data samples and re-calculate $\bar{x}$ and s_x. There is no guarantee, however, the new estimation by this approach would converge to $n \geq N$ and the same process therefore has to be repeated.

b) The second, which is adopted by the MACSC, samples 60 more data points and then re-calculate $\bar{x}$ and s_x from the total of 120 data samples (i.e. $n = 120$ for the 2nd trial). The PE is actually the $n = n + R * n$ repetitive process, which stops when the $n \geq N$ criterion is satisfied.

The MACSC adopts the second compensation method because it converges much faster. Usually $\bar{x}$ and s_x stabilize in the second or third trial as shown by previous experience. The above example, however, has not illustrated the IAT delays among the data points in the $n=n+R*n$ process. For example, sampling the 680 data items may take days, hours or merely seconds. This kind of unpredictable sampling time reduces the cache size tuning precision of the MACSC and makes the hit ratio oscillate in the steady state [Wu2003]. The key measure to resolve the unpredictable PE execution time problem is to make the $n=n+R*n$ process non-repetitive or $n=F$, where F is the fixed number of data points to be sampled. This has implicitly imposed the following "*PE criteria*": a) the alternative solution should have comparable computation time to PE; b) its accuracy should be traffic independent; c) its sensitivity to PD changes should be comparable to PE; and d) the solution should work with only F number of data points to make the sampling time predictable. These criteria led to the *Convergence Algorithm* (CA) adoption as a support for better MACSC performance, thus forming the unique MACSC(M^{3}RT) solution.

5.4.2. The MACSC(M3RT) Solution

In the MACSC(M^{3}RT) framework, the PE statistical computation was replaced by the Convergence Algorithm (CA), which is also known as the M^{3}RT method, to reduce the oscillation problem in MACSC(PE). The CA technique in its basic form is represented by the equations (5.4.4) and (5.4.5) [Wong2001a]. The relevant parameters are defined as follows:

a) M_0 is the first data sample when the M^{3}RT first started.
b) M_i is the mean estimated for the F (*flush limit*) number of data points collected in the time window.
c) M_{i-1} is the feedback of the last estimated mean to the current i^{th} estimation cycle
d) m_j^i is the jth sample in the ith M_i estimation cycle for $j=1,2...(F-1)$.

The simulated results indicated that the F (*flush limit*) range of $9 \leq F \leq 16$ yields faster convergence to M_i and $F=14$ is the fastest. Subsequently, the CA concept was refined and implemented into the macro M^{2}RT (Mean Message Response Time) tool. The M^{3}RT (*Micro Mean Message Response Time*) [Wong2002a] is its micro CA version that runs as an independent object in parallel with the MACSC main body. The CA form in equation (5.4.6) is has included the proportional (P) control to prevent severe oscillation in the M_i convergence process. The f parameter indicates the number of samples (i.e. m_j^i) used in the M_i prediction cycle.

$$M_0 = m_{j=0}^{i=1} \tag{5.4.4}$$

$$M_i = \frac{M_{i-1} + \sum_{j=1}^{j=F-1} m_j^i}{F} ; i > 1 \tag{5.4.5}$$

$$M_i = \frac{P * M_{i-1} + \sum_{j=1}^{j=f} m_j^i}{P + f} ; i > 1 \tag{5.4.6}$$

The use of M^3RT for MACSC support provides the following advantages:

a) It runs in parallel with the MACSC main body, which requires a much longer time to execute. As a result, the M^3RT does not prolong the MACSC execution time.
b) The M^3RT always settles to the mean of the distribution in the time window of interest. For example, figure 5.5 shows how M^3RT has correctly estimated the mean for a RTT trace of a TCP (*Transmission Control Protocol*) channel. This trace [Wong2001a] can be approximated by the gamma function in figure 5.6 with parameters: α_o = 2 and β_o = 5. The symbols in figure 5.5 to provide more information for the interested readers are as follows: *RawIAT* for IAT samples, *CA_EstMean* for "*the mean estimated by* M^3RT", *Raw Mean* for the mathematical average of all the IAT samples in the trace, and *Typical Mean* is the *mode* (i.e. typical value) in the trace.

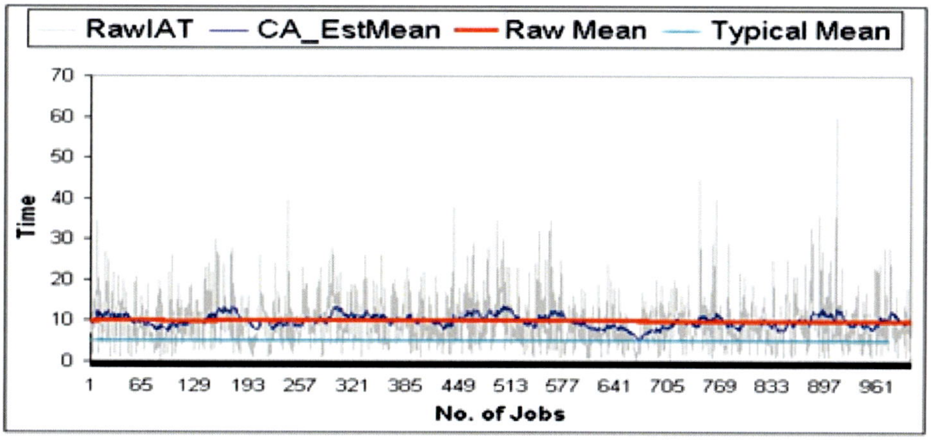

Figure 5.5. Example of actual M^3RT application for a TCP channel.

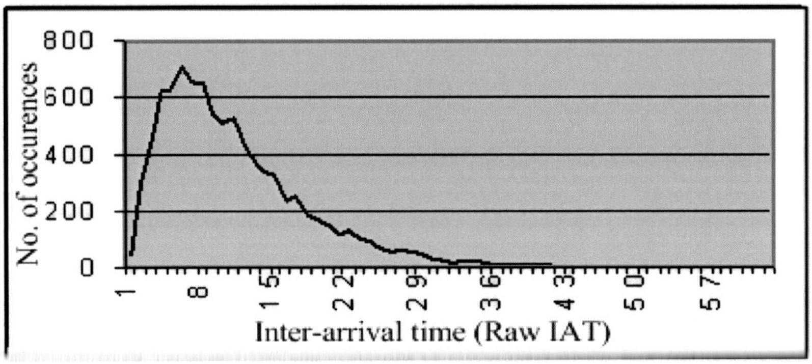

Figure 5.6. Approximated gamma distribution for the trace in figure 5 ($\alpha_o = 2$, $\beta_o = 5$).

Figure 5.5 shows that the convergence to the distribution mean M_i by M^3RT is much smoother than the raw IAT waveform. This convergence smoothness of M_i, however, could be a liability for the MACSC operation because it also requires high sensitivity to the PD changes for accurate estimation of its current standard deviation. Repeated timing analyses of the M^3RT [Wong2001a] in experiments using the *Intel's VTune Performance Analyzer* [VTune] confirmed that intrinsically it requires an average of 250 clock cycles (T cycles) to execute. The physical time for the 250 clock cycles depends on the actual platform that the M^3RT entity is running on. For example, on a platform of 100 Mega hertz (MH) speed (SP) the physical time (PT) per control cycle execution is $PT = T/SP$ or $PT = 250/(100*10^6) \approx 2.5$ micro seconds. The intrinsic execution time is raw and includes no actual IAT delays. In real-time applications, however, the actual M^3RT time depends on the average IAT delay for collecting the F (*flush limit*) or f number of data points.

In the MACSC(M^3RT) solution, the PE computation is replaced by the M^3RT solution and this yields equation (5.4.11). In fact, the equation (5.4.6) for M_i can be rearranged into equation (5.4.7) and then (5.4.8). By assuming $\alpha = \frac{p}{p+f}$ and $(1-\alpha) = \frac{f}{p+f}$, equation (5.4.8) becomes equation (5.4.9) for $\frac{p}{p+f} + \frac{f}{p+f} = 1$. The physical meaning of equation (5.4.9) is that the M_i convergence speed and accuracy depends on p for $p > 0$; a large p makes M_i depend more on the past performance (i.e. M_{i-1}).

$$M_i = \frac{p}{p+f} * M_{i-1} + \frac{1}{p+f}\left(\sum_{j=1}^{j=f} m_i^j\right) \tag{5.4.7}$$

$$M_i = \frac{p}{p+f} * M_{i-1} + \frac{1}{p+f}(f)\left(\frac{1}{f}\right)\left(\sum_{j=1}^{j=f} m_i^j\right) \tag{5.4.8}$$

$$\because \frac{p}{p+f} + \frac{f}{p+f} = 1$$

$$\mathrm{M_i} = \alpha * \mathrm{M_{i\text{-}1}} + (1 - \alpha) * \left(\frac{\sum_{j=1}^{j=f} \mathrm{m_i^j}}{f} \right) \tag{5.4.9}$$

Based on the philosophy of equation (5.4.9), the equation (5.4.10) which calculates the instantaneous PD standard deviation SD_j can be synchronized with the ith M_i prediction cycle. That is, $SD_j = \sigma_i$ is estimated with a sample size of $n = (f - 1)$. The trick is to find the right ζ value for fast, smooth and accurate σ_i convergence. The aim is to set $\alpha = \zeta = \rho / (\rho + f)$ so that M_i and σ_i are predicted on the same basis. The user, however, can choose to set a different value for ζ for whatever valid reasons. With equation (5.4.10), the dynamic cache size tuning mechanism is now represented by equation (5.4.11), where $CacheSize_i$ is the ACS in the ith cycle. To stop propagation of the error in the initialized cache size for MACSC operation, equation (5.4.11) should be rewritten into equation (5.4.12) for implementation. Equation (5.4.12) is different in that it uses the latest PD standard deviation σ_i to compute the new adjusted cache size.

$$\sigma_i = \zeta * \sigma_{i-1} + (1 - \zeta) * \sqrt{\frac{\sum_{j=1}^{j=f} \left(m_i^j - M_i \right)^2}{f - 1}} \tag{5.4.10}$$

$$CacheSize_i = CacheSize_{i-1} * \left(\frac{\sigma_i}{\sigma_{i-1}} \right) \tag{5.4.11}$$

$$CacheSize_i = 2 * \nabla * \sigma_i * OS_{average} \tag{5.4.12}$$

5.4.3. The MACSC(F-PE) Solution

The MACSC(F-PE) approach also alleviates hit ratio oscillations as occurred with the MACSC(PE). These oscillations are caused by inaccurate calculation of the standard deviation of the relative data object profile and they reduce the overall performance of the dynamic cache size tuning mechanism. The F-PE (*fine-tuned point estimate*) computation method builds on the MACSC(M^3RT) experience by using historic information of the data objects as feedback for stability. The feedback in this case makes use of α and ζ in equations (5.4.9) and (5.4.10) respectively. It involves the following steps: 1) compute $\bar{x}$ from the $n \geq N$ samples by using the PE approach, namely, the $\sqrt{N} - equation$, and 2) calculate the standard deviation s_x. These values are then fined-tuned by equations (5.4.13) and (5.4.14), where z is the operation cycle. The adjusted cache size or ACS is conceptually determined by equation (5.4.15) and its implementation is represented by equation (5.4.16) to avoid propagation of any cache size initialization error.

$$\bar{x}_z = \alpha \bar{x}_{z-1} + (1-\alpha)\bar{x}_z \quad (5.4.13)$$

$$s_x^z = \zeta s_x^{z-1} + (1-\zeta) s_x^z \quad (5.4.14)$$

$$CacheSize_z = CacheSize_{z-1} * \left(\frac{s_x^z}{s_x^{z-1}} \right) \quad (5.4.15)$$

$$CacheSize_z = 2 * \nabla * s_x^z * OS_{average} \quad (5.4.16)$$

5.5. Experimental Results

Many experiments were carried out overtime with different prototypes implemented in Java over the controlled Internet environment, with the setup shown in figure 5.7, to verify the following:

a) The MACSC(PE), MACSC(M^{3}RT) and MACSC(F-PE) indeed can determine the popularity ratio of the data objects quickly and accurately on the fly.
b) They can maintain the given hit ratio consistently in a dynamic manner.

The experiments reported in [Wong2003a, Wu2004, Wu2005] first made use of known distributions to set the references, which would then be used for comparisons with those results obtained from using pre-collected Internet traffic traces. These traces are normally composite in nature and embed waveforms that intertwine in an unpredictable manner. The platform for the reported experiments was the Java-based Aglets mobile agent platform [Oshima1998], chosen for its stability, rich user experience, and scalability. The Aglets platform is designed for Internet applications, and this makes the experimental results scalable for the open Internet environment. The replacement algorithm used in all the reported simulations was the traditional basic LRU (*Least Recently Used*) approach supported by the "*twin cache system* (TCS)". The TCS actively filtered out the "*one-timers*", which are caching "*noise*", to concentrate the hot data in the proxy cache so that more meaningful results could be produced [Wu2003]. One-timers are infrequently accessed data objects.

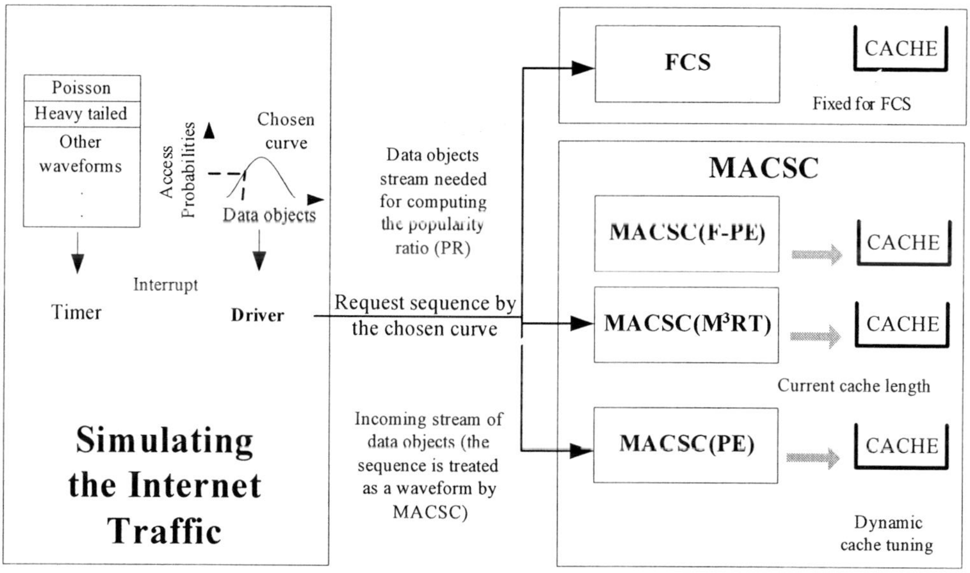

Figure 5.7. The setup for the experiments for verification and comparison.

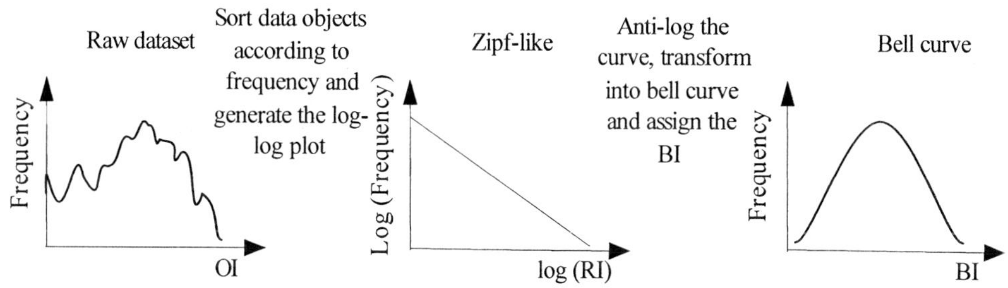

Frequency	10	3	2	6	8
OI	1	2	3	4	5
RI					
BI					

Frequency	10	8	6	3	2
OI	1	5	4	2	3
RI	1	2	3	4	5
BI					

Frequency	3	8	10	6	2
OI	2	5	1	4	3
RI	4	2	1	3	5
BI	1	2	3	4	5

Figure 5.8. Summary of the generation of the bell identifier (BI) value.

To generalize, for the reported experiments, the driver generated the request traffic profile for the operation. The request traffic was generated by one of the following methods: a) choosing a known distribution from the table; b) simulating a request pattern by interleaving different bell curves of known standard deviations [Wong2003a]; and c) using a pre-collected real data trace. The simulation results presented in this section were reproduced with the different MACSC solutions.

In the first method, the chosen curve (in figure 5.7) picked from the table mimics the desired PD distribution and drives the interrupt timer. The PD changes over time are mimicked by interleaving bell-shape curves of different standard deviations. When an interrupt occurs, a random number is generated as the access probability, which is one of the values on the Y axis of the chosen PD curve. On the X-axis of this curve lie the unique integer object identifiers (OI) of the date objects. Each position on the x-axis is also identified by a "bell" identifier (BI), which initially matches the object identifier (OI) in a one-to-one correspondence relationship. The OI position is changed by the ranking process over time as shown in figure 5.8. These bell identifiers are generated at the beginning of an experiment. The procedures for the experiment are as follows:

a) Each data object in a raw dataset is assigned a unique object identifier (OI).
b) The access frequencies of every data object are counted continuously.
c) The access frequencies of the data objects are sorted in the Zipf-like curve generated by a log-log plot. In this plot, each data object has its own rank identifier (RI) for its ranked position.
d) The Zipf-like curve is transformed into a bell curve called the PD (popularity distribution). Then, "bell" identifiers (BI) are assigned.
e) The calculation of the popularity ratio is based on the BI values.

Figure 5.8 shows the summary of the generation of the BI values, and their relationship with RI and OI over time in the continuous operation of the MACSC framework.

For the experimental results presented in this book, the average data object size is 5k bytes. The number of retrievals generated by the driver is 1 million. The cache size is first initialized to meet the prescribed hit ratio. For example, a given hit ratio of 68.3% (confidence level of one standard deviation or one ∇) means that the cache size should be initialized to $5k * 0.683 * 40{,}000$ bytes (or 136.6MB). The basic LRU replacement algorithm deletes aged objects in the cache to accommodate the hot newcomers. The simulation results presented here are SR (*standard deviation ratio*) based (equation (5.1)). The primary goal of the MACSC tuner is to provide more effective dynamic cache size tuning for the substantial number of small caching systems in the field. These inexpensive systems usually cost less than US$1000.

In the reproduced experiments, different http traces were used to verify the performance of the different MACSC dynamic cache size tuning solutions. The 1st dataset was generated by a simulator that interleaves different bell distributions. The 2nd and 3rd were real http traces from ACM SIGCOMM. The 4th was wireless http traces from the Mosquito Net. The experiments with these three real http datasets (two wireline http and one wireless traces) were intended to demonstrate if the tuners indeed work for real environments. The 2nd http dataset, namely NASA-HTTP, is the trace of one month's worth of http requests to the NASA Kennedy Space Center WWW server in Florida. There are 3,461,612 total requests logged with 21,169 different objects. The 3rd http trace, namely the BU-Web-Client, contains roughly a half year's worth of http requests of Mosaic clients running in the Boston University Computer Science Department. There are 1,143,839 requests with 91,546 different objects. The 4th http wireless datasets, namely Mosquito Net, is the trace of WaveLan wireless network in the Gates Computer Science Building of Stanford University. In 84 days it logged a total of 11,739,384 requests among 13,020 data objects.

Table 5.1. Summary of the three traces that yielded the experimental results presented

1st set: The simulated distribution

Simulated dataset (bell-shape distribution)	
No. of transactions	200,000
No. of objects	5000
Combination of S.D.	1k->2.5k->1.5k->2k
Kurtosis values	1.071211589
Skewness values	0.115921141

2nd set: The NASA-HTTP trace

NASA-HTTP (real http dataset)	
No. of transactions	3,461,612
No. of objects	21,169
Duration	31 days
Kurtosis values	40.59381233
Skewness values	-0.012181612

3rd set: The BU-Web-Client trace

BU-Web-Client (real http dataset)	
No. of transactions	1,143,839
No. of objects	91,546
Duration	169 days
Kurtosis values	6.727393489
Skewness values	-0.001931108

4th set: The Mosquito Net trace

Mosquito Net (real http dataset)	
No. of transactions	11,739,384
No. of objects	13,020
Duration	84 days
Kurtosis values	69.52779182
Skewness values	-1.206788887

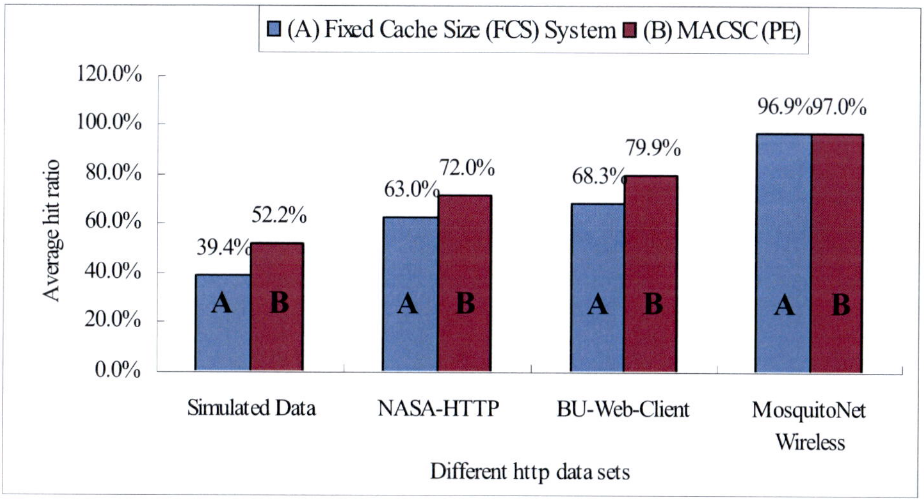

Figure 5.9. Average hit ratios by MACSC(PE) and Fixed Cache Size(FCS) System.

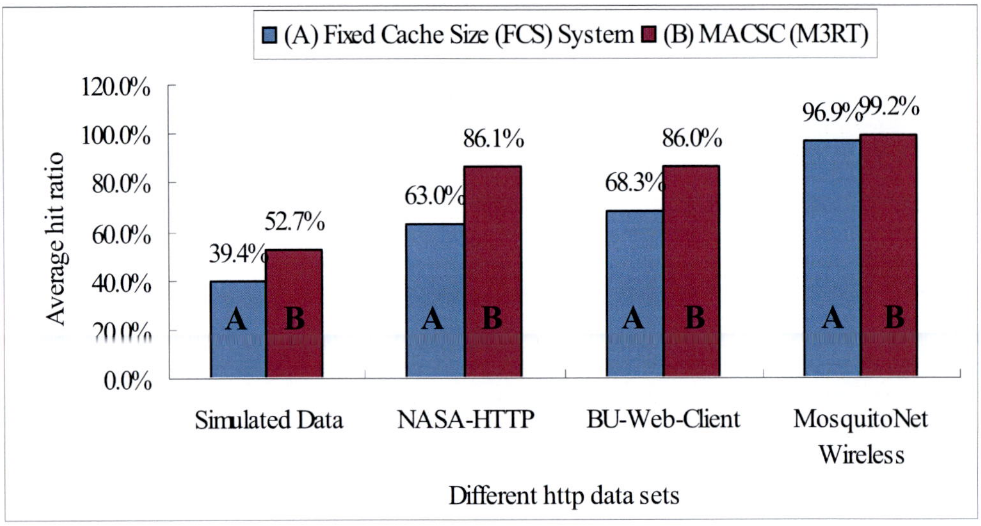

Figure 5.10. Average hit ratios by MACSC(M^3RT) and FCS.

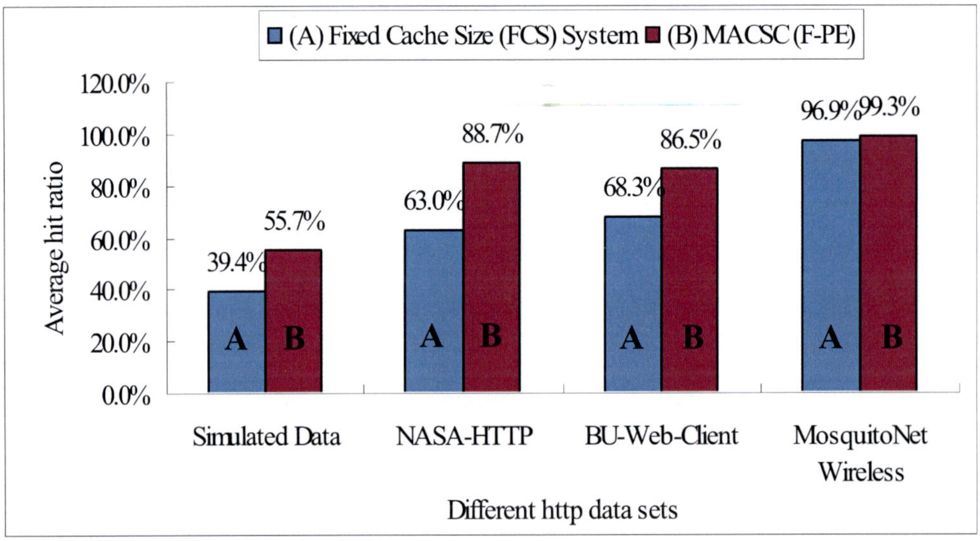

Figure 5.11. Average hit ratios by MACSC(F-PE) and FCS.

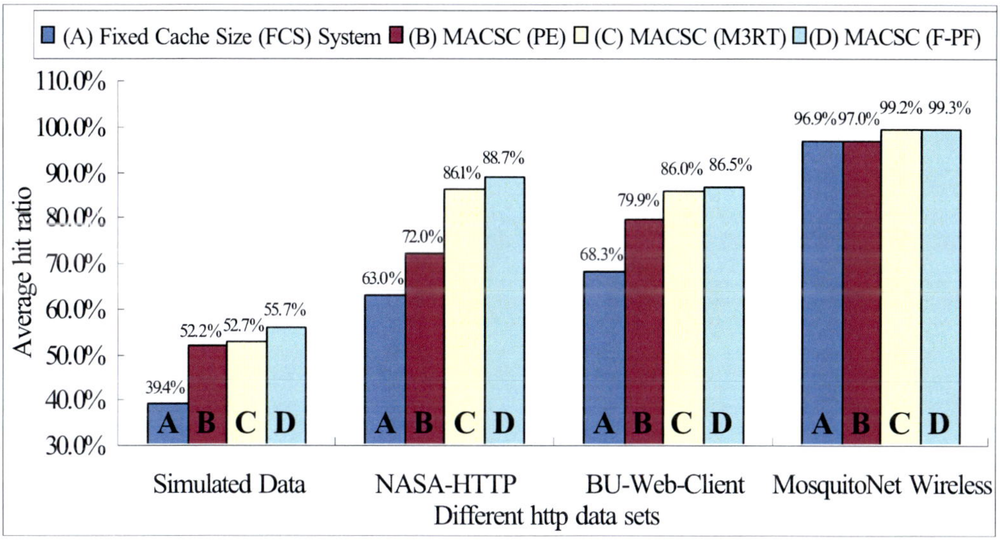

Figure 5.12. Performance comparison of four systems with the four datasets.

For the experimental results presented in this book, the given hit ratio to be maintained was 68.3%. Figure 5.9 compares the results by FCS and MACSC(PE) with the different datasets. The MACSC(PE) consistently produced a higher hit ratio than the FCS. The FCS cannot maintain the given hit ratio in the simulated dataset and the NASA-HTTP dataset. Figure 5.10 compares the FCS and MACSC(M^3RT) performance for the NASA-HTTP, BU-Web-Client, and MosquitoNet Wireless real datasets, showing that the MACSC(M^3RT) tuner had no problem in maintaining the given hit ratio consistently for the different datasets. Comparing the FCS and MACSC(F-PE) performance with the datasets in figure 5.11 we can see that the MACSC(F-PE) dynamic buffer size tuner also consistently yielded and maintained the given hit ratio for the NASA-HTTP, BU-Web-Client, and MosquitoNet Wireless real datasets. All three dynamic buffer size tuners, however, failed to maintain the given hit ratio for the simulated dataset, which is formed by interleaving different bell distributions characterized by their standard deviations. Yet, they still could maintain a much better hit ratio compared with the FCS. Our analysis showed that the failure was caused by the rapid changes in the IAT traffic pattern over time due to the interleaving operations. This indicates that some kind of compensation is needed to counteract possible traffic ill effects, which could impede the dynamic cache size tuning efficiency. Figure 5.12 compares the performance of the four caching systems. In addition, all the solutions maintain the given hit ratio for the wireless dataset. The MACSC(F-PE) obviously yielded the best hit-ratio maintenance followed by MACSC(M^3RT).

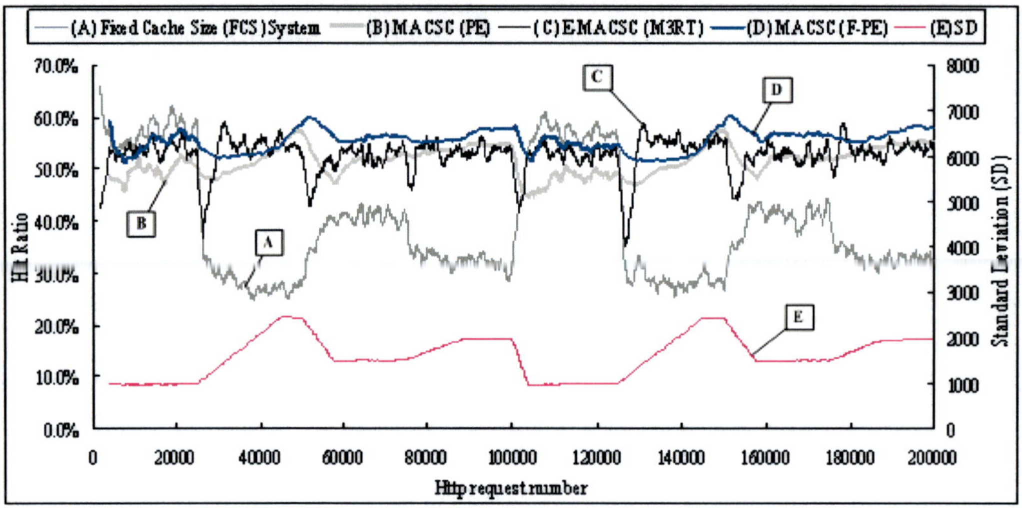

Figure 5.13. Changes of hit ratios by different caching systems - simulated data.

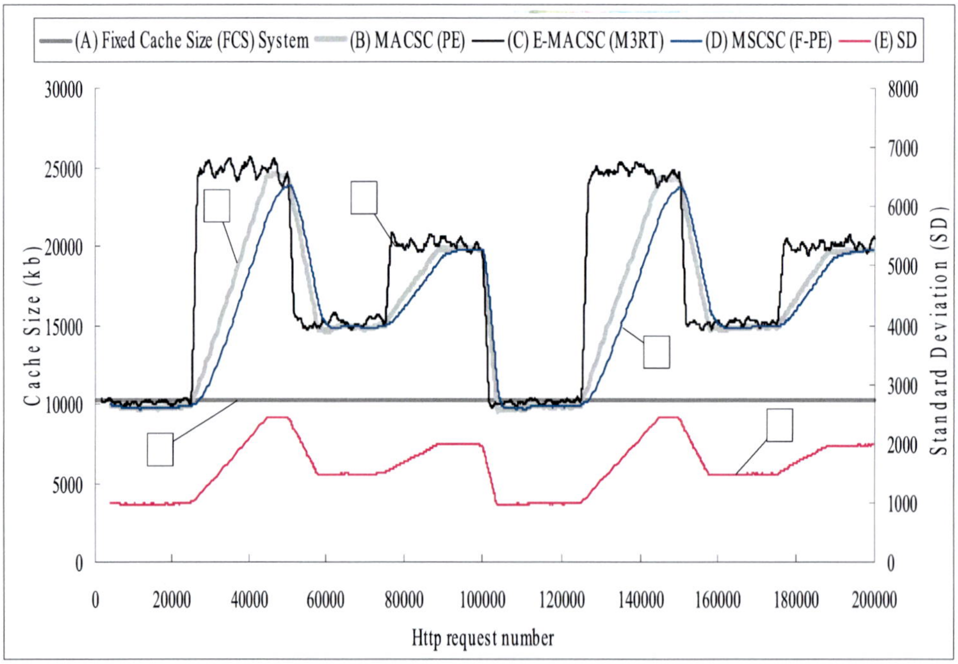

Figure 5.14. Changes of memory usage by different caching systems - simulated data.

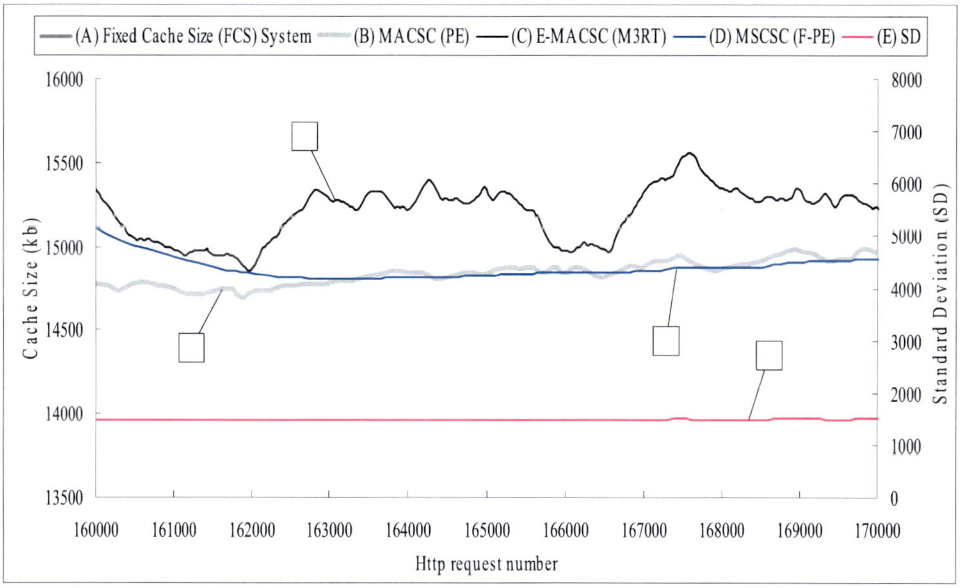

Figure 5.15. Magnified view of changes in memory usage in figure 5.13.

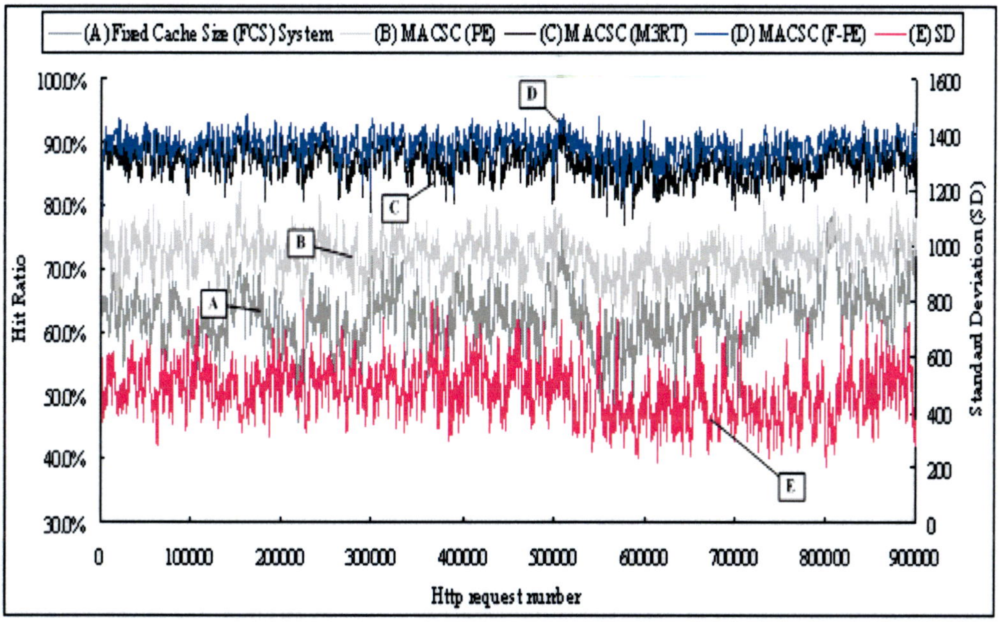

Figure 5.16. Changes of hit ratios by the caching systems - NASA-HTTP dataset.

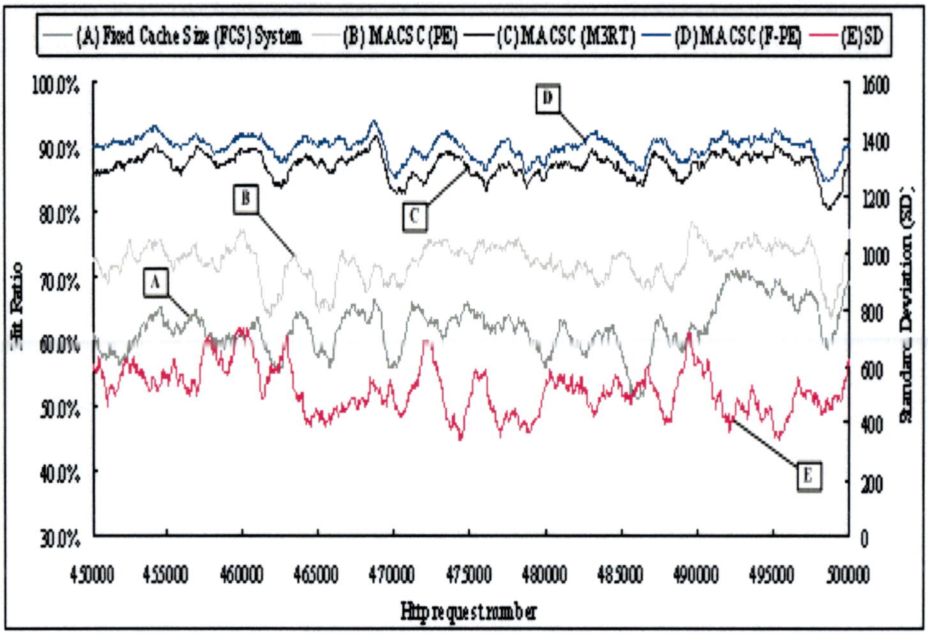

Figure 5.17. Magnified view of changes in hit ratios in figure 5.16.

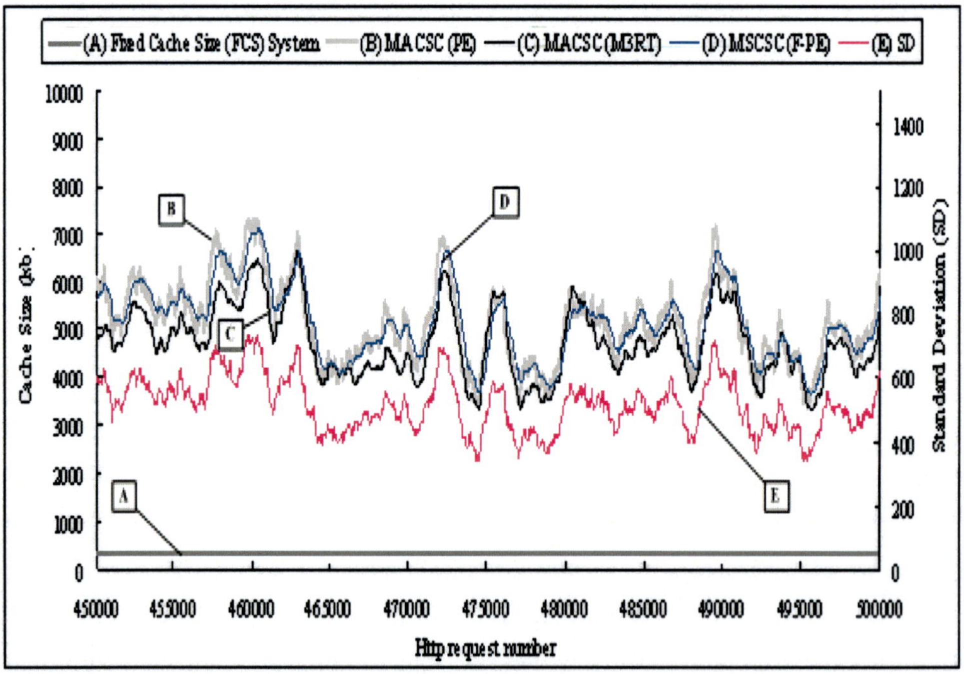

Figure 5.18. Magnified view of changes in memory usage in figure 5.16.

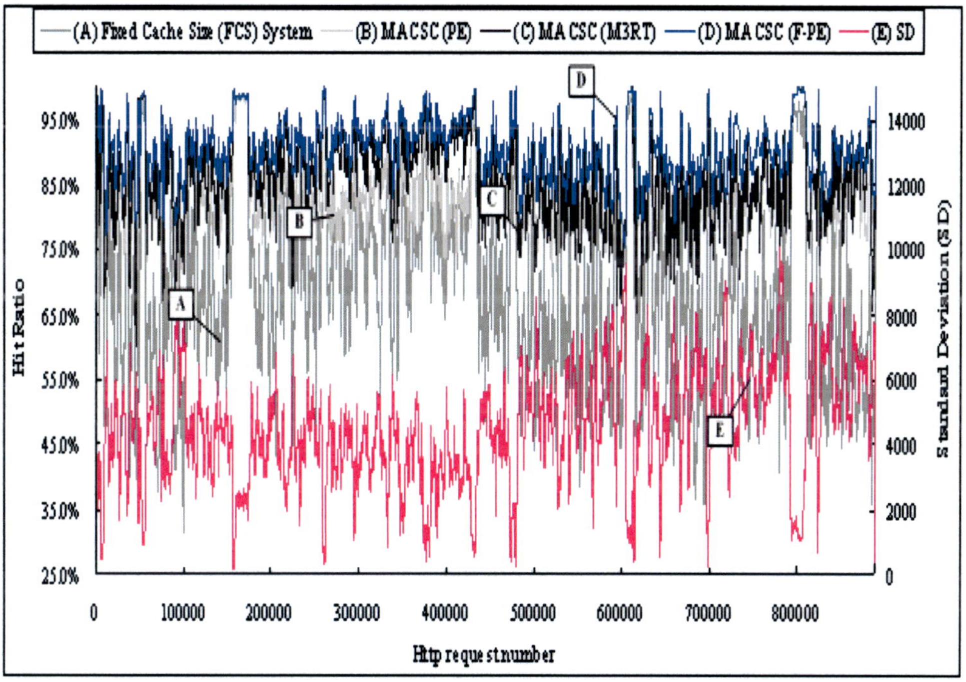

Figure 5.19. Hit ratio changes in different caching systems - BU-Web-Client dataset.

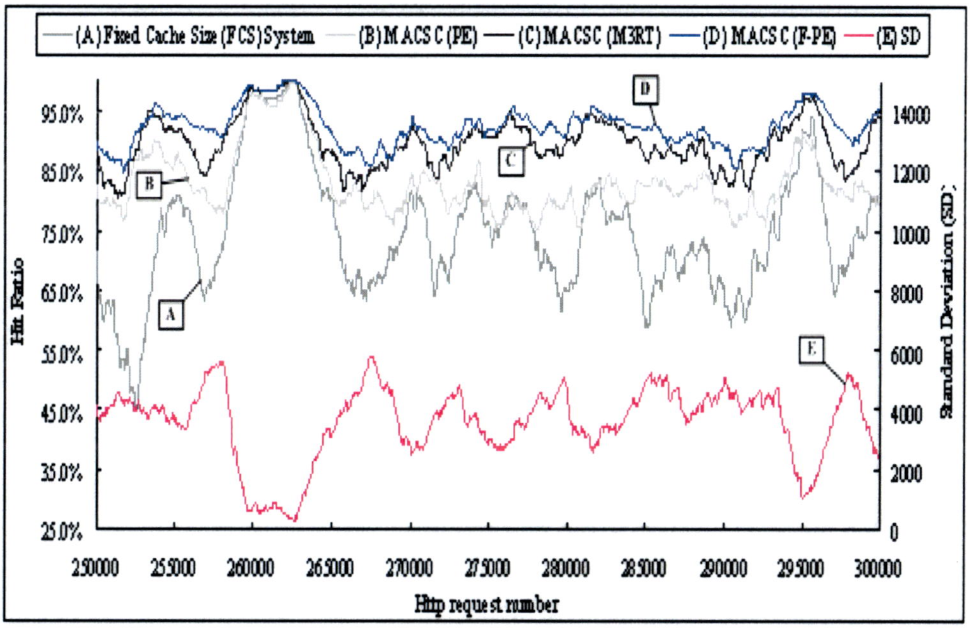

Figure 5.20. Magnified view of changes in hit ratios in figure 5.19.

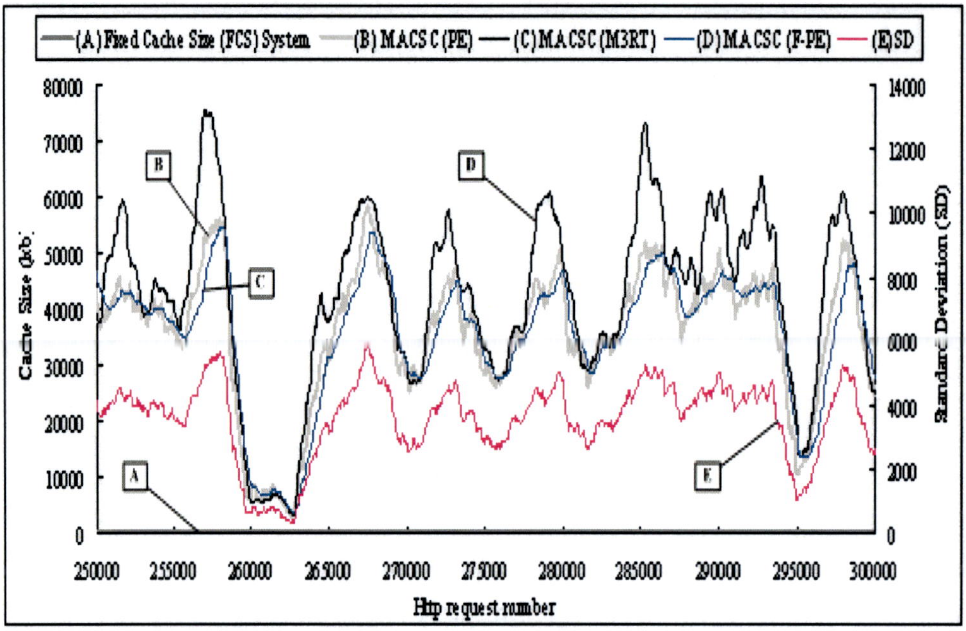

Figure 5.21. Magnified view of changes in memory usage for figure 5.19.

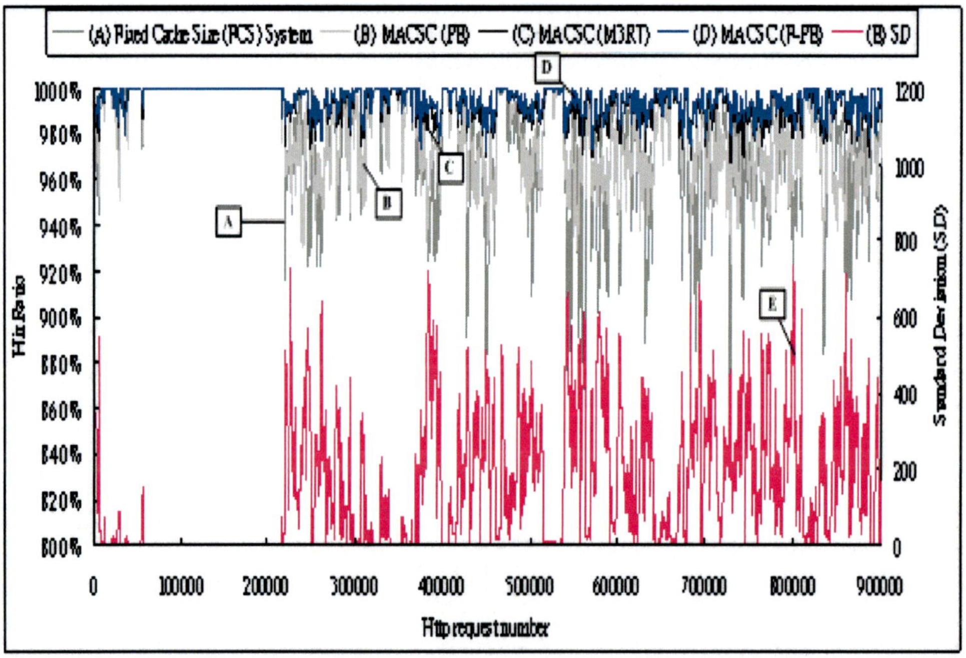

Figure 5.22. Changes of hit ratios by the caching systems - the Mosquito Net dataset.

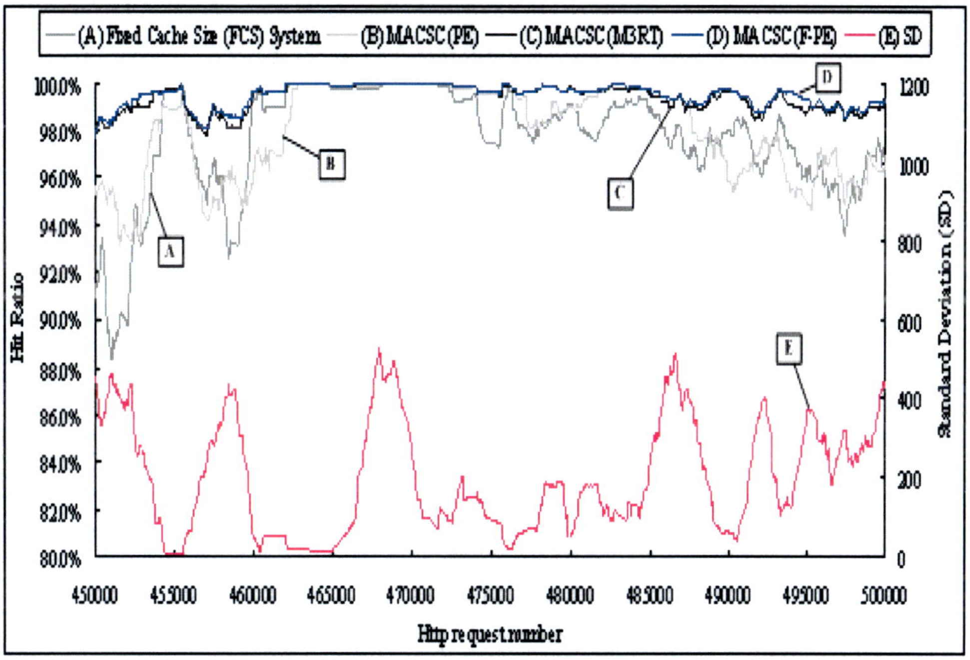

Figure 5.23. Magnified view of changes in hit ratios in figure 5.20.

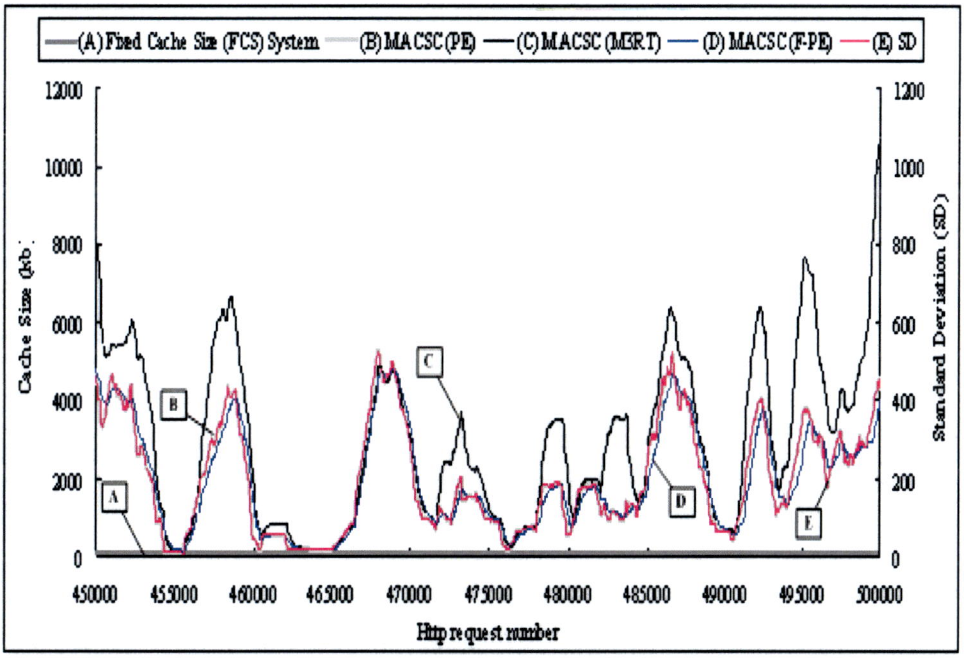

Figure 5.24. Magnified view of changes in memory usage for figure 5.20.

Figures 5.13, 5.16, 5.19 and 5.22 show the changes in hit ratios in the control processes by the four caching systems with respect to the four datasets: simulated, NASA-HTTP, BU-Web-Client and MosquitoNet Wireless. The FCS hit ratio suddenly dropped steeply when the standard deviation or SD increased. This was due to the lack of cache space to store enough hot data objects that were equivalent to the given hit ratio. The three MACSC dynamic cache size tuner versions, however, were still able to upkeep higher hit ratios. Figures 5.14, 5.18, 5.21 and 5.24 show the corresponding changes in memory usage for the cache tuning processes for the different datasets. These plots also show that the dynamic cache size adjustment process by the MACSC(F-PE) fluctuated much less than the MACSC(PE)'s. Therefore, with the same amount of memory usage, the MACSC(F-PE) should yield and maintain a much higher hit ratio. The MACSC(F-PE) consistently used the same amount of memory as the MACSC(PE) but it still produced and maintained a much higher hit ratio. For example, in figure 5.12 with the NASA-HTTP trace the MACSC(F-PE) yielded a hit ratio of 88.7%, which is 16.7% higher than the MACSC(PE). Empirically, the MACSC(F-PE) used around 20% less memory than the MACSC(M^3RT) in a consistent manner as observed in all the experiments conducted. Therefore, it can be concluded from the experimental results that the MACSC(F-PE) solution should have the best performance among all the MACSC solutions.

5.6. SUMMARY

In this chapter, the novel MACSC (*Model for Adaptive Cache Size Tuning*) framework is introduced. It maintains the given proxy cache hit ratio by leveraging the relative data object popularity as the sole parameter. By doing so, it shortens the roundtrip time for information retrieval over the Internet. The present MACSC research focuses on how to make the framework applicable to small caching systems, which are inexpensive and therefore substantial in number in the field. It uses the two most current successive standard deviations (SD) that represent changes in the popularity distribution to compute the adjusted cache size (ACS).

The key issue in realizing MACSC is to compute relative data object popularity quickly, accurately and independent of the IAT traffic patterns. For this reason, a lot of research effort is focused on finding suitable tools that are based on the *Central Limit Theorem*. At first, the point-estimate or PE approach that works with raw data points without feedback was explained. This approach led to the development of the original MACSC(PE) solution. The problem with the PE approach is the difficulty experienced in controlling real-time computation delay because enough data points must be collected for proper *SD* computation. This led to the M^3RT adoption as a more efficient alternative. The M^3RT is a *micro* version of the *Convergence Algorithm* that is based on the *Central Limit Theorem*. When the PE computation is replaced by the M^3RT mechanism, it is the MACSC(M^3RT) solution that always yields higher hit ratios than the MACSC(PE). The empirical MACSC(M^3RT) experience also indicated that it was possible to further improve the proxy cache hit ratio by using proper feedback. This led to the appearance of the MACSC(F-PE) version. "*F-PE*" stands for *fine-tuned point estimate*, which involves two feedback parameters, namely, α and ζ in equations (5.4.13) and (5.4.14) respectively. Different rigorous experiments over time by the originators of the MACSC solutions, namely, MACSC(PE), MACSC(M^3RT) and MACSC(F-PE), have no problem in maintaining the given hit ratio at all. The MACSC(F-PE), however, consistently yields a higher hit ratio than the MACSC(M^3RT), which performs better than the MACSC(PE). Some of the experiments published by the originators of the MACSC solutions were reproduced and repeated with different traffic waveforms and traces. The reproduced results actually concurred with what were reported, indicating the dynamic cache tuning solutions are indeed effective in shortening information retrieval time over the web.

5.7. KEY REFERENCES

[Aggarwal1999] C. Aggarwal, J.L. Wolf and P.S. Yu, Caching on the World Wide Web, *IEEE Transaction on Knowledge and Data Engineering,* 11(1), 94 – 107

[Breslau1999] L. Breslau, P. Cao, L. Fan, G. Phillips and S. Shenker, Web Caching and Zipf-like Distributions: Evidence and Implications, *Proc. of IEEE INFOCOM'99 Conference,* 126 – 134

[Jin2000a] S. Jin and A. Bestavros, Popularity-Aware Greedy Dual-Size Web Proxy Caching Algorithms, *Proc. of the International Conference on Distributed Computing Systems,* 2000

[Wong2001a] Allan K.Y. Wong, Tharam S. Dillon, Wilfred W.K. Lin and May T.W. Ip , M^2RT: A Tool Developed for Predicting the Mean Message Response Time for Internet Channels, *Computer Networks,* 36(5/6), 557 – 577

[Wong2003a] Allan K.Y. Wong, May T.W. Ip and Richard S.L. Wu, A Novel Dynamic Cache Size Adjustment Approach for better Retrieval Performance over the Internet, *Computer Communications,* 26(14), 2003, 1709 – 1720

[Wu2000a] K.L. Wu and P.S. Yu, Latency-Sensitive Hashing for Collaborative Web Caching, *Computer Networks,* 33(1-6), 633 – 644

[Wu2004] Richard S.L. Wu, Allan K.Y. Wong and Tharam S. Dillon, RDCT: A Novel Reconfigurable Dynamic Cache Size Tuner to Shorten Information Retrieval Time over the Internet Computer Systems, *Science and Engineering,* 19(6) 363 – 372

[Wu2005] Richard Wu, Allan K.Y. Wong and Tharam S. Dillon, E-MACSC: A Novel Dynamic Cache Tuning Technique to Reduce Information Retrieval Roundtrip Time over the Internet, *Computer Communications,* 2006

Chapter 6

Case Studies – Using Real-Time Traffic Pattern Detection to Harness the Service Roundtrip Time over the Internet

6.1. Background

All the experience so far indicates that the following strategies, specifically designed for user-level applications, can indeed harness service roundtrip time (RTT) over the Internet:

a) Dynamic buffer size tuning (DBST) [Lin2005a]: The aim is to ensure that the buffer length always covers the queue length by a safety margin Δ. By doing so, the chance of retransmission by clients due to server buffer overflows is eliminated. As a result, it shortens the service roundtrip time between the client and the server, and this contributes toward making the Internet more usable for time-critical applications.
b) Dynamic cache size tuning (DCST) [Wu2005]: The aim is to maintain the given hit ratio, which represents the expected performance by the user. This hit ratio reduces the involvement of the Internet Domain Name Server (DNS), and thus also reduces the significant time delay in the information retrieval process. If the proxy server cannot find the data requested by the client, then it has to search the remote data source or web server. The side effect of this is that any frequent transfer of large volumes of data across the network by the remote data sources would consume the network bandwidth. Since the dynamic cache size tuning mechanism alleviates such voluminous transfers, it frees backbone bandwidth, which would otherwise be consumed by the transferring process, for public sharing. The fringe benefit is a lessening of potential network congestion.

The researchers in both the DBST and DCST areas observed that the stability and performance of the tuners are affected by the Internet traffic patterns. The Internet follows the power laws [Medina2000] and therefore its traffic pattern can change over time from short-range dependence (e.g. Poisson) to long-range-dependence (e.g. heavy-tailed and self-similar) [Molnar1999, Crovella1997]. This observation led to the proposal of the novel real-time traffic pattern detection (RTPD) [Lin2004] approach. This approach is basically the combination of three elements, "$M^3RT + R/S + filtration$" as described in Chapter 3 (R/S means *rescaled adjusted statistics*).

In this chapter, two case studies are presented. The first case demonstrates how the RTPD mechanism helps the FLC dynamic buffer tuner reconfigure effectively on the fly to ward off traffic ill effects. The second case shows how the RTPD mechanism is effectively used by the MACSC dynamic cache tuner for reconfiguration on the fly. During the reconfiguration process, the RTPD element included as part of the tuner identifies the current traffic pattern. The tuner then uses the detected result to adjust its control process spontaneously to neutralize the negative impact by traffic patterns on its performance and stability [Wu2006].

6.2. Case 1 – Reconfigurable Dynamic Buffer Tuning

This case study is for the FLC[4x6] dynamic buffer tuner in figure 6.1. The "*dot*" marks the reference point (i.e. "0" of the $\{0, \Delta\}^2$) as 0.8. This point is the given "*queue length over buffer length*" reference (i.e. called QOB_R). The X marks the "*don't care*" state, and the linguistic variables are as follows:

a) *Current QOB ratio (or QOB_i)*: ML for *M*uch *L*ess than QOB_R, L for *L*ess than QOB_R, G for *G*reater than QOB_R, and MG for *M*uch *G*reater than QOB_R.
b) *Current* dQ/dt : NL for *N*egative and *L*arger than the threshold, NM for *N*egative but *M*edium to the threshold, NS for *N*egative and *S*maller than the threshold, PS for *P*ositive and *S*maller than the threshold, PM for *P*ositive and *M*edium to the threshold, and PL for *P*ositive and *L*arger than the threshold.

QOB			dQ/dt					
			NL	NM	NS	PS	PM	PL
		ML	-	-	-	-	-	-
0.7		L	-	-	X	X	+	+
0.8		G	-	-	X	X	+	+
0.9		MG	+	+	+	+	+	+

Figure 6.1. An FLC design/configuration example, FLC[4x6].

The control decision depends on the current QOB_i and dQ/dt. It may be *Addition (buffer elongation) or* "+", *Subtraction (buffer shrinkage) or* "-", or *don't care*. The FLC[4x6] prototype is supported by fuzzy rules (L_{new} and L_{old} denote the adjusted buffer length and the buffer length before tuning respectively), exemplified by the following five:

Rule 1: If (QOB_i is ML) AND (dQ/dt is NL) Then Action is "-"(Subtraction) AND $L_{new} = L_{old}$ - ICM
Rule 2: If (QOB_i is ML) AND (dQ/dt is NM) Then Action is "-"(Subtraction) AND $L_{new} = L_{old}$ - ICM
Rule 3: If (QOB_i is ML) AND (dQ/dt is NS) Then Action is "-"(Subtraction) AND $L_{new} = L_{old}$ - ICM
Rule 4: If (QOB_i is ML) AND (dQ/dt is PS) Then Action is "-"(Subtraction) AND $L_{new} = L_{old}$ - ICM
Rule 5: If (QOB_i is ML) AND (dQ/dt is PM) Then Action is "-"(Subtraction) AND $L_{new} = L_{old}$ – ICM

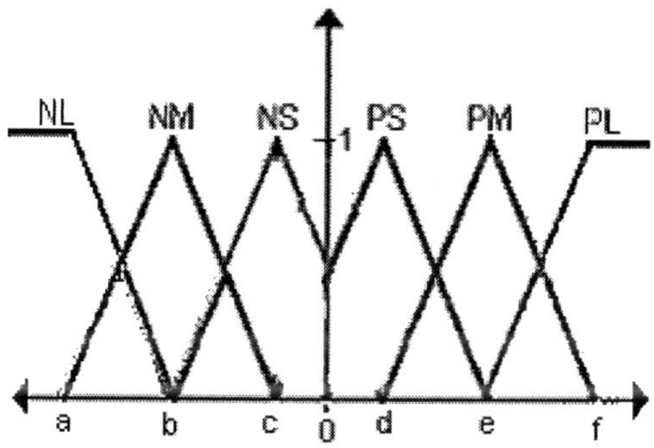

Figure 6.2. Membership function for dQ/dt.

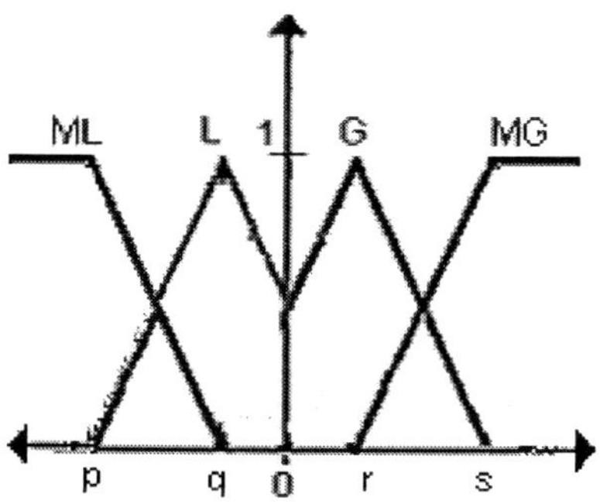

Figure 6.3. Membership function for QOB.

As mentioned in Chapter 4, the FLC[4x6] design has two control parameters: QOB and dQ/dt. The dQ/dt membership function is gradient, and the y-axis of figure 6.2 is the degree of membership measurement. The x-axis is the gradient difference between two successive dQ/dt measurements. For this design the values from a to f are: a=0.003, b=0.002, c=0.001, d=0.001, e=0.002 and f=0.003. Figure 6.3 shows the QOB membership function for the same design, and the x-axis is the QOB ratio that changes in a dynamic manner. The values for the p, q, r and s are respectively: 0.7, 0.75, 0.85 and 0.9. The current dQ/dt and QOB values decides which fuzzy region to be operated by the FLC. For example, if the degree of the dQ/dt membership function is between b and c (i.e. $y = 0.5$) and that for QOB is between p and q, the following four fuzzy regions are possible candidates: [ML,NM], [ML,NS], [L,NM] and [L,NS]. Therefore, the possible actions are: -, -, - and X. The majority rule in the FLC framework selects the minus (-) operation.

6.2.1. The FLC Reconfiguration Scheme and Traffic Patterns

The FLC reconfiguration scheme is also known as the adaptive/reconfigurable FLC model (A-FLC or R-FLC). It works by squeezing the range-threshold of the "*don't care*" region. The scheme has three conceptual elements: RTPD, FLC, and "*don't-care region's range-threshold auto-tuning capability, or simply RAC*". The PIDC component in the FLC framework works with the proportional (P), integral (I) and derivative (D) controls, as well as the two thresholds, *Th1* (i.e. Δ of the objective function for the P or QOB control) and *Th2* (i.e. Δ for the D or dQ/dt control). The PIDC working alone has four conceptual control regions, defined by different $\pm Th1$ and $\pm Th2$ combinations. The FLC fuzzy logic divides these thresholds into the finer membership functions. There are *range-thresholds* among them (e.g. the *range-threshold* between $a = 0.003$ and $b = 0.002$ is 0.001 in figure 6.2) for refined control actions. In figure 6.3, *Th1* covers the range-thresholds for the finer QOB control regions: ML, L, G, and MG regions. Similarly, *Th2* covers the NL, NM, NS, PS, PM and PL regions. When the FLC model is operating in a specific fuzzy control region, in this setup there will be an intrinsic time delay before a corrective action is activated. For example, if the increased dQ/dt value is less than the *range-threshold* of the current "*don't care*" region, no immediate action is taken. By the time the action is activated, there could be significant overshoot or undershoot already.

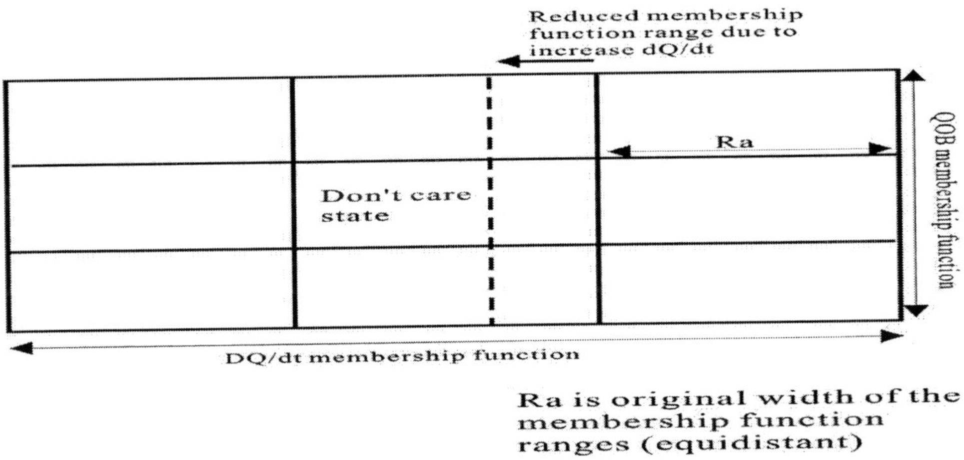

Figure 6.4. Adjusting the membership function range of *don't care* state on the fly.

The overshoot/undershoot accumulation contributes to the oscillations in the FLC convergence process in the steady state. The proactive step by the novel A-FLC model to prevent significant overshoot/undershoot is to adjust the *range-thresholds* of the current "*don't care*" fuzzy regions on the fly. Normally, if the increase (or decrease) of dQ/dt is more than (or less than) the given "*gradient threshold* (GT)", the RAC adjusts the *range-threshold* by the "*given percentage* (GP)". Figure 6.4 shows how the "*don't care*" *range-threshold* of a growing dQ/dt value is "*squeezed*" to enlarge the *range-threshold* on the right side. This enlargement, in effect, prompts the A-FLC to take immediate action instead of waiting passively for the condition "$dQ/_{dt}$ > *predefined range-threshold*" to materialize. The "*squeezing*" action, which quickens the tuner response and shortens the service roundtrip time, is reconfiguration in the A-FLC context.

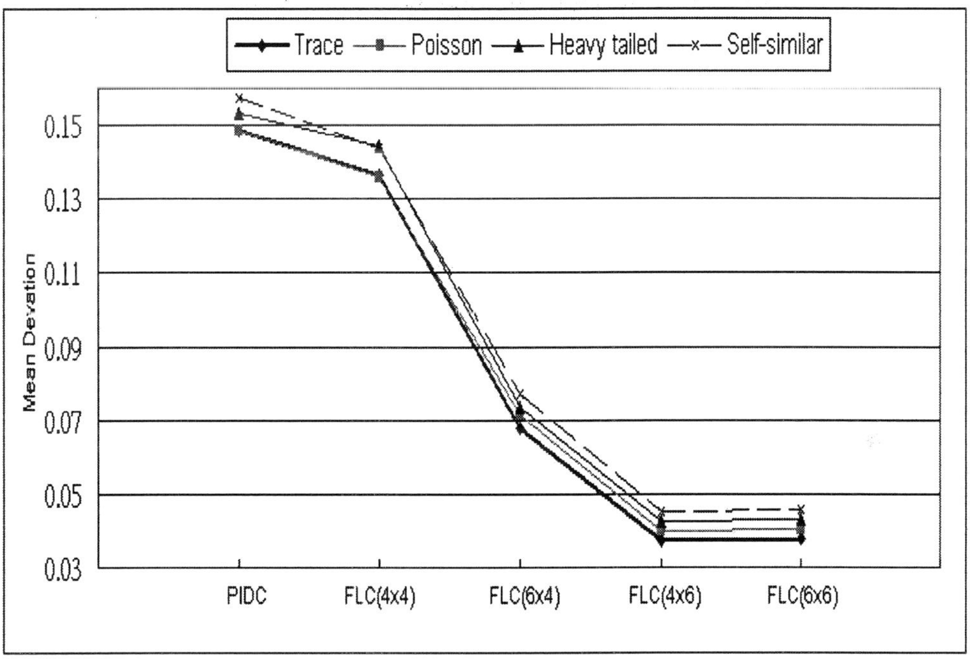

Figure 6.5. Mean Deviation Errors of different FLC designs versus traffic patterns.

Figure 6.5 shows the mean deviations from the given QOB_R reference by different FLC designs. It demonstrates how these designs (without RTPD support) react to the different traffic patterns, namely, Poisson, self-similar, and heavy-tailed (a Pareto distribution in this case). The "*trace*" in the plot is for a set of RTT data that exhibited the LRD character, for comparison purposes. It is the data set pre-collected for a TCP channel that interconnected the Hong Kong PolyU Intranet and the remote Latrobe University in Australia. For the same data sets, figure 6.5 shows that the A-FLC produces more accurate dynamic buffer tuning by yielding less mean deviation (MD) from the QOB_R reference. Figure 6.6 compares the MD profiles for the FLC, which works with the given/static range-threshold, and the A-FLC supported by limited dynamic *range-threshold adjustments*. It is limited because the A-FLC adjusts the range-threshold only by the "*given percentage* (GP)". It does not use the RTPD output to further fine-tune the GP as part of the reconfiguration process. Even with limited range-threshold adjustment, the A-FLC produces less MD than the FLC. For figure 6.6 static GT and GP values are 0.003 radians and 5 % respectively.

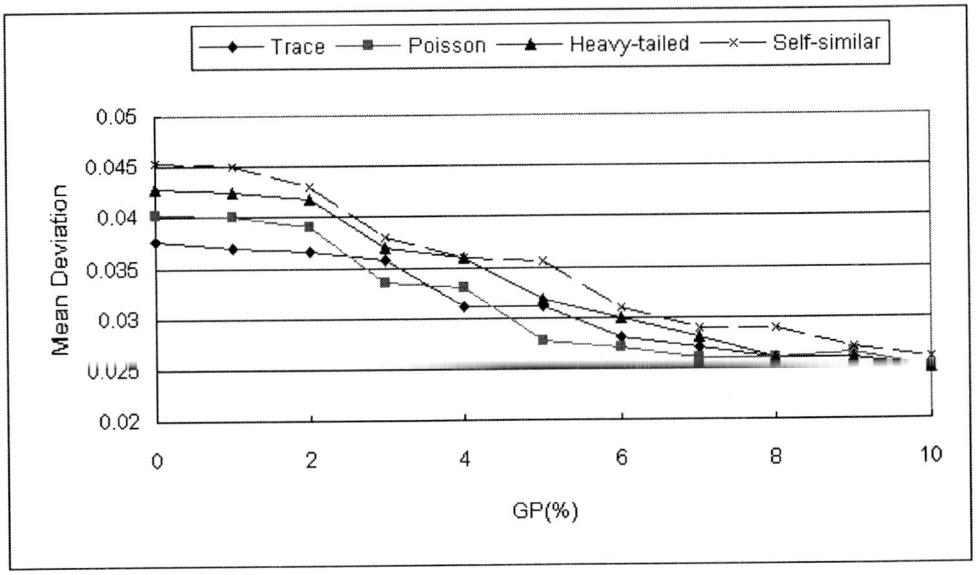

Figure 6.6. Mean deviations by A-FLC for different traffic patterns and GP values.

The *Th1* and *Th2* thresholds in the A-FLC model are not statically assigned by the user, but are generated by the system automatically from past performance. A unique A-FLC salient feature is its *MD-vs-Thresholds* graph, which accumulates all the previous A-FLC experience. When the A-FLC has stopped running, it contributes a new point which is defined by the following: the MD (mean deviation), and the *Th1* and *Th2* values last used. After the A-FLC tuner has operated for a number of occasions, the [MD, (*Th1*, *Th2*)] points will yield a good estimate of the best starting *Th1* and *Th2* values for the next application. The best choice is always the pair that yields the minimum MD value on the *MD-vs-Thresholds* graph. The A-FLC also invokes the $M^3 RT$ logical entity to compute MD quickly and accurately.

6.2.2. More Refined FLC Reconfiguration with RTPD

Without RTPD support, the RAC element in the A-FLC model operates with the given static GP value. The RTPD enables the A-FLC to reconfigure on the fly with respect to the instantaneously detected traffic type. Then, the RAC selects the most effective GP value with respect to the type. In action, the logical RTPD object/entity runs in parallel with the A-FLC main body. Since the RTPD execution time (891 clock cycles measured by Intel's VTune Performance Analyzer [VTune]) is longer than A-FLC's (less than 400 clock cycles), it becomes the A-FLC *de facto* cycle time. Figure 6.6 shows how different GP values affect the A-FLC performance for different data sets shown in figure 6.5. The significant indication is that different traffic patterns need different GP values to produce the same mean deviation. For example, producing a mean deviation of 0.0026 the A-FLC needs GP=0.7 for Poisson, GP=0.8 for the heavy-tailed (Pareto) trace and GP>10 for the self-similar trace. The significance of this is that different GP values should be used for different traffic patterns. The trade-off is longer A-FLC cycle times for higher GP values, as was confirmed by previous experiments.

Figure 6.7 shows the A-FLC execution times for the Poisson and heavy-tailed traces. The static GP values needed for these two cases to produce the same mean deviation of 0.027 are 5% and 7% respectively. The VTune measurements show that A-FLC needs 280 clock cycles for the Poisson trace but 340 clock cycles for the heavy-tailed dataset. If the RTPD has detected that the traffic pattern has changed from heavy-tailed to Poisson, then the host A-FLC should respond by reconfiguring itself. This means squeezing the GT by 5% instead of 7% to improve the dynamic tuning cycle time by (340 - 280)/340 or 17.65 percent. This greatly reduces the chance of deleterious effects on the tuning process. For successful A-FLC operation, it is necessary to calibrate the relationship among the following parameters: MD, GP, and traffic pattern. The calibration enables the A-FLC to select the correct GP value with respect to the desired MD and the current Internet traffic instantaneously detected by the RTPD mechanism. Many different experiments showed that the A-FLC is consistently more accurate than the FLC by producing smaller MD values, which are indicative of lessened traffic ill effects. Figure 6.8 shows the performance difference between A-FLC(4x6) and FLC(4x6] for three traffic cases, all with GP=5%.

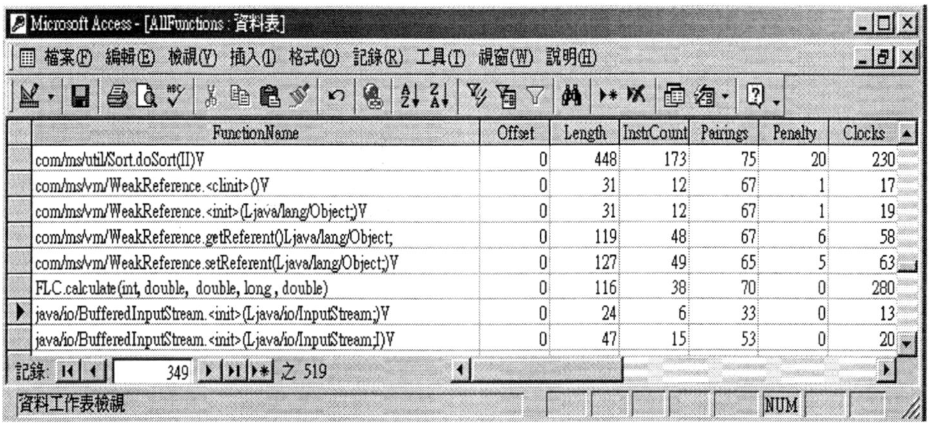

FunctionName	Offset	Length	InstrCount	Pairings	Penalty	Clocks
com/ms/util/Sort.doSort(II)V	0	448	173	75	20	230
com/ms/vm/WeakReference.<clinit>()V	0	31	12	67	1	17
com/ms/vm/WeakReference.<init>(Ljava/lang/Object;)V	0	31	12	67	1	19
com/ms/vm/WeakReference.getReferent()Ljava/lang/Object;	0	119	48	67	6	58
com/ms/vm/WeakReference.setReferent(Ljava/lang/Object;)V	0	127	49	65	5	63
FLC.calculate(int, double, double, long, double)	0	116	38	70	0	280
java/io/BufferedInputStream.<init>(Ljava/io/InputStream;)V	0	24	6	33	0	13
java/io/BufferedInputStream.<init>(Ljava/io/InputStream;I)V	0	47	15	53	0	20

Figure 6.7 (a). for GP=5% and MD=0.027 the R-FLC execution time is 280 clock cycles for the Poisson distribution in figure 6.5.

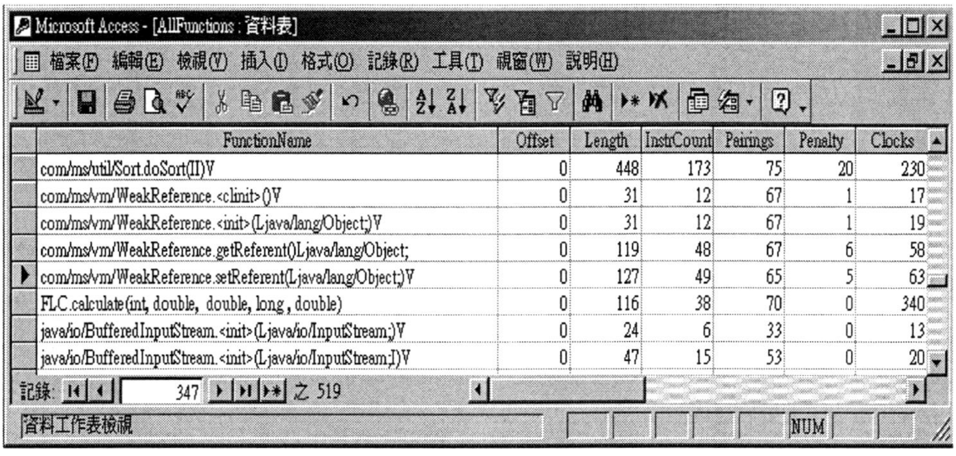

FunctionName	Offset	Length	InstrCount	Pairings	Penalty	Clocks
com/ms/util/Sort.doSort(II)V	0	448	173	75	20	230
com/ms/vm/WeakReference.<clinit>()V	0	31	12	67	1	17
com/ms/vm/WeakReference.<init>(Ljava/lang/Object;)V	0	31	12	67	1	19
com/ms/vm/WeakReference.getReferent()Ljava/lang/Object;	0	119	48	67	6	58
com/ms/vm/WeakReference.setReferent(Ljava/lang/Object;)V	0	127	49	65	5	63
FLC.calculate(int, double, double, long, double)	0	116	38	70	0	340
java/io/BufferedInputStream.<init>(Ljava/io/InputStream;)V	0	24	6	33	0	13
java/io/BufferedInputStream.<init>(Ljava/io/InputStream;I)V	0	47	15	53	0	20

Figure 6.7 (b). for GP=8% and MD=0.027 the R-FLC execution time is 340 clock cycles for the heavy-tailed distribution in figure 6.5.

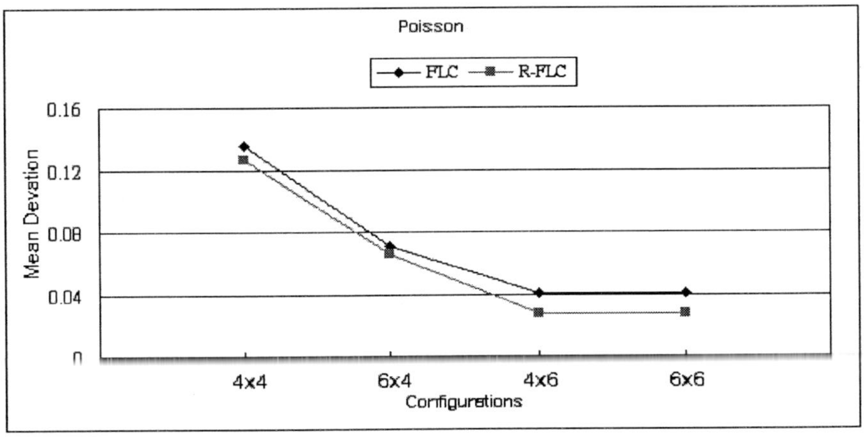

Figure 6.8(a). FLC(4x6) and R-FLC(4x6) [or A-FLC(4x6)] performances for the Poisson trace, GP=0.05.

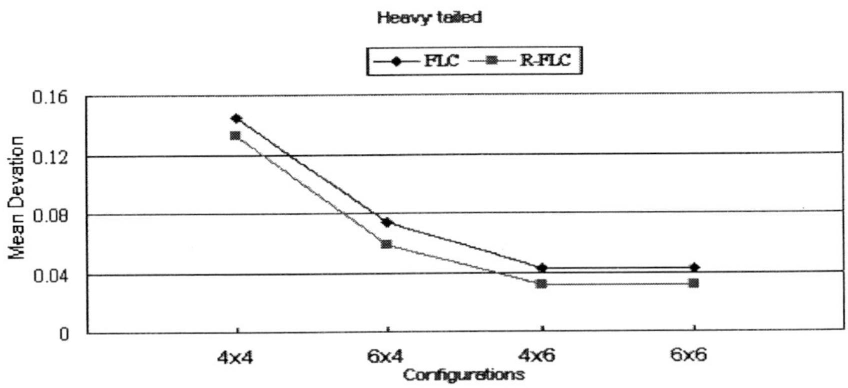

Figure 6.8(b). FLC(4x6) and A-FLC(4x6) [or R-FLC(4x6)] performances for the heavy-tailed trace, GP=0.05.

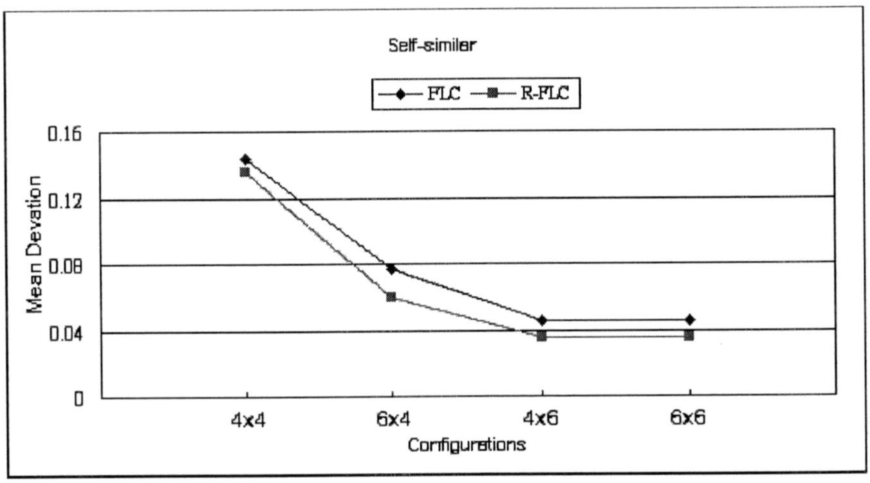

Figure 6.8(c). FLC(4x6) and A-FLC(4x6) [or R-FLC(4x6)] performances for the self-similar trace, GP=0.05.

6.3. Case 2 – Reconfigurable Dynamic Cache Tuning

This case study demonstrates how reconfigurable dynamic cache size tuning can be achieved by including the RTPD mechanism into the MACSC (Model for Adaptive Cache Size Control) framework. As explained in Chapter 5, MACSC works with equations (5.1) and (5.2). The symbols in these equations are: a) the suffixes "VR" for "variance ratio based" and "SR" for "standard deviation ratio based" (SR $=\sqrt{VR}$), b) CS for cache size, and c) SD for standard deviation [WongIp2003]. The dynamic maintenance process tunes the corresponding popularity ratio, which is defined by the VR or the SR ratio. The equation (6.1) and (6.2) are different forms for equation (5.1) and (5.2) respectively.

$$CS_{Adjusted\_VR} = CS_{Old\_VR} * \left(SD_{ThisSample} / SD_{LastSample} \right)^2 \ldots\ldots\ldots\ldots(6.1)$$

$$CS_{Adjusted\_SR} = CS_{Old\_SR} * \left(SD_{ThisSample} / SD_{LastSample} \right) \ldots\ldots\ldots\ldots(6.2)$$

If it is assumed that currently measured $SD_{ThisSample}$ = S_b and $SD_{LastSample}$ = S_a (as shown by Figure 5.2c), then $(S_b / S_a)^2$ and (S_b / S_a) are the instantaneous VR and SR ratios respectively. The experimental results presented in this section for demonstration purposes are based on equation (6.2). To compute accurate VR and SR ratios on the fly, the MACSC needs to predict the true mean μ and the true standard deviation SD or δ from the current popularity distribution (PD). It is a prediction process because μ and δ should be estimated from limited available data points. This implies the *Central Limit Theorem* because a curve plotted with a collection of sample means would indicate the approximate location of μ and δ. The PD in the MACSC context is a distribution of objects' access frequencies versus the individual objects. It is a real-time entity because its shape is determined by the user preference at the time. The user preference dictates the more popular or hotter objects currently being accessed more than others. The direct measurement approach adopted by MACSC to predict μ and δ on the fly involves the following:

a) *Estimated mean* $(\bar{x})$: For a sample of arbitrary size n, and in accordance with normal practice, the minimum value for n should be equal to or greater than 10.
b) *Estimated standard deviation* s_x: The SD calculated from the n data points above.

According to the *Central Limit Theorem*, if $\delta_{\bar{x}}$ is the standard deviation of the real-time curve plotted with many $\bar{x}$ values, then the relationship, $\delta_{\bar{x}} = \delta / \sqrt{n}$ should hold, for a large n and a sufficient number of $\bar{x}$ values. The statistical s_x value, however, differs from $\delta_{\bar{x}}$ normally. Finding the mean and standard deviation of any unknown waveform is usually a guessing game. The degree of accuracy of a statistical estimation depends on whether the result satisfies the given tolerance. The MACSC works with the "$\sqrt{N}$ *-equation*", namely, $E\mu = k\delta_{\bar{x}} = k(\delta_x / \sqrt{N})$ [Chis1992], which has the following tolerance parameters:

a) *Fractional error tolerance* (E): This is the fractional error about μ (ideal/true mean value) by $\bar{x}$ (estimated mean for a sample of arbitrary size n on the fly).
b) *SD tolerance* (k): This is the number of standard deviations that $\bar{x}$ is away from the true mean μ and that can be tolerated.

The aim of the $\sqrt{N}$ *-equation* is to find the minimum sample size N that would yield acceptable μ and δ predictions with respect to the specified k and E tolerances. The first step is to derive $N = (\frac{k\delta_x}{E\mu})^2$ from the $\sqrt{N}$ *-equation*, and this is called the "*point estimate* (PE)" basis. For real-life applications $\bar{x}$ and s_x, which are calculated on the fly statistically, should be used instead of μ and $\delta_{\bar{x}}$. That is, $N = (\frac{ks_{\bar{x}}}{E\bar{x}})^2$ should be used instead of $N = (\frac{k\delta_{\bar{x}}}{E\mu})^2$. The following example shows how the conversion actually works.

The $N = (\frac{ks_{\bar{x}}}{E\bar{x}})^2$ example for demonstration purposes:

a) For a sample of 40 response times (i.e. sample size n is 40), the following are estimated: $\bar{x} = 20$ and $s_x = 8$.
b) The given SD tolerance is two standard deviations (i.e. k=2 or 95.4%), and the allowed fractional error tolerance E is 5% (E=0.05).
c) The values above together yield $N = (\frac{2*8}{0.05*20})^2$ or N=256.

The computed N in this case indicates that in order to satisfy the $E\mu = k\delta_{\bar{x}}$ criterion, the sample size must be at least 256. This means that the sample size of n=40 initially used for the data collection process is not good enough. In the PE context, the initial n value is the "*PE seed*". As explained in Chapter 5, the *PE seed* problem can be rectified by either one of the following approaches:

a) *First approach*: Collect at least another (256 – 40) or 216 response times and then estimate $\bar{x}$ and s_x again.
b) *Second approach*: Collect another n=40 additional response times and estimate $\bar{x}$ and s_x again, and if the newly computed N is less than 2n (or 80 for one

additional round) then stop; otherwise, repeat the same process with additional n samples.

Practical experience shows that the second approach normally converges to the expected N value much faster. In many cases $\bar{x}$ and s_x would stabilize in the second or third trial.

6.3.1. RTPD as the Basis for Dynamic MACSC Reconfiguration

The basis for the MACSC reconfiguration is to choose the best PE seed value in a real-time and adaptive manner. The choice is tied in with the traffic pattern detected by its RTPD element. Different timing analyses of the MACSC Java prototype with various pre-collected traffic data traces (i.e. inter-arrival times (IAT)). These analyses made use of the Intel's VTune Performance Analyzer [VTune] and indicate that the MACSC intrinsically needs 1673100 clock cycles to execute [WongIp2003]. For a node operating at 143 mega hertz, the physical execution time is $(1/143)*10^{-6}*1673100$ or 11.7ms. The intrinsic execution assumes that there is no actual IAT delay in fetching data points for the calculation. This is true only when all the data points are already available as in a pre-collected trace. In real-life deployments, however, the PE has to wait for the IAT delay before the next data point can be fetched. For correct operation, the average IAT delay of the traffic in the actual MACSC operation should be more than 11.7ms. As this delay shortens $CS_{Adjusted\_SR}$, accuracy would deteriorate because of missing data points in the sampling process. It was observed that such data losses are more serious for the self-similar traffic, which can have high-frequency bursts.

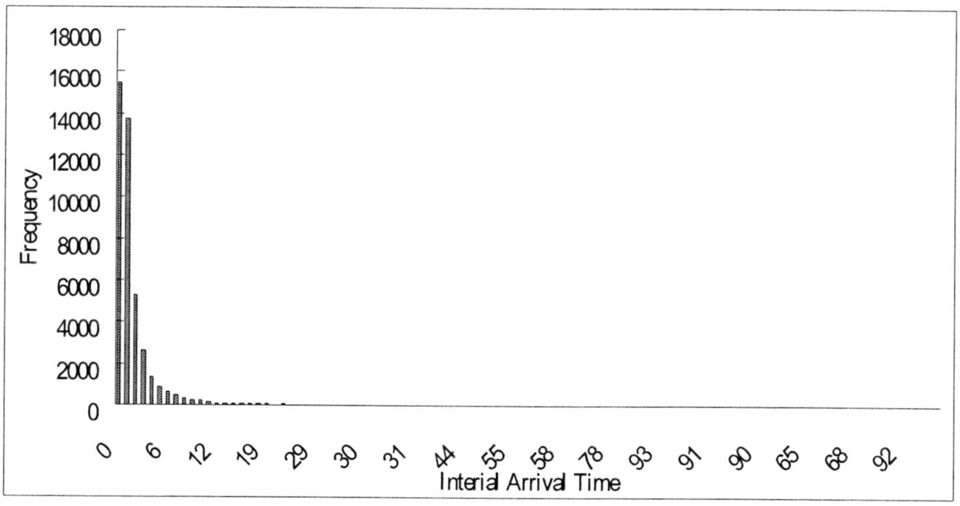

Figure 6.9. LRD frequency distribution of http request to the EPA dataset, mean IAT is 2.

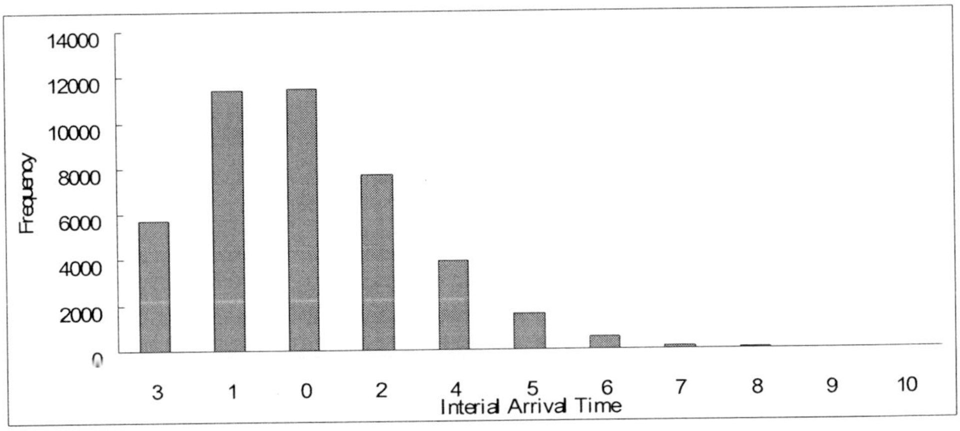

Figure 6.10. SRD Poisson IAT distribution with mean equal to 2 as the mixer.

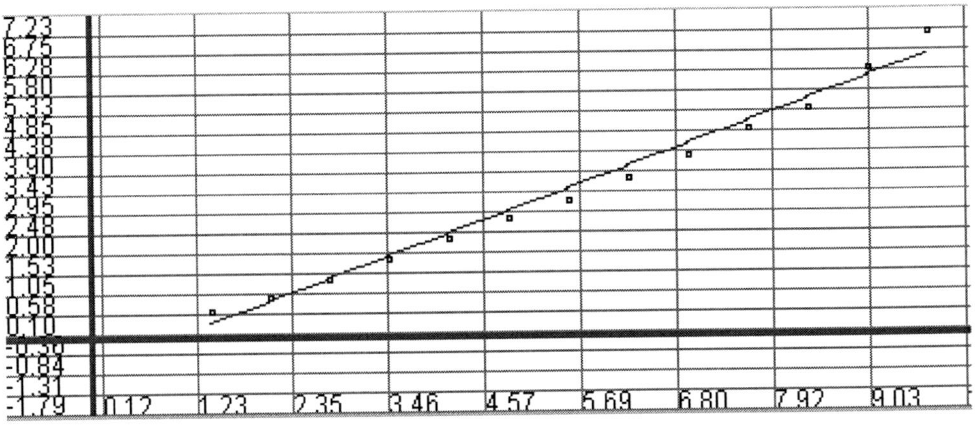

Figure 6.11(a). R/S plot confirms LRD for EPA trace, H=0.761 of 99.3% confidence.

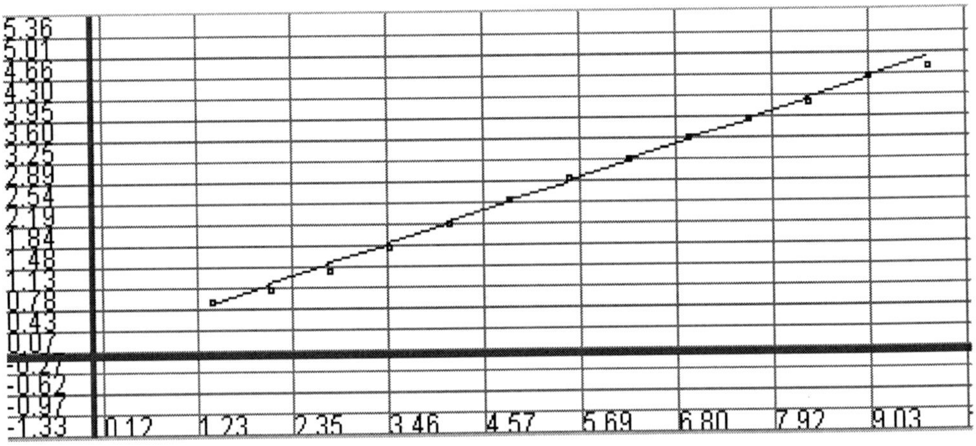

Figure 6.11(b). R/S confirms SRD for Poisson trace, H=0.491 of 99.8% confidence.

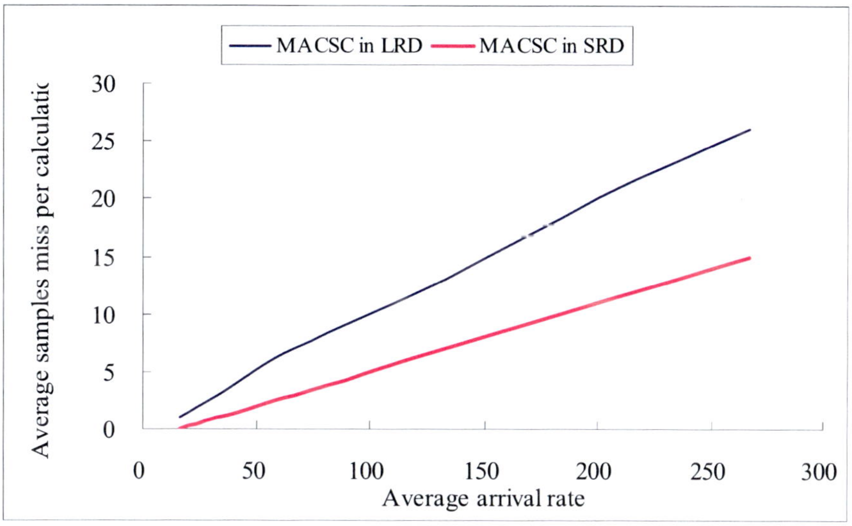

Figure 6.12(a). Data sample loss versus IAT for the EPA and Poisson traces.

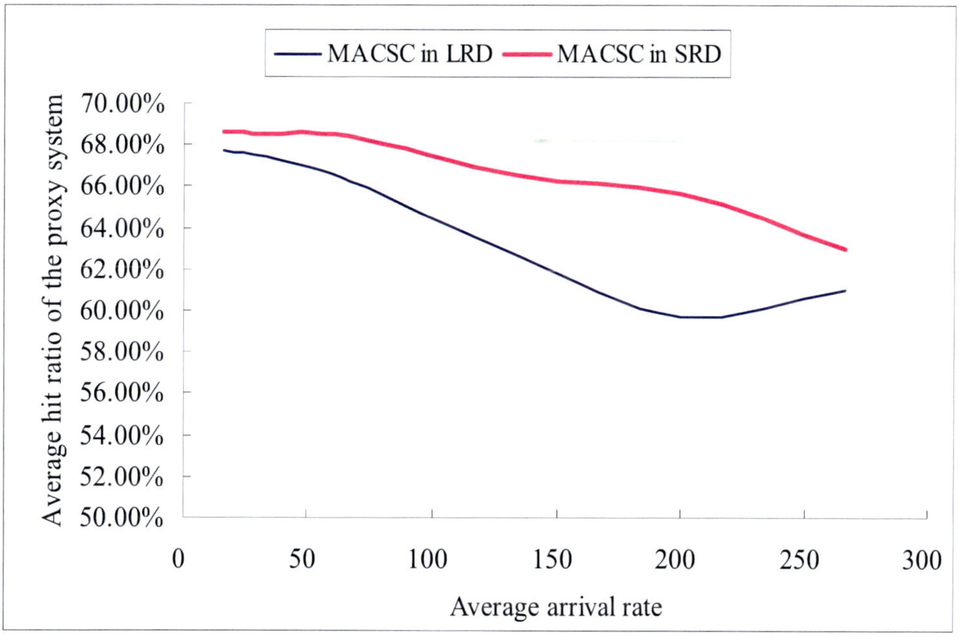

Figure 6.12(b). Hit ratio versus IAT for the EPA and Poisson traces.

To demonstrate the correlation between IAT and data loss the MACSC results, the actual LRD caching trace of 42438 http requests from the US EPA (Environmental Protection Agency) (figure 6.9) and a SRD Poisson trace (figure 6.10) are compared. The Hurst (H) values from the R/S plots of the two different traces processed by the RTPD prototype confirm their LRD (H = 0.761 in figure 6.11(a)) and SRD (H=0.491 in figure 6.11(b)) characters respectively. Figure 6.12 (a) shows data loss against the IAT rate, and figure 6.12(b) shows the respective changes in hit ratio.

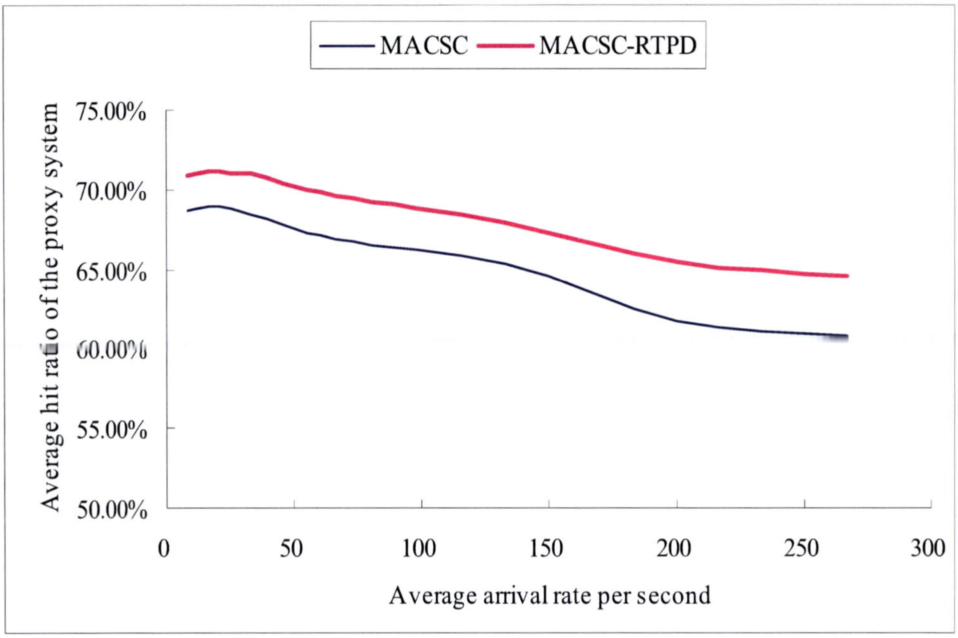

Figure 6.13. MACSC-RTPD generally yields a higher hit ratio.

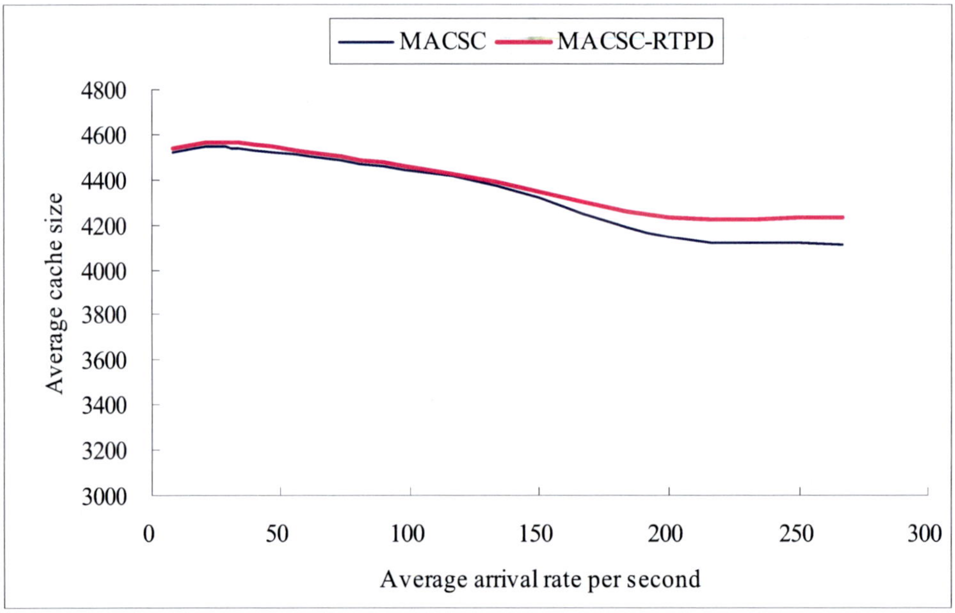

Figure 6.14. MACSC-RTPD does not consume excessive caching memory.

In the reconfigurable MACSC scheme, the best "*PE seed*" value should be picked for the new control cycle that computes $N = (\frac{ks_x}{Ex})^2$ with respect to the current traffic pattern for the purpose of fast convergence. At this moment, the method for calibrating the *n* values against specific traffic patterns is still an open issue. The "RTPD and MACSC" combination forms the new MACSC-RTPD framework, which is called the R-DCST (*Reconfigurable Dynamic Cache Size Tuner*) model [Wu2004]. Since the MACSC main body and the RTPD object are two parallel logical entities, the RTPD does not burden the MACSC execution. The experimental results with R-DCST on the Aglets mobile agent platform confirm that the RTPD element indeed helps the MACSC achieve its objective of effective reconfiguration. The Aglets platform is chosen because it is designed for Internet applications. This allows the experimental results to be scaled for the open Internet. As shown by figure 6.13, the R-DCST indeed maintains the given hit ratio of 68.3% (one SD) much better than the MACSC that has no RTPD support. The extra on-line MACSC "adaptive capability" gained from the RTPD mechanism, however, does not consume caching memory excessively for its more efficient hit ratio maintenance operation. Both figures 6.13 and 6.14 were produced from the same IAT traffic trace.

6.4. Summary

In this chapter, two case studies are presented. The first case study demonstrates how dynamic buffer tuning can make use of the RTPD results to carry out reconfiguration on the fly. The experimental results for the FLC[4x6] controller provided the basis for discussion. The second case shows how the RTPD mechanism can be included as part of the MACSC framework. Then, the traffic pattern detected by the RTPD element provides the necessary basis for the MACSC to reconfigure spontaneously to ward off traffic ill effects affecting its performance.

The RTPD construct is basically the "$M^3RT + R/S + \textit{filtration}$" combination. All experimental results empirically indicate that the RTPD mechanism is unquestionably an effective means for enhancing the FLC and MACSC performance. In effect, RTPD makes the Internet more friendly and usable for time-critical applications because it helps harness the client/server service RTT.

6.5. Key References

[Crovella1997] M.E. Crovella and A. Bestrvros, Self-similarity in the World Wide Web Traffic: Evidence and Possible Causes, *IEEE/ACM Transactions on Networking,* 5(6), December 1997, 835-846

[Lin2004] Wilfred W. K. Lin, Richard S.L. Wu, Allan K. Y. Wong, and Tharam S. Dillon, A Novel Real-Time Traffic Pattern Detector for Internet Applications, Proc. of the Australasian Telecommunication Networks and Applications Conference, Sydney, Australia (ATNAC'04), December 2004, 224-227

[Lin2005a] W. K. Lin, Allan K. Y. Wong, and Tharam S. Dillon, Application of Soft Computing Techniques to Adaptive User Buffer Overflow Control on the Internet, *IEEE Transactions of Systems, Man and Cybernetics, Part C*

[Medin2000] A. Medina, I. Matta and J. Byers, On the Origin of Power Laws in Internet Topologies, *ACM SIGCOMM,* 30(2), 2000, 18-28

(A), (B) and (C) shown in figure 7.1 depicts the process in the second leg. In step (A) the proxy requests the DNS to locate the data object. The locating operation is represented by step (B). Once the data object is located the DNS informs the proxy to retrieve it directly as step (C). If the following are assumed, RTT1 as the RTT delay of the first leg, RTT2 as the RTT delay of the second leg, and hr the hit ratio of the proxy cache (i.e. miss ratio equal to $(1-hr)$), then $S = \frac{RTT2 + RTT1}{RTT1 + [0 * RTT2 + (1-hr)RTT2]}$ represents the speedup due to caching. Assuming RTT2=10RTT1 and $hr = 0.8$, then S can be computed as $\frac{11RTT1}{RTT1 + 0.2RTT2} = \frac{11}{3} \approx 3.67$. This shows that maintaining a high hr is imperative for shorter information retrieval RTT. The only known mechanism from the literature that can achieve this is the MACSC framework for dynamic cache size tuning (Chapter 5). It is true that many different extant caching approaches can help yield a high hit ratio, but they do not maintain it. The GreedyDual-Size replacement algorithm, which works with a fixed-size cache, is one example [Aggarwal1999, Cao1997].

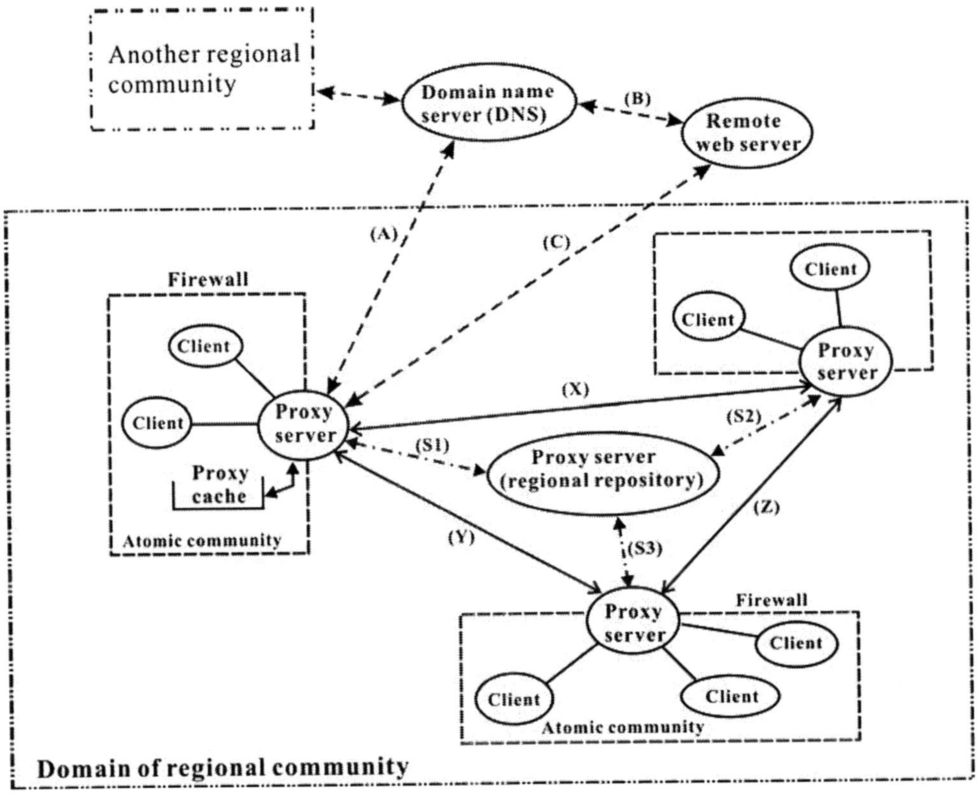

Figure 7.1. Domain of a regional community.

Although a high hr value shortens the information retrieval RTT, it has its limit. To transcend this limit, the concept of caching architecture emerged [Wang1999], the rationale of which is to make different proxy servers collaborate. There are many possible collaborating schemes including the following: a) hierarchical, such as the unique Harvest system

[Chankhunthod1996]; b) distributed, such as the ICP (Internet Cache Protocol [RFC2186]) architecture; and c) hybrid setup ("distributed + hierarchical") which aims to reduce the chance of involving distant or slower caches [Rabinovich1998].

So far, it has been difficult to determine the best collaborative caching scheme. In fact, every scheme is found to have pros and cons. For example, it was shown by researchers that the hierarchical schemes usually have lower retrieval latency for small data objects than their distributed counterparts. The latter, however, usually have shorter information transfer time and higher bandwidth usage [Rodriguez1999]. In theory, a hybrid scheme should combine the best features of the hierarchical and distributed schemes, but finding an efficacious hybrid scheme is still an elusive and open issue. Previous experience shows that, unless the following open problems are resolved, it will not be easy to improve the performance of the hierarchical schemes significantly [Rodriguez1999]:

1. Placement of proxy servers: It is difficult to decide where to place the proxy servers in the different hierarchical levels in the network for optimal performance. A possible solution is to let the servers have the intelligence to decide when and where to migrate. This involves mobile agent/object technologies and sophisticated network management techniques, which have been explored only sparsely [Lo2006, Bieszczad1998].
2. Levels of hierarchy: Since every level in the hierarchy of proxies introduces some delays, a highly hierarchical structure of many levels would cause a significant service RTT delay for the information retrieval process.
3. Performance bottlenecks: Since there are usually more lower-level proxies, which would request the higher level for the data objects that could not be found locally, long queuing delays at the high-level proxies turn the latter into performance bottlenecks.
4. Unusable copies: Multiple copies of supposedly the same data objects are usually stored at the different levels to facilitate access and retrieval. With time, some of these copies may become outdated thereby leading to data incoherence. To resolve this problem, a mechanism should be in place to ensure the coherence of all the multiple copies wherever they are located in the network.

The main challenge of the distributed scheme is to locate a data object quickly if it is absent from the home proxy cache. The relevant solutions to this challenge include:

1. IP multicast: If the data object is absent locally, the proxy multicasts the request to its collaborators. In figure 7.1, the three distributed proxy servers in the three atomic communities are collaborating. If the object is not cached anywhere within the group, then the request is forwarded to the remote data source and this may involve the DNS.
2. Cache routing: A proxy passes a request to the local proxy, which may relay it to another proxy according to a routing table or hashing function. The routing process repeats until the original source of the data object is reached. It is useful for the proxy server to keep a summary of what data objects the collaborating proxies/caches have. This "summary cache" approach directs the request to the cache that most likely has the requested data [Fan1998].

3. Adaptive multicast [Michel1998]: This is a form of adaptive web caching, which includes other approaches [Wang1999]. The core of this approach is to grow a distribution tree for every proxy in a mesh of proxies. These proxies are arranged into overlapping multicast groups so that a request traverses through them in search of the needed data. A distribution tree, which starts from a server and fans out towards sources of high demand, is encoded in a routing table. This tree normally would be updated and reconfigured in a real-time manner. In this scheme, a request for a more popular object, which is close to the "root" of the distribution (i.e. the proxy server), would traverse fewer proxies for a successful data object hit. The issue of how to grow a useful distribution tree is still waiting to be explored.

In fact, figure 7.1 is a simple distributed caching system which, if properly supported, can attain the nearest cache effect. The core elements are the multicast protocol and the "regional repository (RR)". The proxy operation can make use of the techniques of IP multicast, cache routing and distribution tree. Those data objects flushed out from each proxy by the local replacement operation are retained in the RR, which is managed by a dedicated proxy server. Any proxy could locate a data object within the regional community of proxies (including that for the repository) by multicast. Only when the object cannot be found, does the proxy search through the DNS. If the repository always retains the more popular data objects wanted by the regional community, then the chance of involving the DNS is greatly reduced.

The success of the scheme in figure 7.1, however, depends on whether open issues such as the following are resolved satisfactorily:

a) Data incoherence: The RR should have a large cache for keeping potentially hot data based on past experience, for the regional community. This enhances the chance of data incoherence because the RR may keep out-dated data objects. Practically, it is unrealistic for all the data sources in the Internet to broadcast and announce the data objects that have been updated because of the sheer size of the Internet and unexpected network faults. The alternative is to give proxy servers the power to invalidate old copies by replacing them with updated ones (a validation process). As yet, there is limited experience in the area of cache data coherence [Belloum2002], particularly in relation to the invalidation process.
b) Time to live: One viable approach to resolve the data incoherence problem is to allow a data object to "live" in a proxy cache only in the defined period. If this period can be accurately estimated and leveraged as a parameter for a replacement algorithm, then data objects can be removed from the proxy cache proactively to prevent data incoherence. So far, there is little published experience in this area.
c) Zipf-like behavior: Evidence was found for Zipf-like behavior [Breslau1999], which is presented by the log-log plot of the access frequencies versus the ranked position of the objects in descending order. That is, the Zipf-like behavior at anytime is the linear regression (log-log), $y(r) \propto r^{-\beta}$, where r is the ranked position of the object, $y(r)$ the log value of this object's current total access frequency from the time of consideration, and β is the slope of the linear curve or regression. The MACSC framework for dynamic cache size tuning uses the Zipf-like behavior in a real-time manner (see Chapter 5). In fact, this behavior may be used to reduce the

chance of data incoherence by enabling faster replacement of unpopular objects. However, there is little experience so far in how to achieve faster replacement as such.

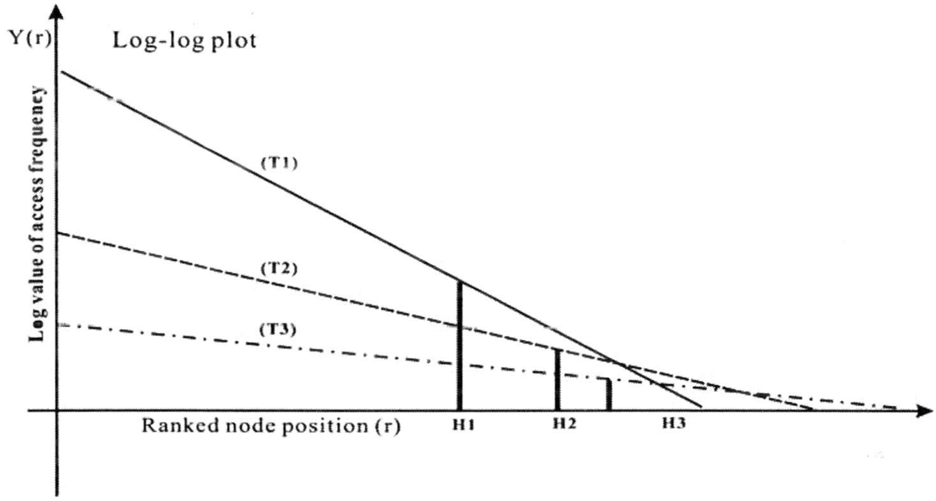

Figure 7.2. Using the Zipf-like behavior to augment replacement.

Figure 7.2 illustrates a scheme whereby the Zipf-like behavior can be used to enhance replacement efficacy. At the three different time points, T1, T2 and T3, β assumes different values that affect the caching dynamics at that time. As time passes, some data objects could suddenly become more popular (higher access frequency) than others. This means the same r (ranked) positions may not represent the same object as before because more popular data objects have now assumed lower r values. The regression, however, does not reflect such swaps in object positions. The β value always reflects the concentration of the hot data, which congregates at the higher end (the left side of the X axis). If thresholds are preset to determine which objects are not "en par", they can be flushed out in one shot in the replacement process. In figure 7.2, the threshold for the regression at T1 is H1 and only those objects on the left side of H1 are "en par". The steeper the regression, the more objects would be flushed out due to the higher concentration of hot data on the left of H1. Therefore, the replacement operation leverages β and the respective threshold. The way to compute β and the corresponding threshold on the fly is still an open issue.

7.2. Adaptive Replacement

From the service speedup up equation, $S = \dfrac{RTT2 + RTT1}{RTT1 + [0 * RTT2 + (1 - hr)RTT2]}$, which we discussed before, the hit ratio hr plays an important role. Therefore, it is imperative for any caching system to keep a high hr value in a relatively consistent manner. And, producing a high S value is a way to enhance the quality of service (QoS) because it leads to short client/server information retrieval RTT. In fact, service RTT is one of the many QoS indicators for time-critical applications. The ultimate QoS issue for these applications is to ensure short RTT so that the service result is consistently returned before the deadline [Lin2006]. The ability to maintain a high *hr* value efficaciously is especially important for small systems because of their limited memory resources. A small system cannot allocate excessive memory for caching purposes because this would lead to suspension of other tasks due to lack of recyclable memory. The result is poor system throughput. Therefore, for a small system, the ultimate goal is to use the minimum memory resources in a dynamic manner to achieve the highest *hr* value and thus the shortest possible RTT. The excess memory from caching is then recycled backed to enhance the overall system throughput. This is exactly what the MACSC principle is [Wu2004].

The quality of a caching system is usually measured and judged by its average hit ratio [Podlipnig03]. A high hit ratio would reduce the following:

a) Network bandwidth congestion as a fringe benefit.
b) User-perceived RTT delays, for example, in telemedicine a higher *S* value or shorter response time enhances the chance of saving patients in contingent cases.
c) Loading of the original data sources (web servers) because, if the data objects are found locally, no services from the web servers are needed.

This is why the primary goal of any caching strategy is either the yielding of a high hit ratio and/or maintaining the given one. The given hit ratio represents the level of caching performance expected by the user. Therefore, maintaining the given hit ratio is tantamount to satisfying the "contracted" quality of service (QoS) [Podlipnig2003]. It is unfortunate that most of the extant caching strategies are "best effort" approaches. They may produce a high hit ratio, but not necessarily maintain it. The appearance of the MACSC dynamic cache tuner recently [Wu2004] has changed this situation. The MACSC tuner is a form of adaptive web caching that is more an "exact" method than a "best-effort" approach. It adjusts the cache size with respect to the given *hr* on the fly so that the given hit ratio is consistently maintained as the minimum. The MACSC framework can include different replacement strategies for maximum effects. The proposal of this framework aimed to eliminate the following two major problems encountered by previous replacement strategies:

a) Static cache size: Previous strategies predominately work with a fixed-size cache, which frequently cannot hold enough data objects to produce the expected hit ratio.
b) Heavy parameterization: Different replacement strategies enhance the cache hit ratio in different ways by leveraging different parameters. Leveraging too many parameters or heavy parameterization by a strategy is counterproductive in two ways [AbSA1995, Yu1999]. The first is long computation delay, and the second is that parameters may counteract one another in different conditions.

The desire to produce a high hit ratio and maintain it consistently led to the adaptive replacement school of thought [Podlipnig03]. This is one of the issues under the umbrella of adaptive caching [Wang1999], which is defined as "*methods that make the caching system adapt to the dynamic changing of user demands and the network environment to essentially achieve optimal performance, such as a high or given hit ratio*".

In the literature, two adaptive replacement strategies can be identified, but they represent emerging thoughts:

a) Invoking different replacement algorithms at different times in an on-line manner [Aguilar2001]: The argument is that the best replacement algorithm in the predefined list should be invoked for the particular situation. The problem is how to calibrate an algorithm against the "so-called" best working condition. At this moment, there is little progress being made on this open issue.
b) Tuning parameters on the fly [Niclausse1998]: The rationale is to give more weight to different parameters at different times in an on-line manner. The rationale is to accentuate the effects of the best parameter(s) at the time to yield the highest hit ratio [Jin2000]. So far, there has been little success regarding this open issue.

7.3. Traffic Analysis

The negative impact of Internet traffic on system performance was reported in the early 1990s [Paxson1999, Jamijoon2004]. The conclusion was that Internet based systems and applications should not be designed with a preconceived mathematical model in mind, otherwise they would fail easily. The cause of failure is the ever-changing traffic pattern in the Internet, which follows the power laws. For example, the Internet traffic pattern may change from short-range dependence (SRD) such as Markovian patterns to long-range dependence (LRD) that includes self-similar and heavy-tailed waveforms. Therefore, contemporary tools aimed at Internet applications would try to take dynamic traffic pattern changes into account. The Convergence Algorithm (CA) is one such example, which works with accuracy that is traffic independent because it is derived from the *Central Limit Theorem* [Wong2001b].

The CA is an IEPM (Internet End-to-End Performance Measurement [Cottrel1999, Cottrel2001]) technique that predicts the mean response time of a communication channel. It differs from other extant techniques for being the only IEPM method designed for real-time application. For example, CA can be used by real-time applications to measure the mean RTT of all the potential servers within their domain. As a result, these applications can pick the nearest server to provide the necessary services. In this way, the client applications could get the service results in the shortest possible RTT. Around the same time as the emergence of the IEPM school of thought, some researchers started to analyze how Internet traffic could impede system performance. The analyses, however, were exclusively offline (i.e. postmortem) and worked with IP traffic traces [Molnár1999] pre-collected over the wireline infrastructure. The findings showed that SRD, LRD and multifractal could interleave within a single trace. Some researchers argued that there was a correlation between the ON/OFF activities in the network and self-similar traffic patterns because such a correlation exists in the local area networks (e.g. Ethernet). Table 7.1 shows some of the useful statistical techniques that are suitable for identifying particular traffic patterns [Molnár1999, Lin2005b].

In the traffic analysis process, the first step is to ensure that the traffic trace being scrutinized is stationary [Taqqu2003]. This is achieved by ensuring that the Hurst (H) value is between 0 and 1; $0 < H < 0.5$ indicating SRD and $0.5 < H < 1$ for LRD. The hierarchy in figure 7.3 generalizes the postmortem traffic analysis steps involved. A distribution $F(x)$ is heavy-tailed provided that $1 - F(x) = x^{-\alpha} L(x)$ holds, where $L(x)$ varies slowly at ∞. This implies $\lim_{x \to \infty} F(x)/L(x) = 1$ for $t > 0$. The Pareto distribution is the simplest heavy-tailed case for $L(x) \equiv 1$. A process $Y(x)$ is self-similar if the finite-dimensional distributions $Y(ax)$ are identical to $\alpha^H Y(x)$, where the scaling factor is the Hurst(H) exponent; that is, $\{Y(\alpha x_1), Y(\alpha x_2), ..., Y(\alpha x_d)\} \equiv \{\alpha^H Y(x_1), \alpha^H Y(x_2), ..., \alpha^H Y(x_d)\}$.

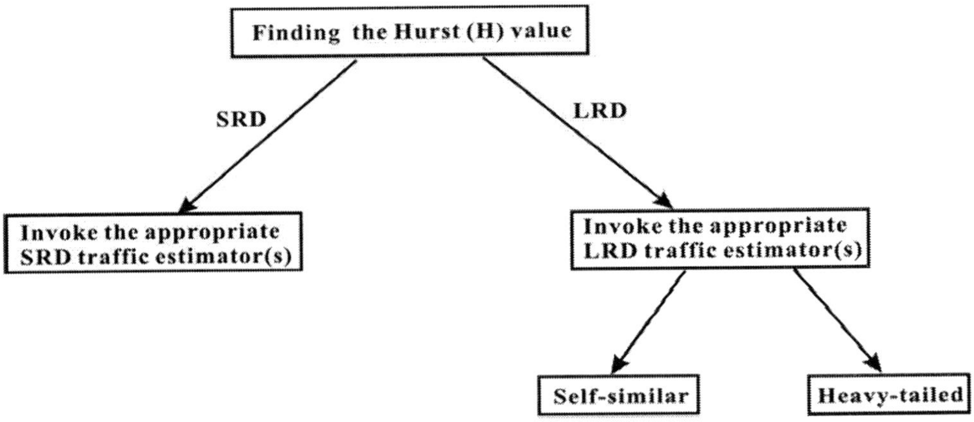

Figure 7.3. A simple hierarchy for Internet traffic analysis.

Table 7.1. Methods and traffic pattern identifications

Methods for heavy-tailedness	Methods for self-similarity	Methods for H value/effect
Modified QQ-plot	Variance-time plot	R/S (readjusted scaled statistics) plot
Hill estimator	Self-similarity (S^2) filter [Lin2005b]	Periodogram
De Haan's moment		

Although there have been extensive studies of wireline IP traffic behavior, there is still little experience published for the wireless sector. At this moment, it is difficult to come to the same conclusion that the IP traffic behavior in the wireline sector applies to the wireless counterpart. There is a lack of sufficient empirical evidence, and findings [Lin2005c, UTS, MosquitoNet] indicate that the methods listed in table 7.1 may be applicable. In fact, it was argued that the "after-the-fact" results from the post-mortem or off-line analyses may not be useful in improving system performance in a dynamic fashion. As a result, some researchers concentrated on real-time traffic analysis with a technique called *real-time traffic pattern detection* (RTPD). Although the research direction is new, the findings so far indicate that the

RTPD can indeed help improve system performance (see Chapter 6). The representative work in the literature in the RTPD direction is by Lin *et al* [Lin2004], and one application example of this technique is shown in the paper by Wu *et al* [Wu2005c]. The S^2 filter in table 7.1 works equally well for off-line and real-time applications.

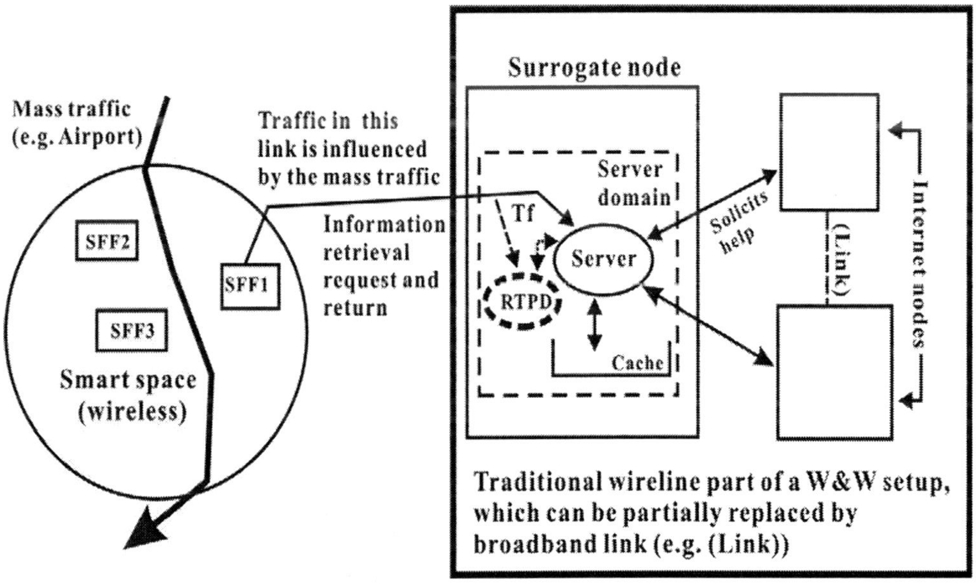

Figure 7.4. A generic view of a pervasive computing or WandW environment.

Wireless traffic analysis is still an open issue because there are two basic categories: close-range and wide-range. The close range-categories include part of the IEEE 802.11 protocol stack (and others such as Bluetooth or IEEE 802.15 (table 7.2)), which are generally known as "*WiFi*". The wide-range (broadband) category includes the family of IEEE 802.16 standards and is usually represented by its associated industry consortium "*WiMax*". WiFi and WiMax have different purposes. Other than supporting wireless LAN, which is modeled after the Ethernet operation, WiFi provides the basis for traditional pervasive computing with client mobility in mind. Clients in this case are the small form factor devices such as the PDA (personal digital assistant). Figure 7.4 depicts a pervasive computing environment of two parts, wireless smart space(s) and the wired Internet infrastructure. Traditionally, these two parts are connected via the base stations into a complete "wireless + wireline (WandW)" architecture. Since the emerging broadband wireless technology is aimed at replacing cables and wires (partially or totally) in general, the wired portion in the supposedly wireline infrastructure in the WandW framework would shrink [Ghosh2005]. The wireline infrastructure in figure 7.4 will gradually become more composite in nature as time progresses. The changing nature would affect the meaning of pervasive computing, which at this moment is still evolving [Garlan2002].

The IEEE Working Group for the 802.16 broadband wireless standards has been trying to tap the 10 to 66 gigahertz (GHz) range that includes licensed and unlicensed spectrums. Different products keep appearing and claim to operate with wireless broadband, but they usually have interoperability problems, especially at the medium access control (MAC) and physical (PHY) levels. To deal with these problems the associated industry consortium with

IEEE 802.16, WiMax, created profiles. Adherence to a profile improves interoperability among vendors. Today, the bulk of the WiMax focus is on the frequency band below 11 GHz. In fact, the IEEE 802.16 effort is spent on finding a deployable alternative to replace the cabled network technologies such as fibre optic links and digital subscriber lines (DSL). There is still a long way to go before this replacement potential can be realized because there are many unresolved difficult problems. They include the following: a) up to 25 percent of a broadband cell may have communication blackout for single-antenna users; b) poor reception if the user is traveling more than 80 miles an hour; and c) high loss rate. The high loss rate problem is serious because it is the source of widespread retransmissions and thus long service roundtrip time (RTT). Many researchers try to resolve this problem in reality by modifying the automatic repeat request (ARQ) technique [Ghosh2005, Lin1982].

Table 7.2. Part of the IEEE 802.11 protocol stack and Bluetooth (IEEE 802.15)

802.11 protocols →	Infrared	FHSS (Frequency Hopping Spread spectrum	OFDM (Orthogonal Frequency Division Multiplexing), two versions: 802.11a and 802.11g
802.15 → (Bluetooth)	Piconet as the basic unit		

If the traditional pervasive computing infrastructure becomes more wireless supported by a rich mix of WiFi and WiMax setups, it will be difficult to harness the service RTT between the client and the server. To understand the reasons behind this, a close look at figure 7.4 is warranted. Let us start first with a traditional WandW setup without the broadband presence. It is assumed that the smart space or cell, which is located in an airport and supported by IEEE 802.11 type of wireless operations, is where mobile clients (e.g. SFF1 and SFF2) can communicate with the wired Internet. The traffic pattern of this cell depends on the mass transit traffic (especially during peak rush hours) by clients passing through it. The surrogate server node, which is the front end computer assigned to serve this cell, would receive the same traffic pattern (e.g. *Tf*) that is transcribed laterally. In fact, this traffic pattern and its real-time changes can be measured by the RTPD technique (see Chapter 3). If the request by a client is information retrieval, then the surrogate would try to find the data locally (e.g. from its own cache)). If the data is absent, then it solicits help from other server nodes in the wireline Internet infrastructure by cyber foraging [Garlan2002].

The traffic patterns and intensity among the collaborating nodes in the wired portion of WandW can be monitored by well established IEPM techniques such as Convergence Algorithm and RTPD. These techniques have been validated with traditional IP traffic. If the wired portion is partly or wholly replaced by broadband wireless, then the extant techniques that detect the traffic patterns may fail because there is still a lack of knowledge about broadband traffic. It is dangerous to assume that the previous knowledge in postmortem and wireless traffic analyses [Molnár1999, Lin2005c] would apply. Therefore, the methodology for identifying the broadband wireless traffic patterns is an urgent open issue. Otherwise, it will be difficult to ensure stable, good system performance through harnessing of the traffic. In this aspect, it becomes necessary to understand the meaning of mixed traffic types to system behavior. In the next generation of WandW setups, the surrogate will be supported in future by nodes arbitrarily interconnected by cables and broadband wireless means. This implies that the traffic between any two monitoring points/ends can come from a composite link/channel of mixed technologies. For example, the communication link may be interleaving wireline IEEE 802.11 and wireless IEEE802.16 hops.

7.3.1. Fractal Breakdown and Implications

If an Internet traffic time series is stationary, then it is either short-range dependence (SRD) or long-range dependence (LRD). The novel real-time traffic pattern detection (RTPD) technique, which is supported by the CAB (continuous aggregate based) mechanism [Lin2004, Lin2005, Lin2006, Wu2005], can detect SRD and LRD. It can also identify if the LRD traffic is heavy-tailed, self-similar or multifractal [Willinger1994]. If a self-similar or non-differentiable time series embeds different self-similarity or fractal dimensions (e.g. Cantor set in Chapter 3), it is multifractal. In a multifractal aggregate X^m, where m is the aggregate size, different fractality may exist for different local data points. The local fractality should be inside the Holder exponent range between 0 and 1. If the computed Holder exponent is outside this range, fractal breakdown is indicated. In reality, any stationary process may go into an unexpected chaotic, unstable condition. If the condition is persistent, the system will break down. Therefore, techniques that can detect fractal breakdown on the fly are useful for system reliability and safety. Yet, there is little experience published in the literature in the following areas:

a) Effective technique(s) for detecting fractal breakdown in a dynamic manner.
b) Correlations between fractal breakdown and possible causes.
c) Solutions to circumvent or prevent fractal breakdowns.

It was observed that a chaotic, irregular point in a function would have a low Holder exponent (HE) [Daoudi1999]. This means that it is natural for different data points in a time series to have varied HE values to reflect the local fractalities. The HE or local fractality for point t of function $f(t)$ in the continuous domain is shown by equation (7.1). This equation, however, is not suitable for real-time application over the Internet because: a) Internet operation is in the discrete domain, and b) to detect fractal breakdown on the fly means that the Holder exponent has to be computed quickly for small aggregates (i.e. X^m with a small m).

$$HE(t) = \lim_{h\to 0} \frac{\log(|f(t+h)-f(t)|)}{\log(|h|)} \quad ....(7.1)$$

With the aim of computing the Holder exponent on the fly for real-time applications, a group of researchers [Shereshevsky2003] proposed a new statistical technique. The rationale is to calculate the Holder exponent, HE_i for the data point x_i in X^m, where m is the number of sampled data points, x_0, x_1, ... x_i, x_{i+1}, ... x_{m-1}. The calculation is controlled by the parameter λ in the range (0,1). It was shown that $m = 20$ is sufficient to yield a reasonable HE_i value. The statistical technique can be summarized in three steps represented by equations (7.2), (7.3) and (7.4). Equation (7.4) can be generalized as equation (7.5). The criteria for applying these equations, which together form a *discrete tool for detecting fractal breakdown* (DT-DFB) on the fly, are as follows:

a) In the first step, the l integer must satisfy the $0 \le i+l \le m$ condition, where m is the aggregate size for data sampling on the fly. For each integer $l \ne 0$ the calculation of $R_{i,l}$ goes from $-s$ to $+s$ about the chosen x_i data point for $s = m/2$.

b) In the second step, k represents the absolute integer distance $|s|$ about x_i, $1 \le k \le l$. The aim is to find the minimum value between the R_{i-l} and R_{i+l}.

c) The third step computes the weighted average of the $h_{i,k}$ approximations.

$$R_{i,l} = \frac{\log|x_{i+l} - x_i|}{\log(\frac{|l|}{m})} \text{.......(7.2)}$$

$$h_{i,k} = \min(R_{i,l} : |l| \le k) \text{......(7.3)}$$

$$HE_i = \frac{(1-\lambda)}{(1-\lambda^l)}(h_{i,1} + \lambda h_{i,2} + \lambda^2 h_{i,3} + ... + \lambda^{l-1} h_{i,l}) \text{......(7.4)}$$

$$HE_i = \frac{(1-\lambda)\sum_{i,q=1}^{q=l}(\lambda^{q-1} h_{i,q})}{(1-\lambda^l)} \text{........(7.5)}$$

Table 7.3. An excerpt of table 3.2 in Chapter 3

Time series (rows)	β	$H = (1 - \beta/2)$	R^2 (coefficient of determination)	Loading Factor ψ	Kurtosis	Skewness
5	0.4685	0.766	0.959 (95.9%)	0.5	-0.58417	0.892037
6	0.3762	0.812	0.885 (88.5%) (less than Th_{R^2})	0.6 (rejected)	-1.01033	0.446756

It was shown empirically that the detection of fractal breakdowns can indeed be achieved by applying equations (7.2), (7.3) and (7.5). For example, the R^2 value for row 6 in table 7.3, which is a shorter version of table 3.2, is less that 90%. When this is compounded by the sudden change in the Hurst (H) value, something unusual such as fractal breakdowns might have occurred. Figure 7.5 shows how the calculations by the above equations confirm fractal breakdowns in different regions of the time series. All the chaotic regions have negative Holder exponent values. The data points of interest in this example range from the 250th to the 450th. In between the chaotic regions of a rapidly oscillating nature (e.g. the section from around the 295th data point to the 380th sample) are the smooth parts of the distribution. The experience gained by the authors (of this book) about the DT-DFB approach is significant. It was confirmed empirically that this approach can be combined with the RTPD technique. Then, the RTPD element would inform the host real-time application if the operating environment has suddenly become turbulent. With this knowledge, the application can take proactive steps to prevent failure. Therefore, it is absolutely worthwhile to explore the open issue of real-time fractal breakdown detection.

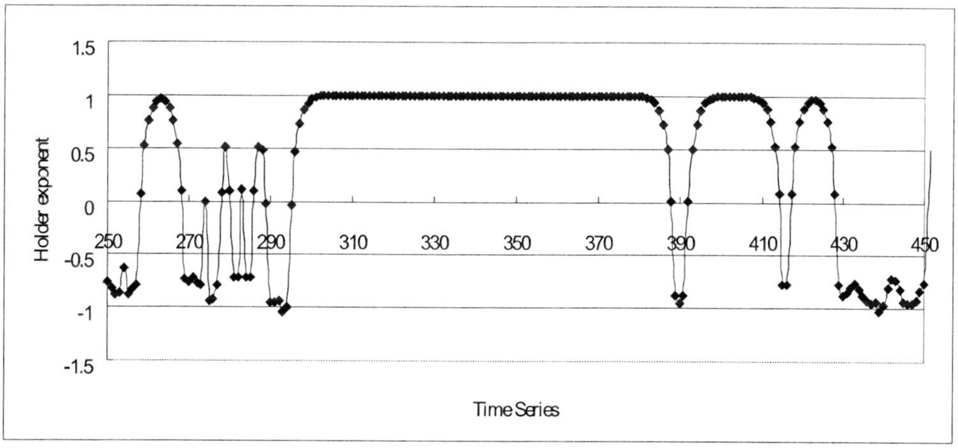

Figure 7.5. Fractal breakdowns in row 6 of table 3.2 (Chapter 3) detected by DT-DFB.

7.4. Improving Replacement Efficacy with Dynamic Cache Size Tuning

Caching is important for Internet based applications because of the following:

a) It helps produce a shorter service information retrieval roundtrip time (RTT), making the customer satisfied. A happy customer is a return customer and this is fundamental to e-commerce success.
b) Since the data objects to be retrieved are located locally (i.e. in the proxy cache), there is less data to be transferred across the open network. This effectively frees more of the Internet bandwidth for sharing and lessens the chance of network congestion.

There are two factors that determine the communication distance between the client and the data source: the actual service RTT and the proxy cache hit ratio. In fact, as explained earlier, there are two legs in every information retrieval. The first is between the client and the proxy and the second is between the proxy and the remote data source. If the delay in the first leg is RTT_1 and RTT_2 for the second, the extent to which the total RTT, namely,

"$RTT_1 + RTT_2$" can be shortened depends on the proxy cache hit ratio (hr). That is, the roundtrip speedup S can be defined by $S = \dfrac{RTT_1 + RTT_2}{RTT_1 + [0 * hr + (1 - hr) * RTT_2]}$.

For $RTT_2 = 10RTT_1$ and $hr = 0.8$ the speedup is $S = \dfrac{11RTT_1}{(1+2)RTT_1} \approx 3.67$.

The value of S, however, does depend on hr, but it is always important to make RTT_1 and RTT_2 short in time-critical applications. This led to the concept of fetching from the nearest cache(s) and the emergence of collaborative caching, which is a process of sharing web caches through a specific protocol. The first known cache sharing strategy was proposed by the Harvest project [Danzig1993, ICP1998] using the Internet Cache Protocol (ICP), which discovers and retrieves data objects from collaborating neighboring caches. The basic concept is to organize the neighboring caches into a mesh or hierarchy. If a proxy has missed a hit, it will multicast the same request to its supposed close neighbors (i.e. low RTT_2). Therefore, the scheme is basically speculative in the sense that the proxy would keep only one of the same return data objects. In the process, a substantial amount of effort has been wasted by those proxies that bothered to serve the request. If we assume the following for an ICP system: n proxy neighbors, r is the average number of requests received by every proxy per unit time, and the average hit ratio is hr, the ICP request rate in the collaborative system is $(n-1)(1-hr)r$. At anytime the system needs to handle $n(n-1)(1-hr)r$ ICP requests. For a reasonably large n letting $k = (1-hr)r$ the bandwidth consumption (BC) is proportional to kn^2: $BC \propto kn^2$.

One way to prevent such heavy consumption of bandwidth is to use summary caches. In this case, every proxy has a summary cache or directory that records the data objects that other neighboring proxies could possibly have [Fan2000]. If the ICP inquiries can be sent to only those neighbors that are most likely to have the needed data object, then bandwidth can be reduced because of the much smaller n value; $n = 1$ in the ideal case.

The importance of caching to Internet performance has spawned different areas of research aimed at producing a high hr and a low RTT_2. The literature confirms that the most researched topic in caching is replacement strategy. The extant algorithms, in this respect, work exclusively with a fixed-size cache. Among them the five "champions", which yield high hit ratios (but do not necessarily maintain them), are: LRV (Lowest Relative Value), SIZE, LRU (Least Recently Used), Hybrid, and GDS (Greedy Dual-Size). Different trace-driven simulations indicate that GDS consistently produces the highest hit ratio [Cao1997] among the five. Yet, these simulations also indicate that under certain conditions, the hit ratio obtained by these strategies/algorithms can drop seriously. Some subsequent detailed analyses show that the sudden dips in hit ratio are caused by the variations in object sizes during the caching process. There will be a dip in the hit ratio if the fixed-size cache has to store more sizeable data objects. Therefore, maintaining a given hit ratio is equivalent to keeping the "given number of standard deviations of objects". This is physically difficult unless the cache size is self-tuned on the fly. This is exactly what the novel MACSC dynamic cache tuner has achieved (see Chapter 5). That is, the cache size always accommodates the changes in the "*popularity spread of the data objects*".

Figure 7.6 shows the changes of the relative object popularity profile at two different time points (i.e. A and B). The changes are reflected in the spread or variance of the data objects within the same set over time. *Sa* and *Sb* indicate the standard deviations for the timely popularity profile A and B. If a cache of a fixed size is able to keep enough hot data for the given confidence of one-standard deviation δ (or 68.4%) about the mean (i.e. δ = *Sa*), then it would not work for *Sb*. Physically, the wider *Sb* needs a bigger cache to hold extra data objects in order to satisfy the same given 68.4% confidence.

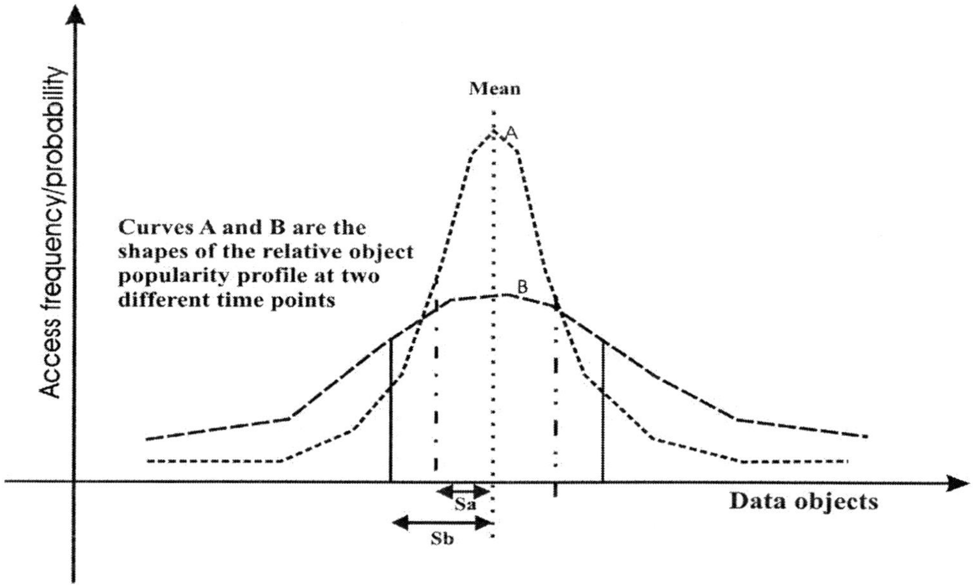

Figure 7.6. Changes in the spread of the relative data object popularity profile.

From the perspective of the changeable popularity spread (figure 7.6), any replacement algorithm designed to gain a high hit ratio with a cache of static size *S* works well only when the size required by the given number of standard deviation $\sigma = n\delta$ (i.e. S_δ) is smaller than S, or $S_\delta \leq S$, where δ is the standard deviation. To maintain the given hit ratio under all conditions, for example 68.4% (i.e. one δ of the popularity profile), the cache size should be timely and adaptively adjusted by leveraging the chosen system parameters. The MACSC (Model for Adaptive Cache Size Control) achieves dynamic cache size tuning by using the log-log plot of the "*access frequencies versus the ranked positions of the data objects within the set*". A higher frequency has a higher rank (in descending order); this is called the Zipf-like behavior. It leverages this behavior by transforming it into a bell-shape relative object popularity profile (figure 7.6). The key for computing the popularity ratio (PR) is to use either the standard-deviation ratio (SR) or variance ratio (VR), $SR = \sqrt{VR} =$ $(\sigma_{ThisSample} / \sigma_{LastSample})$. The MACSC tunes the cache size S_t to satisfy the $S_\sigma \leq S_t$

condition. For Figure 7.6 $(S_b/S_a)^2$ and (S_b/S_a) are the VR and SR respectively. The equations, $CS_{Tuned\_SR} = CS_{Old\_SR} * (\sigma_{ThisSample}/\sigma_{LastSample})$ and $CS_{Tuned\_VR} = CS_{Old\_VR} * (\sigma_{ThisSample}/\sigma_{LastSample})^2$ represent the SR and VR based tuning approaches.

The MACSC implementation can make use of different statistical techniques for computing the standard deviation of the relative object popularity profile on the fly. For example, MACSC(PE) uses the point-estimate (PE) approach but MACSC(M^3RT) relies on the Convergence Algorithm (CA). All the successful MACSC implementations so far (see Chapter 5) entail the LRU replacement algorithm. In effect, the MACSC mechanism provides a variable cache size for the LRU to work in a dynamic manner.

The issue of how effectively the MACSC solutions would work with the four other champion replacement strategies, LRV, Hybrid, GDS and SIZE [Cao1997], is still open.

7.5. Summary

In this chapter, several open issues related to time-critical cases on the Internet were explored. These include nearest cache, adaptive replacement, traffic analysis of mixed wired/wireless vehicles, fractal breakdown, and improved replacement efficacy through dynamic cache size tuning. They all need considerable further exploration, analysis and experimentation before the aforementioned issues can be properly addressed.

7.6. Key References

[ABSA1995] M. Abrams, C. Standridge, G. Abdulla, S. Williams and E.A. Fox, Caching proxies: limitations and potentials, Proc. of the 4th International World Wide Web Conference, MA, December 1995

[Aggarwal1999] C. Aggarwal, J. L. Wolf and P. S. Yu, Caching on the World Wide Web. In *IEEE Transactions on Knowledge and Data Engineering,* v. 11, 1999, 94-107

[Aguilar2001] J. Aguilar and E. Leiss, A Web Proxy Cache Coherency and Replacement Approach, Proc. of the 1st Asia-Pacific Conference on Web Intelligence, 2001

[AWC] Adaptive Web Caching, http://www.nrg.ee.lbl.gov/floyd/web.html

[Belloum2002] A.S.Z. Belloum and L.O. Hertzberger, Concurrent Evaluation of Web Cache Replacement and Coherence Strategies, *Simulation,* 78(1), January 2002, 28-35

[Beslau1999] L. Breslau, P. Cao, G. Philips and S. Shenker, Web Caching and Zipf-like Distributions,: Evidence and Implications, *Proc. of IEEE INFOCOM,* 1999, 126-134

[Bieszczad1998] A. Bieszczad, B. Pagurek and T. White, Mobile Agents for Network Management, *IEEE Communication Surveys,* 1(1), 1998

[Cao1997] P. Cao and S. Irani, Cost-aware WWW Proxy Caching Algorithms, Proc. of USENIX Symposium on Internet Technologies and Systems, December 1997, 193-206

[Cao1997] P. Cao and S. Irani, Cost-Aware WWW Proxy Caching Algorithm, *Proc. of the 1997 USENIX Symposium on Internet Technology and Systems,* December 1997, 193-206

[Chankhunthod1996] A. Chankhunthod1996, P.B. Danzig, C. Neerdaels, M.F. Schwartz and K.J. Worrel, A Hierarchical Internet Object Cache, *Proc. of Usenix'96,* January 1996

[Cottrel1999] L. Cottrel, M. Zekauskas, H. Uijterwaal and T. McGregor, Comparison of Some Internet Active End-to-End Performance Measurement Projects, http://www.slac.stanford.edu/comp/net/wan-mon/iepm-cf.html, 1999

[Cottrel2001] L. Cottrel, Passive vs. Active Monitoring, http://www.slac.stanford.edu/comp /net/wan-mon/passive-vs-active.html, March 2001

[Danzig1993] P.B. Danzig, R.S. Hall and M.F. Schwartz, A Case for Caching File Objects inside Internetworks, *Proc. of SIGCOMM*, 1993, 239-248

[Daoudi1999] K.Daoudi, A.B. Frakt and A.S. Willsky, Multiscale Autoregressive Models and Wavelets, *IEEE Transactions on Information Theory,* 45(3), April 1999, 828-845

[Fan1998] L. Fan, P. Cao, J. Almeida and A.Z. Broder, Summary Cache: A Scalable Wide-Area Web Caching Protocol, Proc. of SIGCOMM'09, 1998

[Fan2000] L. Fan, P. Cao, J. Almeida and A.Z. Broder, Summary Cache: A Scalable Wide-Area Web Cache Sharing Protocol, IEEE/ACM on Networking, 8(3), June 2000, 281-293

[Garlan2002] D. Garlan, D.P. Siewiorek, A. Smailagic and P. Steenkiste, Project Aura: Toward Distributed-Free Pervasive Computing, Pervasive Computing, April-June, 2002, 22-31

[Ghosh2005] A. Ghosh, D.R. Wolter, J.G. Andrews and R. Chen, Broadband Wireless Access with WiMax/802.16: Current Performance Benchmarks and Future Potential, *IEEE Communications Magazine,* February, 2005, 129 - 136

[ICP1998] ICP Working Group Report, National Laboratory for Applied Network Research, htt[://ircache.nlanr.net/Cache/ICP/

[Jamjoom2004] H. Jamjoom, P. Pillai and K.G. Shin, Resynchronization and Controllability of Bursty Service Requests, *IEEE/ACM Transactions on Networking,* 14(4), August 2004, pp. 582- 594

[Jin2000] S. Jin and A. Bestavros, Popularity-Aware Greedy Dual-Size Web Proxy Caching Algorithms, Proceedings of the International Conference on Distributed Computing Systems, 2000

[Lin2004] Wilfred W. K. Lin, Richard S.L. Wu, Tharam S. Dillon and Allan K. Y. Wong, A Novel Real-Time Traffic Pattern Detector for Internet Applications, Proc. of the 2004 Australian Telecommunication Networks and Applications Conference(ATNAC), Sydney, Australia, December 2004, 224-227

[Lin2005] Wilfred W. K. Lin, Allan K. Y. Wong, Richard S.L. Wu , and Tharam S. Dillon, A Novel Real-Time Self-Similar Traffic Detector/Filter to Improve the Reliability of a TCP Based End-to-End Client/Server Interaction Path for Shorter Roundtrip Time, ICETE'05, Reading UK, October 2005, vol. 1, 94 – 101

[Lin2005b] Wilfred W. K. Lin, Allan K. Y. Wong, and Tharam S. Dillon, A Novel R^2-FLC Dynamic Buffer Size Tuner to Support Time-Critical Applications over the Internet by Improving Logical Channel Fault Tolerance, Proc. of the 11th International Symposium on Pacific Rim Dependable Computing (PRDC'2005) Changsha, PRC

[Lin2005c] Wilfred W.K. Lin, Tharam T. Dillon and Allan K.Y. Wong, Using the Novel FLC Dynamic Buffer Size Tuning Technique to Support More Dependable Location-Aware, Proc. of the 4th International Conference on Mobile Business (MBusiness2005), July, Sydney, 507-513

[Lin2006] Wilfred W. K. Lin, Allan K.Y. Wong, Tharam S. Dillon and Wong Hok Leung, A Novel Self-Similarity (S^2) Traffic Filter to Enhance the Success of E-Business, the WSEAS Transactions on Systems, 8(5), 2006, 1895-1900

[Lin2006] Wilfred W.K. Lin, Allan K.Y. Wong and Tharam S. Dillon, Application of Soft Computing Techniques to Adaptive User Buffer Overflow Control on the Internet, *IEEE Transactions on Systems, Man and Cybernetics,* Part C, 36(3), May 2006, 397 -410

[Lin82] S. Lin and P. Yu, A Hybrid ARQ Scheme with Parity Retransmission for Error Control of Satellite Channels, *IEEE Transactions of Communications,* 30(7) July 1982, 1701 - 1719

[Lo2006] Jason L.T. Lo, Allan K.Y. Wong and Wilfred W. K. Lin, SDITPM: A Novel Transfer Policy Model to Facilitate Object Mobility that Shortens Service Roundtrip Time by Load Balancing over the Internet, to appear in the *International Journal of Computer Systems, Science and Engineering,* 2006

[Michel1998] S. Michel, K. Nguyen, A. Rosenstein, L. Zhang, S. Floyd and V. Jacobson, Adaptive Web Caching: *Towards a New Caching Architecture, Computer Network and ISDN Systems,* November 1998

[Molnár1999] S. Molnár, T.D. Dang and A. Vidács, Heavy-Tailedness, Long-Range Dependence and Self-Similarity in Data Traffic, Proceedings of 7th International Conference on Telecommunication Systems, Modelling and Analysis, March 1999, Nashville, USA, 18-21.

[MosquitoNet] Stanford University CSL, http://mosquitonet.stanford.edu/

[Niclausse1998] N. Niclausse, Z. Liu and P. Nain, A New Efficient Caching Policy for the World Wide Web, Proc. of the Workshop on the Internet Server Performance, 1998, 119-128

[Paxson1995] V. Paxson and S. Floyd, Wide-Area Traffic: The Failure of Poisson Modeling, *IEEE/ACM Transactions on Networking,* 3(3), June 1995, 226-244

[Paxson1999] V. Paxson, End-to-end Internet Packet Dynamics, *IEEE/ACM Transactions on Networking,* 7(3), June 1999, 277 -292

[Podlipnig03] S. Podlipnig and L. Boszormenyi, A Survey of Web Cache Replacement Strategy, *ACM Computing Surveys,* 35(4), 374-388

[Poplipng2003] S. Poplipng and L. Boszormenyi, A Survey of Web Cache Replacement Strategies, *ACM Computing Surveys,* 35(4), December 2003, 374 - 398

[Rabinovich1998] M. Rabinovich, J. Chase and S. Gadde, Not All Hits Are Created Equal: Cooperative Caching over a Wide-Area Network, *Computer Networks and ISDN Systems,* November 1998

[RFC2186] D. Wessels and K. Claffy, *Internet Cache Protocol* (ICP), Ver. 2, RFC2186

[Rodriguez1999] P. Rodriguez, C. Spanner and E.W. Biersack, Web Caching Architectures: Hierarchical and Distributed Caching, *Proc. of WCW'99,* 1999

[Shereshevsky2003] M. Shereshevsky2003, J. Crowell, B. Cukic, V. Handikota and Y. Liu, Software Aging and Multfractality of Memory Resources, *Proc. of the 2003 IEEE International Conference on Dependable Systems and Networks* (DSN'03), 2003

[Taqqu2003] M.S. Taqqu, Fractional Brownian Motion and Long-Range Dependence, in *Theory and Applications of Long-Range Dependence,* P. Doukhan et al., Eds., Birkhuser 2003, 5-38

[UTS] Wireless LANs Traffic Traces, Faulty of Technology, University of Technology, Sydney, http://www4.comp.polyu.edu.hk/~cswklin/research/traces/

[Wang1999] J. Wang, A Survey of Web Caching Schemes for the Internet, Computer Communication Review, *ACM SIGCOMM,* 29(5), 1999, 36-46

[Willinger1994] W. Willinger, D. Wilson, W. Leland , M. Taqqu, On the self-similar nature of Ethernet traffic, *IEEE/ACM Transactions on Networking,* vol. 2, 1-15, 1994

[Wong2001b] Allan K.Y. Wong and Joseph H.C. Wong, A Convergence Algorithm for Enhancing the Performance of Distributed Applications Running on Sizeable Networks, *The International Journal of Computer Systems, Science and Engineering,* 16(4), 2001, 229-236

[Wu2004] Richard S.L. Wu, Allan K.Y. Wong and Tharam S. Dillon, RDCT: A Novel Reconfigurable Dynamic Cache Size Tuner to Shorten Information Retrieval Time over the Internet, *International Journal of Computer Systems, Science and Engineering,* 19(6), 2004, -372

[Wu2005] Richard S.L. Wu, Wilfred W.K. Lin, Allan K.Y. Wong,and Tharam S. Dillon, An Experimentally Based Real-Time Traffic Pattern Detector for the Internet, the GESTS (Global Engineering, Science, and Technology Society) *International Transactions on Computer Science and Engineering,* 9(1), June 2005, 79-94

[Wu2005c] Richard S.L. Wu, Tharam T. Dillon and Allan K.Y. Wong, RTPD/MACSC: A Novel Approach for Effective Pervasive Information Retrieval, Proc. of the 4th International Conference on Mobile Business (MBusiness2005), Sydney, Australia, July 2005, 514 - 520

[Yu1999] Philip S. Yu and Edward A. MacNair, Performance Study of a Collaborative Method for Hierarchical Caching in Proxy Servers, IBM Watson Research Center, Research Report, http://www7.scu.edu.au/programme/fullpapers/1829/com1829.htm

BIBLIOGRAPHY

[Abrams1996] Abrams, M., Standridge, C. R., Abdulla, G., Fox, E. A. and Williams, S. (1996). Removal Policies in Network Caches for WWW Documents, *ACM SIGCOMM Computer Communication Review*, 26(4).

[Aguilar2001] J. Aguilar and E.L. Leiss, A Web Proxy Cache Coherency and Replacement Approach, Proc. of the 1st Asia-Pacific Conference on Web Intelligence: Research and Development, 2001, 78 – 84.

[Alex2001] Alex Ma, Skitter, http://wwwdev.caida.org/tools/measurement/skitter/index.xml, 2001

[Amp1] Active Measurements, http://watt.nlanr.net/active//

[Amp1999] Monitoring for the NLANR Active Measurement Program, http://www-iepm.slac.stanford.edu/monitoring/amp/, June 1999 [Mah2001] Bruce A. Mah, http://www.mirrors.wiretapped.net/security/network-mapping/pchar

[Anjum1999] F.M. Anjum, L. Tassiulas, Balanced-RED: An Algorithm to Achieve Fairness in the Internet, *Infocom 1999,* March 1999

[Arlitt1999] M. Arlitt, L. Cherkasova, J. Dilley, R. Friedrich and T. Jin, Evaluating Content Management Techniques for Web Proxy Caches, *Proc. of the 2nd Workshop on Internet Service Performance,* 1999

[Avizienis2004] A. Avizienis, J. Laprie, B. Randell and C. Landwehr, Basic Concepts and Taxonomy of Dependable and Secure Computing, *IEEE Transactions on Dependable and Secure Computing,* 1(1), 2004, 11-33

[Barford1999] A. Barford, A. Bestavros, A. Bradley and M.E. Crovella, Changes in the Web Client Access Patterns: Characteristics and Caching Implications, World Wide Web (Special Issue on Characterization and Performance Evaluation), 1999

[Belloum1998] A.Belloum and L.O. Hertzberger, Dealing with One-Timer-Documents in Web caching, *Proc. of the 24th Conference on EUROMICRO,* 1998

[Bennet1997] J.C. Bennet and H. Zhang, Hierarchical Packet Fair Queuing Algorithms, *IEEE/ACM Transactions on Networking,* 5(5), October 1997

[Bharat] Bharat and A. Broder, Measuring the Web, http://www.research.digital.com/SRCwhatsnew/sem.html

[Bjarat1998] K. Bjarat and A. Broder, Estimating the Relative Size and Overlap of Public Web Search Engines, Proc. of the 7th International World Wide Web Conference (WWW7), 1998

[Braden1998] Braden et.al, Recommendations on Queue Management and Congestion Avoidance in the Internet, *RFC 2309,* April 1998

[Braden1998] Braden et.al., Recommendations on Queue Management and Congestion Avoidance in the Internet, *RFC 2309,* April 1998

[Brakmo1994] L. Brakmo, S. O'Malley and L. Peterson, TCP Vegas: New Techniques for Congestion Detection and Avoidance, *Proc. of the ACM SIGCOMM, 1994*

[Case1996] J. Case, K. McCloghrie, M. Rose and S. Waldbusser, Protocol Operations for Version 2 of the Simple Network Management Protocol (SNMPv2), RFC1905, January 1996

[CERT] CERT Coordination Center, Software Engineering Institute, Carnegie Mellon University, http://www.cert.org/advisories/CA-1996-21.html

[Chankhunthod1996] A. Chankhunthod, P.B. Danzig, C. Neerdaels, M.F. Schwartz and K.J. Worrell, A hierarchical Internet Object Cache, *Proc. of USENIX Annual Technical Conference,* 1996, 153-64

[Chao2002] H. J. Chao, Quality of Service Control in High-speed Networks, Wiley, 2002

[Chatranon2004] G. Chatranon, M.A. Labrador and S. Banerjee, A Survey of TCP-friendly Router-Based AQM Schemes, *Computer Communications,* v. 27, 2004

[Chisman1992] Chisman, J.A. (1992) *Introduction to Simulation and Modeling Using GPSS/PC.* New Jersey, Prentice Hall

[Cisco] Strategies to Protect against Distributed Denial of Service (DDoS) Attacks, http://www.cisco.com/warp/public/707/newsflash.html

[Cottrel1999] L. Cottrel, M. Zekauskas, H. Uijterwaal and T. McGregor, Comparison of Some Internet Active End-to-End Performance Measurement Projects, http://www.slac.stanford.edu/comp/net/wan-mon/iepm-cf.html, 1999

[Cottrel2001] L. Cottrel, Passive vs. Active Monitoring, http://www.slac.stanford.edu/comp/net/wan-mon/ passive-vs-active.html, March 2001

[Demers1995] A. Demers, S. Keshav and S. Shenkar, Analysis and Simulation of a Fair Queuing Algorithm, *ACM Computer Communication Review,* 25(1), January 1995

[Dingle1996] A. Dingle and T. Partl, Web Cache Coherence, *Proc. of the 5th Word Wide Web Conference*, Paris, 1996

[Duska1997] B.M. Duska, D. Marwood and M.J. Feeley, The Measured Access Characteristics of World-Wide-Web Client Proxy Caches, *Proc. of the USENIX Symposium on Internet Technology and Systems,* 1997

[Fan2000] L. Fan, P. Cao, J.M. Almeida and A.Z. Broder, Summary cache: a scalable wide-area web cache sharing protocol. *IEEE/ACM Transactions on Networking,* 2000, 8(3), 281-293

[Floyd1993] S. Floyd and V. Jacobson, Random Early Detection Gateways for Congestion Avoidance, *IEEE/ACM Transactions on Networking,* 1(4), August 1993, 397-413

[Floyd1995] S. Floyd and V. Jacobson, Link-Sharing and Resource Management Models for Packet Network, *IEEE/ACM Transactions on Networking,* 3(4), August 1995

[Floyd1999] S. Floyd and K. Fall, Promoting the Use of End-to-End Congestion Control in the Internet, *IEEE/ACM Transactions Networking* 7(4), 1999

[Garlan2002] D. Garlan, D. P. Siewiorek, A. Smailagic and P. Steenkiste, Project Aura: Toward Distraction-free Pervasive Computing, *IEEE Pervasive Computing,* 1(2), April 2002, 22 – 31

[Gartner1999] F. Gartner, Fundamentals of Fault-tolerant Distributed Computing in Asynchronous Environments, *ACM computing surveys,* 31(1), March 1999, 1-26

[Gnutella] The Gnutella Website: http://gnutella.wego.com

[Goldsmith2005] Andrea Goldsmith, *Wireless Communications,* Cambridge University Press, 2005

[Han1998] S. Han and K.G. Shin, A Primary-Backup Channel Approach to Dependability Real-Time Communication in Multihop Networks, *IEEE Transactions on Computers,* 47(1), January 1998

[Hightower2001] J. Hightower and G. Borriello, Location-Aware Systems for Ubiquitous Computing, *IEEE Computer,* 34(8), August 2001, 57-66

[Hwang1985] K. Hwang and F.A. Briggs, *Computer Architecture and Parallel Processing,* McGraw Hill, 1985

[Ip2001]May T.W. Ip, Wilfred W.K. Lin, Allan K.Y. Wong, Tharam S. Dillon and Dian Hui Wang, An Adaptive Buffer Management Algorithm for Enhancing Dependability and Performance in Mobile-Object-Based Real-time Computing, *Proc. of the IEEE ISORC'2001,* Magdenburg, Germany, May 2001, 138-144

[Ip2002] Allan K.Y. Wong, May T.W. Ip and Tharam S. Dillon, M^3RT: An Internet End-to-End Performance Measurement Approach for Real-Time Applications with Mobile Agents, *Proc. of the ISPAN''002,* 2002, 119-124

[Jacobson1988] V. Jacobson, Congestion Avoidance and Control, *Proc. of the ACM SIGCOMM'88 Conference, 1988*

[Jacobson1990] V. Jaconson, Berkeley TCP Evolution from 4.3-Tahoe to 4.3-Reno, *Proc. of the 18th Internet Engineering Task Force, 1990*

[Jain1999] R. Jain, A. Durresi and G. Babic, Throughput Fairness Index: *An Explanation, ATM Forun/99-0045*

[Jalote1994] P. Jalote, Fault Tolerance in Distributed Systems, Prentice-Hall, Inc. *Upper Saddle River, NJ, USA,* 1994

[Jensen1985] E. D. Jensen, C. D. Locke, and H. Tokuda, A Time-Driven Scheduling Model for Real-Time Operating Systems, *Proc. of IEEE real-Time Systems Symposium,* 1985

[Jin2000] S. Jin and A. Bestavros, Temporal Locality in Web Request Streams: Sources, Characteristics, and Caching Implications, *Proc. of the International Conference on Measurement and Modeling of Computer Systems*, 2000

[Jin2000a] S. Jin and A. Bestavros, Popularity-Aware Greedy Dual-Size Web Proxy Caching Algorithms, *Proc. of the Int'l Conf. on Distributed Computing Systems,* 2000

[Jin2000b] S. Jin, and A. Bestavros, Temporal Locality in Web Request Streams: Sources, Characteristics, and Caching Implications, *Proc. of the International Conference on Measurement and Modeling of Computer Systems,* 2000

[Jonckheere2002] E. Jonckheere, K. Shah and S. Bohacek, Dynamic Modeling of Internet Traffic for Intrusion Detection, *Proceedings of the 2002 American Control Conference,* Volume 3, 8-10 May 2002, 2436 - 2442

[Karp1975] R.M. Karp, *On the Computational Complexity of Combinatorial Problems, Networks,* 5(1), January 1975

[Karray2002] F. Karray, W. Gueaieb and S. Al-Sharhan, The Hierarchical Expert Tuning of PID Controllers Using Tools of Soft Computing, *IEEE Trans. on Systems, Man, and Cybernetics,* Part B, 32(1), February 2002, 77-90

[Kelly1999] T.P. Kelly, S. Jamin and J.K. MacKie-Mason, Variable QoS from Shared Web Caches: User Centered Design and Value-Sensitive Replacement, *Proc. of the MIT Workshop on Internet Service Quality Economics,* 1999

[Kim1998] W.J. Kim and B.G. Lee, FRED-fair random early detection algorithm for TCP over ATM networks, *Electronics Letters,* 34(2), January 1998, pp.152-154

[Kim2001] J. Kim and K.G. Shin, Performance Evaluation of Dependable Real-Time Communication with Elastic QoS, *Proc. of the IEEE DSN2001 Conference,* 2001

[Knadlur1994] D.D. Kandlur, K.G. Shin and D. Ferrari, Real-Time Communication in Multi-hop Networks, *IEEE Transactions on Parallel and Distributed Systems,* 5(10), October 1994

[Knight1999] G. Knight and R. Hazemi, Mobile Agents-Based Management in the INSERT Project, *Journal of Networks and System Management, Special Issue on Mobile Agent-Based Network and Service Management,* 7(3) September 1999

[Krishna2003] G.P. Krishna, M.J. Pradeep and C. Siva Ram Murthy, A Segmented Backup Scheme for Dependable Real-Time Communication in Multihop Networks, *IEEE/ACM Transactions on Networks,* 11(1), February 2003

[Krishnamurthy2002] R. Krishnamurthy, S. Yalamanchili, K. Schwan, R. West and M. Rosu, Architecture and Hardware for Scheduling Gigabit Packet Streams, *Proc. of the 10th IEEE Conference on High-Performance Interconnects,* August 2002

[Kroeger1997] T.M. Kroeger, D. Long D and C. Jeffrey, Exploring the Bounds of Web Latency Reduction from Caching and Prefetching, *Proc. of the USENIX Symposium on Internet Technology and System,* 1997

[Laamanen1999] R.H Laamanen, T. Alanko and K. Raatikainen, Dependability Issues in Mobile Distributed System, *Proc. of the Pacific Rim International Symposium on Dependable Computing,* 1999, 7-14

[Lakshman1996] T. Lakshman, A. Neidhardt, and T. Ott, The Drop from Front Strategy in TCP over ATM and its Interworking with other Control Features, *Proc. INFOCOM'96,* 1242-1250

[Laprie1995] J. Laprie, Dependable Computing: Concepts, Limits, Challenges, Proc. of the IEEE 25th International Symposium on Fault-Tolerant Computing, 1995

[Lewandowski1998] S.M. Lewandowski, Frameworks for Component-based Client/Server Computing, *ACM Computing Surveys*, 30(1), 1998, 3-27

[Lewis1996] Ted Lewis. The next 10000^2 Years: Part I, *Computer,* vol. 29 no.4, April 1996, 64–70

[Li2002] C.L. Li, Z.D. Lu and L.Y. Li, Design and Implementation of a Distributed Computing Environment Model for Object-oriented Networks Programming, *Computer Communications,* 25(5), March 2002

[Lin2004] Wilfred W. K. Lin, Richard S.L. Wu Allan K. Y. Wong, and Tharam S. Dillon, A Novel Real-Time Traffic Pattern Detector for Internet Applications, *Proc. of the Australasian Telecommunication Networks and Applications Conference, Sydney, Australia (ATNAC'04),* Dec 2004, 224-227

[Lin2004] Wilfred W. K. Lin, Richard S.L. Wu, Tharam S. Dillon and Allan K. Y. Wong, A Novel Real-Time Traffic Pattern Detector for Internet Applications, *Proceedings of the 2004 Australian Telecommunication Networks and Applications Conference(ATNAC),* Sydney, Australia, December 2004, pp. 224-227

[Lin2005] Wilfred W.K. Lin, Allan K.Y. Wong and Tharam S. Dillon, Application of Soft Computing Techniques to Adaptive User Buffer Overflow Control on the Internet, *IEEE Transactions on Systems, Man and Cybernetics,* Part C, 36(3), May 2006, 397 -410

[Locke1986] C.D. Locke, Best-Effort Decision Making for real-Time Scheduling, Ph.D. Thesis, Department of Computing, Department of Computer Science, Carnegie Mellon University, *CMUCS-86-134,* 1986

[LWD2005] Wilfred W.K. Lin, Allan K.Y. Wong and Tharam S. Dillon, Application of Soft Computing Techniques to Adaptive User Buffer Overflow Control on the Internet, *IEEE Transactions on Systems, Man and Cybernetics, Part C,* 2005

[Mahanti2000] A. Mahanti, C. Williamson, and D. Eager, Traffic Analysis of a Web Proxy Caching Hierarchy, *IEEE Network,* 14(3), 2000

[Malla2003] A. Malla, M El-Kadi, S. Olariu and P. Todorova, A Fair Resource Allocation Protocol for Multimedia Wireless Networks, *IEEE Transactions on Parallel and Distributed Systems,* 14(1), 2003, 63 – 71.

[Mathis] M. Mathis, J. Mahdavi, S. Floyd and A. Romanov, *TCP Selective Acknowledgement Options, RFC 2018*

[Matt2000] Warren Matthews and Les Cottrell, The PingER Project: Active Internet Performance Monitoring for the HENP Community, *IEEE Communications Magazine,* May 2000, 2-8

[Matt2001] Warren Matthews, Les Cottrell and Davide Salomoni, Passive and Active Monitoring on a High Performance Research Network, Presented at Passive and Active Monitoring (PAM) 2001, Amsterdam, The Netherlands, April 2001

[Medina2000] A Medina, I. Matta and J. Byers, On the Origin of Power Laws in Internet Topologies, *ACM SIGCOMM Computer Communication Review,* 30(2), 2000, 18-28

[Millis1995] D.L. Mills, Improved Algorithms for Synchronizing Computer Network Clocks, *IEEE/ACM Transactions on Networking,* 3(3), June 1995, 245-254

[Molnár1999] S. Molnár, T.D. Dang and A. Vidács, Heavy-Tailedness, Long-Range Dependence and Self-Similarity in Data Traffic, Proceedings of 7th International Conference on Telecommunication Systems, Modelling and Analysis, March 1999, Nashville, USA, 18-21

[Moore] Moore's Law, http://www.intel.com/technology/silicon/mooreslaw/

[Oshima1998] M. Oshima, G. Karjoth and K. Ono, Aglets Specification 1.1 Draft, IBM Corp., http://www.trl.ibm.com/aglets/spec11.htm, 1998

[Ott1999] T. J. Ott, T. V. Lakshman, and L. H. Wong, SRED: Stabilized RED, Proceedings *IEEE INFOCOM '99,* New York, March 1999

[OXYGEN] MIT OXYGEN, http://www.oxygen.lcs.mit.edu/

[p4] http://www-fp.mcs.anl.gov/~lusk/p4/

[Padhye1998] J. Padhye, V. Firoiu, D. Towsley and J. Kurose, Modeling TCP throughput: A Simple and Its Empirical Validation, *Proc. of the ACM SIGCOMM'98, 1998*

[Pan1999] R. Pan, B. Prabhakar and K. Psounis, CHOKe, A Stateless Active Queue Management Scheme for Approximating Fair Bandwidth Allocation. *Proc of INFOCOM,* March 2000

[Patterson2003] C.A. Patterson, R.R. Muntz and C.M. Pancake, Challenges in Location-aware Computing, *IEEE Pervasive Computing,* 2(2), April-June 2003, 80 – 89

[Patterson2003] C.A. Patterson, R.R. Muntz, R. R. and C.M. Pancake, Challenges in Location-Aware Computing, *IEEE Pervasive Computing,* 2(2), 2003, 80 – 89

[Paxson1995] V. Paxson and S. Floyd, Wide-Area Traffic: The Failure of Poisson Modeling. *IEEE/ACM Transactions on Networking,* 3(3), June 1995, 226-244

[Paxson1997] V. Paxson, End-to-End Internet Packet Dynamics, ACM SIGCOMM, *Computer Communication Review,* 27(4), October 1997

[Podlipnig2003] S. Podlipnig and L. Böszörményi, A Survey of Web Cache Replacement Strategies, *ACM Computing Surveys,* 35(4), December 2003, 374 – 398

[PVM] Parallel Virtual Machine (PVM), http://www.csm.ornl.gov/pvm/pvm_home.html

[Ramanathan1992] P. Ramanathan, Delivery of Time-Critical Messages Using a Multiple Copy Approach, *ACM Transactions on Computer Systems,* 10(2), 1992

[RFC1712] C. Farrell, DNS Encoding of Geographical Location, RFC 1712, November 1994

[RFC1853] W. Simpson, IP in IP Tunneling, *RFC1853,* 1995

[RFC768] J. Postel, *User Datagram Protocol, RFC 768,* August 1980

[RFC793] RFC 793 - Transmission Control Protocol, *IETF,* September 1981

[RFC896] J. Nagle, Congestion Control in IP/TCP Internetworks, RFC896, January 1984

[Ryu1996] B.K. Ryu and S.B. Lowen, Point process approaches to the modeling and analysis of self-similar traffic .I. Model construction, Proc. of the 15th Annual Joint Conference of the IEEE Computer Societies - *Networking the Next Generation.* Vol. 3, March 1996, 1468 - 1475

[Saty2001] M. Satyanarayanan, Pervasive Computing: Vision and Challenges, *IEEE Personal Communications,* August 2001, 10-17

[Shin2000] K.G. Shin, C.C. Cjou and S.K. Kweon, Distributed Route Selection for Establishing Real-Time Channels, *IEEE Transactions on Parallel and Distributed Systems,* 11(3), March 2000

[Stankovic1998] John A. Stankovic, Marco Spuri, and Krithi Ramamritham, Deadline Scheduling for Real-Time Systems, Kluwer Academic Publishers, 1998

[Stevens2001] W. Stevens, TCP Slow Start, Congestion Avoidance, fast Transmit, and Fast Recovery, *IETF RFC 2001*, 2001

[Sunil1999] Sunil Kalidindi and Matthew J. Zekauskas, Surveyor: *An Infrastructure for Internet Performance Measurements, INET'99,* San Jose, June 1999

[Tanenbaum2003] A. S. Tanenbaum, Computer Networks, 4th Edition, Prentice Hall, 2003

[Taqqu2003] M.S. Taqqu, Fractional Brownian Motion and Long-Range Dependence, in *Theory and Applications of Long-Range Dependence,* P. Doukhan et al., Eds., Birkhuser 2003, 5-38

[Theotokis2004] A. Theotokis and D. Spinnellis, A Survey of Peer-to-Peer Content Distribution Technologies, *ACM Computing Surveys,* 36(4), 2004, 335 – 371

[Tseng2001] Y.C. Tseng, C.C. Tan, Termination Detection Protocols for Mobile Distributed Systems, *IEEE Transactions on Parallel and Distributed Systems,* 12(6), June 2001, 558-566

[Valloppillil1998] V. Valloppillil and K. Ross, Cache array routing protocol v1.0, Internet Draft, http://icp.ircache.net/carp.txt, 1998

[VTune] Intel's VTune Performance Analyzer, http://ww.intel.com/ support/ performancetools/vtune/v5

[Wang1999] Jia Wang, A Survey of Web Caching Schemes for the Internet, *ACM SIGCOMM Computer Communication Review,* 29(5), October 1999, 36 - 46

[Wang2001] Y. Wang and W. Chen, Supporting IP Multicast for Mobile Hosts, *Mobile Networks and Applications,* v.6, Jan/Feb 2001, 57-66

[Wang2004] J. Wang and B. Ravindran, Time-Utility Function-Driven Switched Ethernet: Packet Scheduling Algorithm, Implementation and Feasibility Analysis, *IEEE Transactions on Parallel and Distributed Systems,* 15(2), February, 2004

[Weiser1991] M. Weiser, The Computer for the Twenty-First Century, Scientific American, 1991, 94-104

[Willinger2003] W. Willinger, V. Paxson, R.H. Hiedi and M.S. Taqqu, Long-Range Dependence and Data Network Traffic, in *Theory and Applications of Long-Range Dependence,* P. Doukhan et al., Eds., Birkhuser 2003, 373-408

[WMW2003] Allan K. Y. Wong, May T. W. Ip, Richard S. L. Wu, A Novel Dynamic Cache Size Adjustment Approach for Better Data Retrieval Performance over the Internet, *Journal of Computer Communication,* September 2003, 26(14), 1709-1720

[Wong1999] Allan K.Y. Wong and Tharam S. Dillon, A Fault-Tolerant Data Communication Setup to Improve Reliability and Performance for Internet-Based Distributed Applications, the Proceedings of the 1999 Pacific Rim International Symposium on Dependable Computing (PRDC'99), December 1999, Hong Kong (SAR), P.R. China

[Wong1999b] Allan K.Y. Wong and Joseph H.C. Wong, A Convergence Algorithm to Help Enhance the Performance of Distributed Systems on Large Networks, *Proc. of the 1999 International Symposium on Parallel Architectures, Algorithms, and Networks* (I-Span'99), Fremantle Australia, June 1999, 302-307

[Wong2000] Allan K.Y. Wong and Tharam S. Dillon, A Fault Tolerant Model to Attain Reliability and High Performance for Distributed Computing over the Internet, *Journal of Computer Communications,* vol. 23, 2000

[Wong2001A] A.K.Y. Wong and J.H.C. Wong, A Convergence Algorithm for Enhancing the Performance of Distributed Applications Running on Sizeable Networks, *International Journal of Computer Systems Science and Engineering,* 16(4), July 2001, 229-236

[Wong2001b] Allan K.Y. Wong and Joseph H.C. Wong, A Convergence Algorithm for Enhancing the Performance of Distributed Applications Running on Sizeable Networks, Computer Systems, Science and Engineering, 16(4), 2001, 229-236

[Wong2001B] Allan K.Y. Wong, Tharam S. Dillon, Wilfred K.W. Lin and May T.W. Ip, M^2RT: A Tool Developed for Predicting the Mean Message Response Time for Internet Channels, *Computer Networks.* 36(2001), 557-577

[Wong2002a] Allan K.Y. Wong, May T.W. Ip and Tharam S. Dillon, M^3RT: An Internet End-to-End Performance Measurement Approach for Real-Time Applications with Mobile Agents, *Proc. of the ISPAN conference,* 2002 119 – 124.

[Wong2003] Allan K. Y. Wong, May T. W. Ip, Richard S. L. Wu: A novel dynamic cache size adjustment approach for better data retrieval performance over the internet. *Computer Communications.* 26(14), 2003, 1709-1720

[Wu2003] C.H. Wu, D.C. Su, J. chang, C.C. Wei, K.J. Lin and J.M. Ho, The Design and Implementation of Intelligent Transportation Web Services, *IEEE International Conference on E-Commerce (CEC 2003),* 24-27 June 2003, 49-52

[Wu2003] Richard S.L. Wu, May T.W. Ip and Allan K.Y. Wong, LDC-CM: A Novel Model for Dynamic Cache Size Adjustment, *Proc. of the International Conference on Internet Computing,* 2, 753 – 758.

[Wu2004] Richard S.L. Wu, Allan K.Y. Wong and Tharam S. Dillon, RDCT: A Novel Reconfigurable Dynamic Cache Size Tuner to Shorten Information Retrieval Time over the Internet, *International Journal of Computer Systems, Science and Engineering,* 19(6), 2004, pp. 363-372

[Zhang1993] L. Zhang, S. Deering, D. Estrin, S. Shenker and D. Zappala, RSVP: A New Resource Reservation protocol, *IEEE Network, vol. 7,* September 1993

[Zhu2001] K. Zhu, Y. Zhuang and Y. Viniotis, Achieving End-to-End Delay Bounds by EDF Scheduling without Traffic Shaping, *Proc. of IEEE Infocom2001,* April 2001

[Zipf] Zipf Curves and Website Popularity, http://www.useit.com/alertbox/zipf.html

APPENDIX A: DETAILS OF M^2RT/ M^3RT AS INTERNET END-TO-END MEASUREMENT TOOLS

The M^2RT and M^3RT are both Java implementations of the same Convergence Algorithm (CA) [Wong01B, Ip2002], except that the M^2RT is a macro tool and the M^3RT is a micro one. For macro applications the M^2RT has to be installed at the two nodes that represent the ends of a communication channel. The M^3RT operates at the micro level because it exists as a logical object that can be invoked for service anywhere and anytime by message passing. This appendix aims at providing more details for interested readers in the light of CA verification before implementation. The CA essence is represented by the equations (A1.1, A1.2 and A1.3). The mathematical average of *i* RTT (roundtrip time) samples can be computed theoretically by equation (A1.1). In reality this equation has a serious hidden problem when working with a large volume of data samples because for samples with large values it would lead to computation overflow. To resolve this problem the CA algorithm (A1.2), which is based on the *Central Limit Theorem*, was proposed. The parameter M_0 is the first sample after CA was invoked for the first time.

$$M_i = \frac{\sum_{j=1}^{j=i} m_j}{i} \quad \dots\dots\dots \quad (A1.1)$$

$$M_i = \frac{M_{i-1} + \sum_{j=1}^{j=F-1} m_i^j}{F} \quad \dots\dots\dots (A1.2); i \geq 1$$

$$M_0 = m_{i=1}^{j=1} \quad \dots\dots\dots (A1.3)$$

Equation (A1.2) has resolved the computation overflow problem of equation (A1.1) with the following measures: a) replacing *i* in the denominator of (A1.1) by F, known as the *flush limit*, and (b) making the M_i convergence iterative, where *i* ($i \geq 1$) denotes the current cycle in the convergence computation. The M_{i-1} is the predicted mean value in last cycle. It is included in the next cycle for *integral* effect. The parameter *j* marks the jth sample mean in the ith current convergence cycle. These changes, however, cannot get rid of the serious oscillations in the convergence process, and since these oscillations would lead to system instability and erroneous performance, they have to be damped. This damping process involves the *proportional* (P) control and the resultant CA model (equation (A1.4)).

$$M_i = \frac{PM_{i-1} + \sum_{j=1}^{j=f} m_i^j}{P + f} \quad ....\;.....(A1.4)$$

For those who are interested in verifying the CA against all kinds of possible traffic IAT (inter-arrival time) waveforms, which can be LRD (short-range dependence), LRD (long-range dependence), multifractal or irregular [Willinger2003, Molnár1999, Tsybakov1998] the time Petri net model in figure A1.1 is included. This model was tested successfully many times on the ALPHA/Sim time Petri net platform. This platform, which is up to the Department of Defense (DoD) standard, is a package developed by ALPHATECH, Inc. (Burlington MA, USA; email:alpha.sim@alphatech.com).

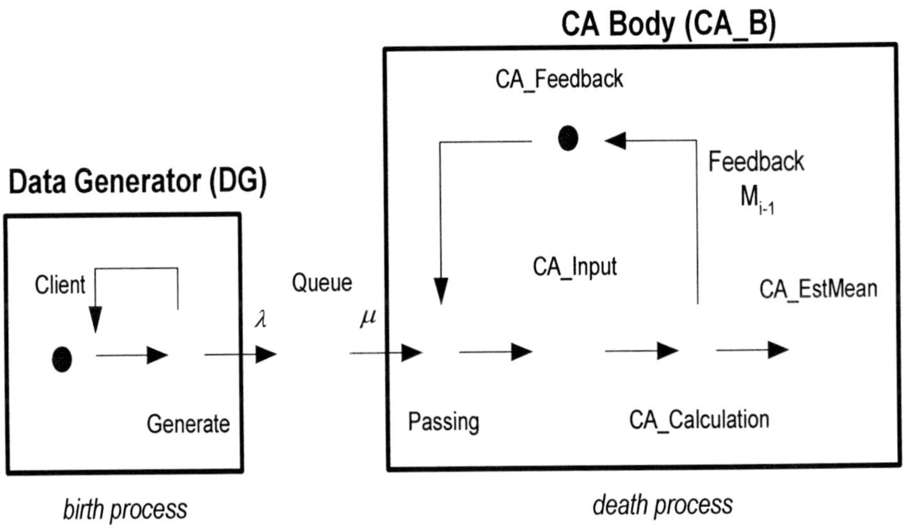

Figure A.1.1 The Time Petri-Net (Alpha/Sim) model for CA simulation.

Figure A1.1 has three basic parts: *Data Generator (DG)*, *Queue*, and the *M^3RT Body* (*CA_B*). To help readers understand the Alpha/Sim operations, relevant symbols and timing rules are shown in figure A1.2 and figure A1.3. In the DG *birth process*, the *Client place* is initialized with one token for starting and perpetuating a simulation. When the *Generate transition* is fired two tokens are generated and one of these (representing a request) goes to *Queue* (the service queue) and the other goes back to *Client* to start another simulation cycle. The transition *Generate* is fired by the chosen waveform/distribution (usually with a known mean for verification and comparison purposes). In the actual simulations different types of waveforms should be used for exhaustive testing. The results from different Gamma distributions in table 1 are presented here for demonstration purposes. The Gamma function of the desired shape is created by setting the parameters α and β. By varying the shape, the birth rate λ can be controlled at will in the different tests. The mean queue length of *Queue* is estimated by the by CA/M^3RT/ M^2RT mechanism, declared as the *CA_B* part in the time Petri net. If the CA (*CA_B*) prediction works correctly, the predicted mean should converge to that of the input Gamma function chosen to drive λ.

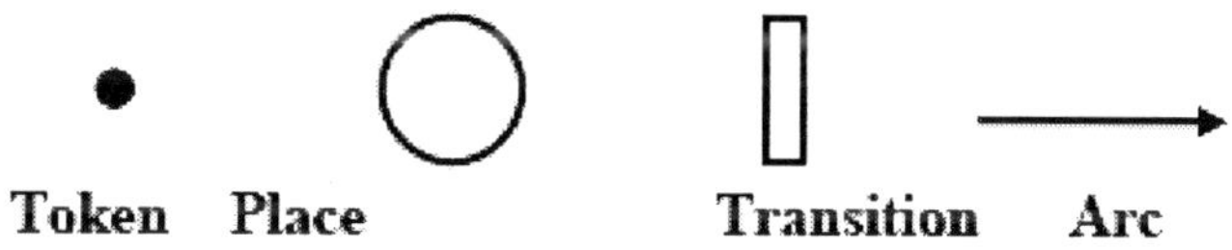

Figure A1.2. Four basic Petri net elements.

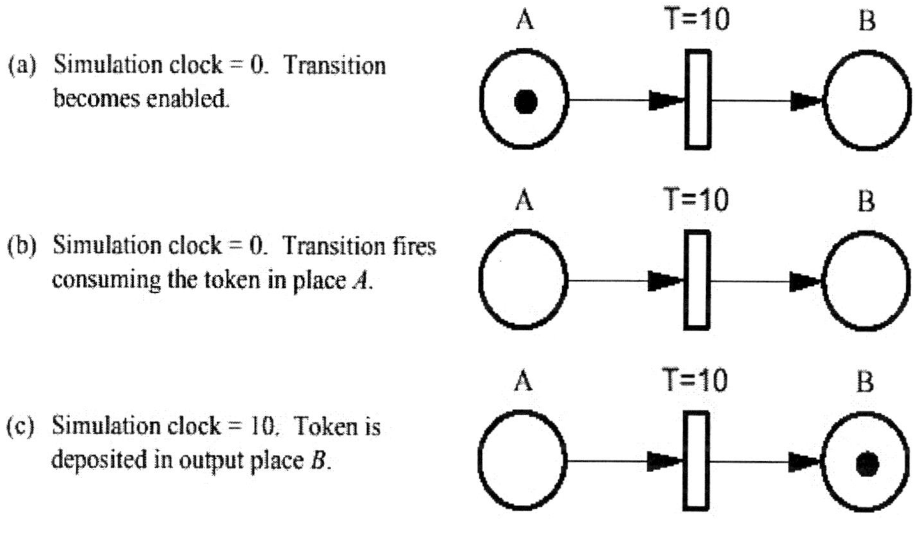

Figure A1.3. Firing/timing rules (modified from the ALPHA/Sim manual).

The requests in the *Queue* are consumed by the *CA_B* one by one, where the *CA_Feedback* place was initialized with one token and M_{i-1} to zero. The *Passing transition* fires to represent the *death/service rate* μ by CA, and the last M_{i-1} drives the *CA_Feedback* place. The *CA_Calculation transition*, which embeds equation (A1.4), fires when there is a token in *CA_Input*. In the simulations the parameters in equation (A1.4) were set to the following optimal values as suggested by [Wong01B]: a) P = 10 (P for *proportional* control), and F = 14 (F for the *flush limit*). The M_i computed at the ith iteration in the Ca convergence process is stored in *CA_EstMean*, which also serves as the M_{i-1} input for the next $((i+1)^{th})$ convergence cycle. Since the *transitions* in time Petri net fire in an indiscriminate manner, the CA behavior in a simulation depends on the instantaneous firing sequence by the *transitions*. For example, the consuming rate μ by the *CA_B* is decided by the two *transitions* within, namely, *Passing* and *CA_Calculation*. It is, however, imperative to ensure that overall system utilization $\delta = \frac{\lambda}{\mu}$ in the model always

Table A1. Different Gamma functions with defined mean values

α	β	Raw mean (mathematical)	Predicted mean
1	10	10	1
2	5	10	5
3	4	12	8

Many experiments of the time Petri net in figure A1.1 were conducted successfully in the Alpha/Sim environment. The results confirmed that the CA output at the steady state always converges to the mean of the chosen input waveform that drives λ. Table 1 lists the characteristics of the driving Gamma waveforms (shown in figure A1.4, A1.5 and A1.6) that produced the M_i distributions in A1.7, A1.8 and A1.9 correspondingly.

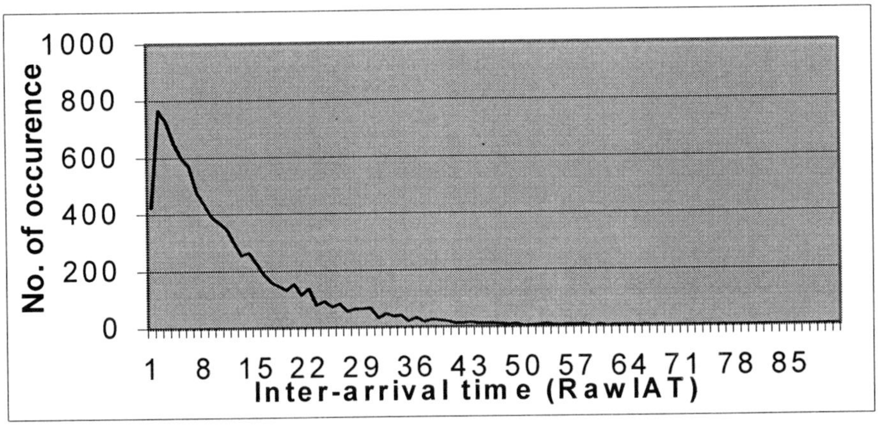

Figure A1.4. Gamma Distribution with α = 1 and β = 10.

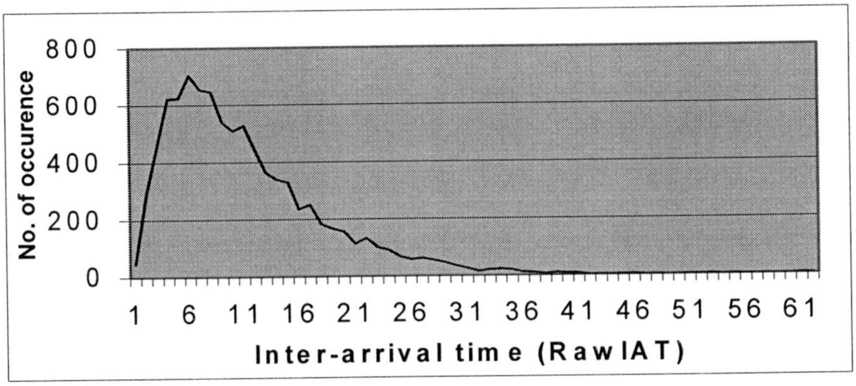

Figure A1.5. Gamma Distribution with α = 2 and β = 5.

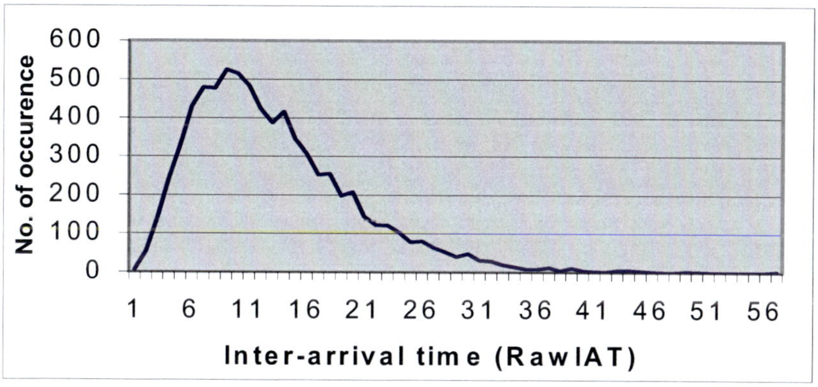

Figure A1.6. Gamma Distribution with $\alpha = 3$ and $\beta = 4$.

The *y-axis* (*Time*) on the graphs (figures A1.7 – A1.9) represents the raw RTT for different requests (*No. of Jobs*) marked on the *x-axis*. Although the fluctuations among the raw RTT are serious for the 1000 *RawIAT* samples scrutinized, the convergence to the given Gamma function mean was always quick and accurate. Other values plotted on figures A1.7 – A1.9 are for comparison purposes:

a) *RawIAT* is the simulated raw RTT by the Data Generator.
b) *CA_EstMean* is mean RTT for the 1000 simulated RTT samples, which converges exactly to the given mean of the chosen Gamma function in table 1.
c) *Raw Mean* is the mathematical average of raw RTT, namely, $[\sum_{i=1}^{1000} RTT_i] / 1000$.
d) *Typical Mean* is the *mode* of the distribution for the 1000 *RawIAT* samples.

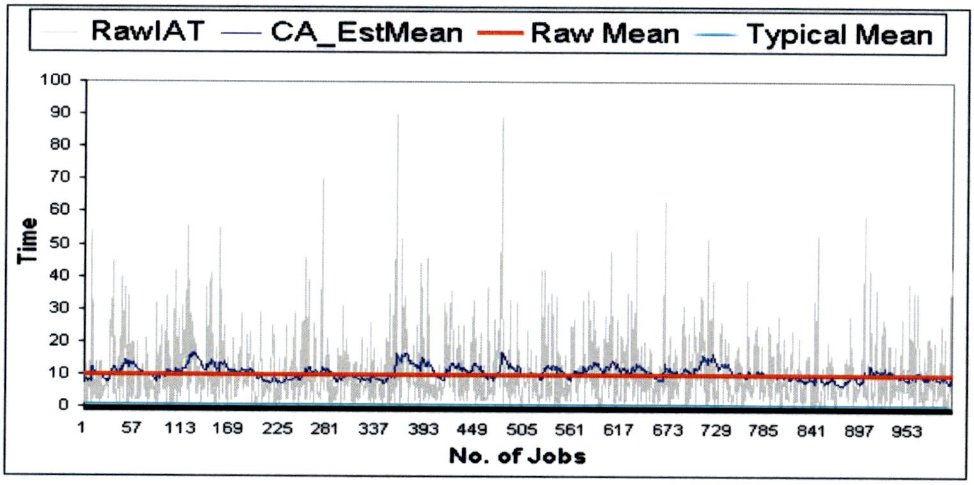

Figure A1.7. Result for Gamma Distribution with $\alpha = 1$ and $\beta = 10$.

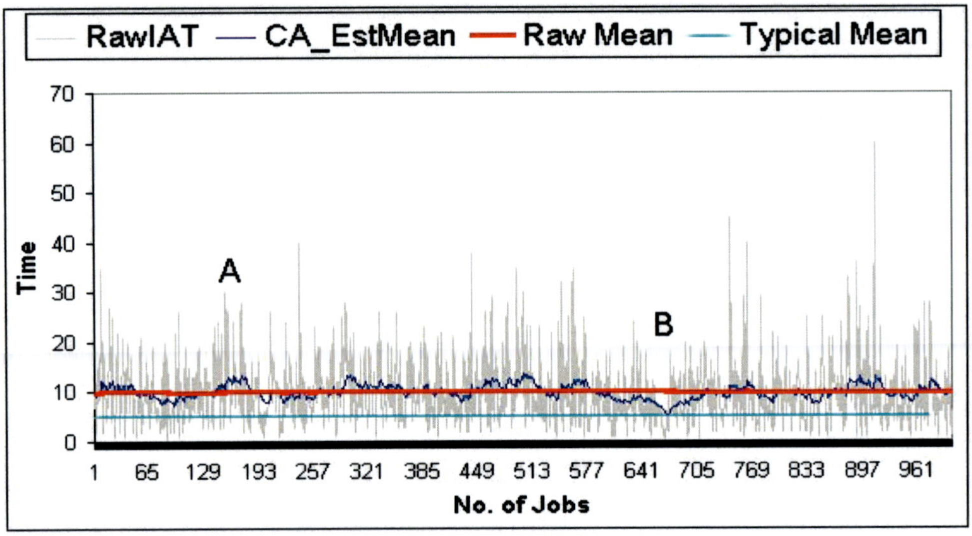

Figure A1.8. Gamma Distribution with α = 2 and β = 5.

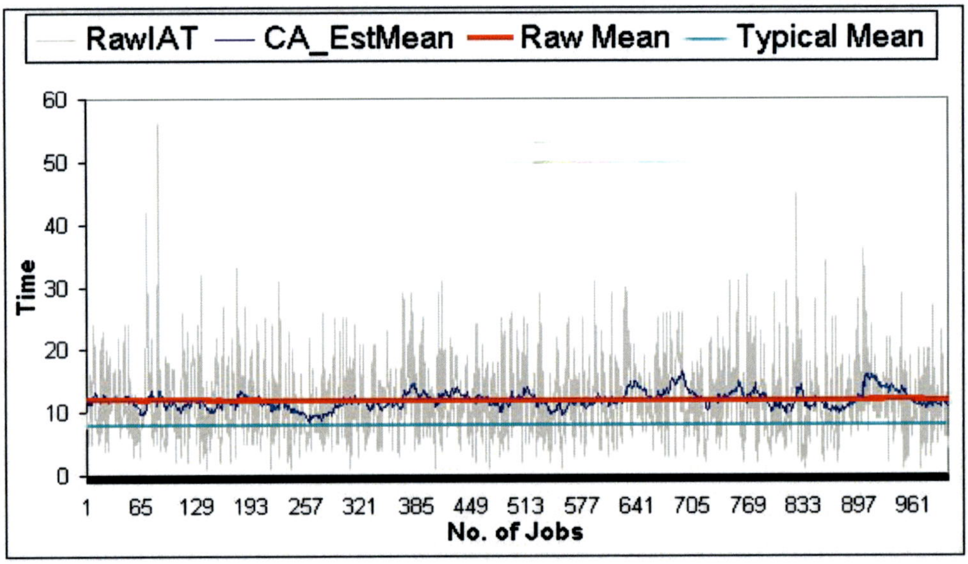

Figure A1.9. Gamma Distribution with α = 3 and β = 4.

The micro CA implementation, namely, M^3RT was deployed successfully in different applications. One example was using M^3RT to measure the difference in time delays between two well-known middleware products: the MPICH (version 1.1.2) for MPI, and the IONA's Orbix 2.3c MT (CORBA 2.0 specification). The setup for this experiment in the Aglets mobile agent environment [Mitsuru1998] is concisely illustrated in figure A1.10. The Aglets platform was especially designed for Internet applications and therefore experimental results obtained in this environment are scalable to the open Internet.

In the setup in figure A1.10, the *driver agent* makes requests, with random inter-arrival time (IAT) intervals, to ask the two local "*Interfaces*" to ping two separate remote server agents: one ping is through the "*CORBA-mediated*" channel and the other is through the "*MPI-mediated*" channel. The same ping, which is finally sent to the other side through the channels, is answered independently by the server agents or aglets (agile applets) running on the same Sun machine. The answers are returned separately through the original channels. The "*ping RTT*" results are received by the local *Interfaces*, which pass them to the two independent dedicated M^3RT APIs. The predicted mean values by the two APIs are then compared. The same experiment is repeated many times with different waveforms as the raw RTTs. The experimental results confirmed that the M^3RT always converged correctly. Figure A1.11 and figure A1.12 are two sets of experimental results for comparison, the MPI and CORBA sets. The M^3RT parameters for the two cases are P=10, and F=14. The comparison indicated that the mean RTT for the CORBA-mediated channel is longer. This concurred with the known fact the ORB (*Object Request Broker*) in CORBA is slow and is therefore inefficient for real-time applications [Lankes2001]. From the experimental results the MPI ping RTT was seemingly faster than the CORBA's by at least 300%.

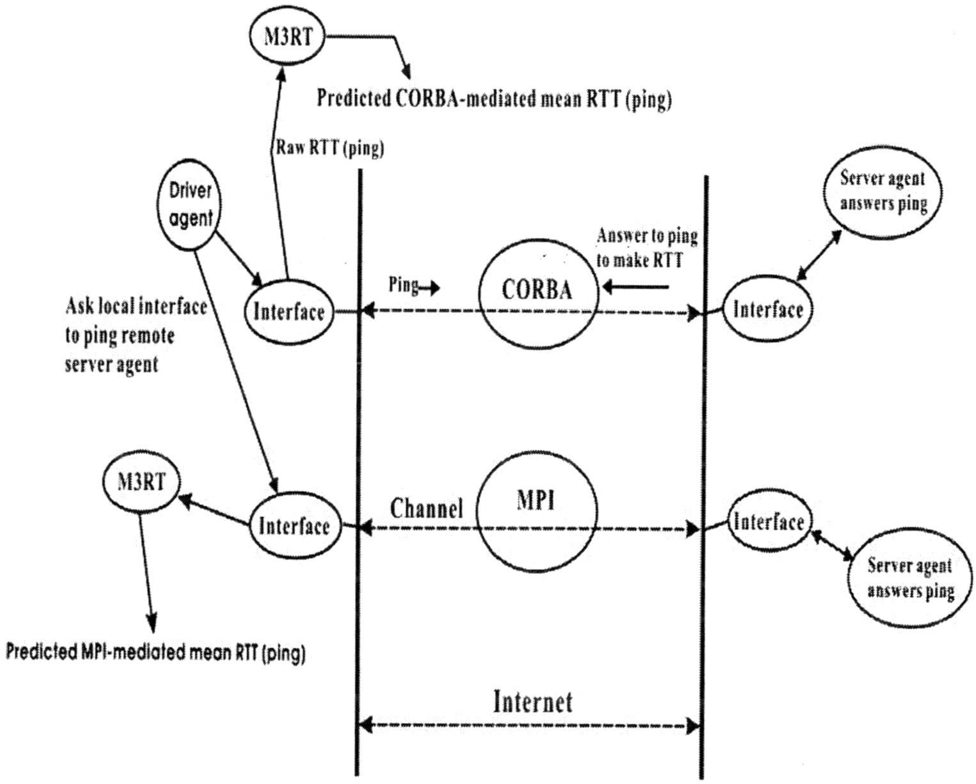

Figure A1.10. The mobile-agent setup for comparing the RTT of CORBA and MPI.

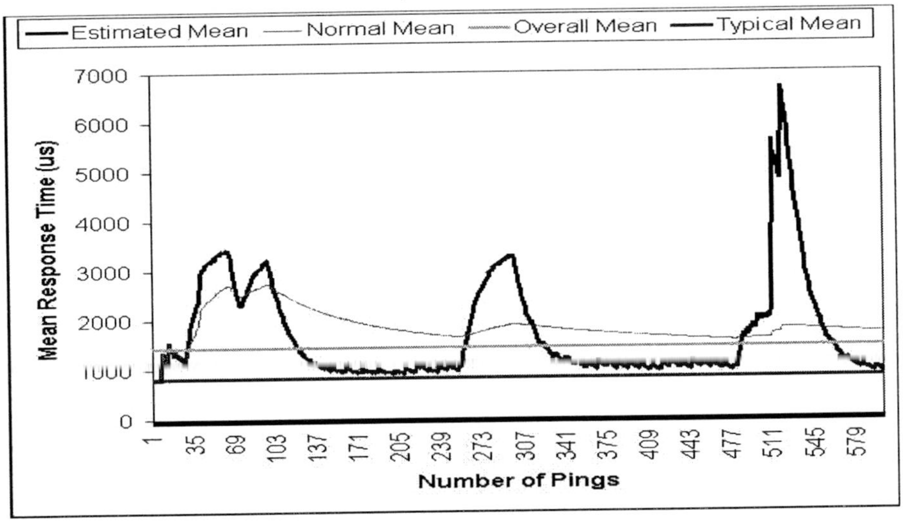

Figure A1.11. Predicted mean ping RTT by M³RT (typical mean ≅ 900) –MPI.

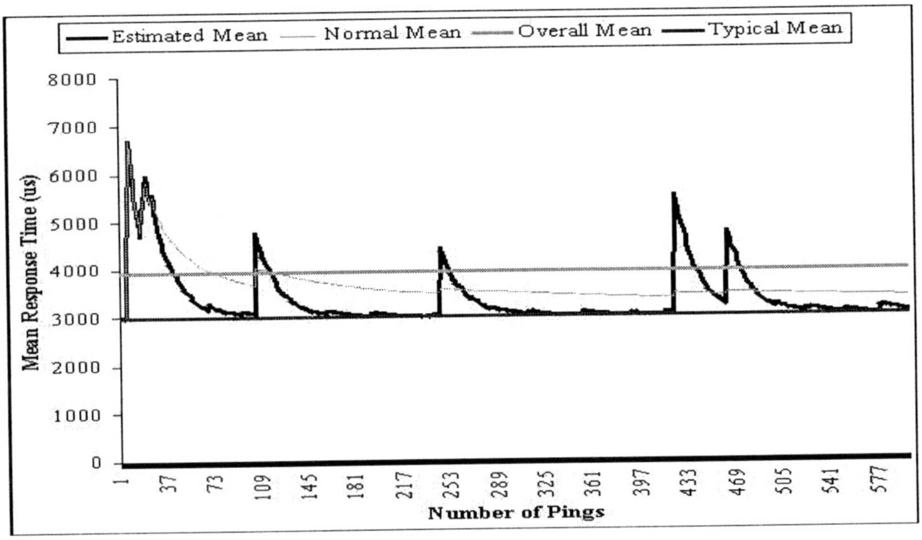

Figure A1.12. Predicted mean ping RTT M³RT (typical mean ≅ 3000) – CORBA.

This example comparing the performance by MPI and CORBA is just the tip of the iceberg for the spectrum of possible CA applications. The CA time Petri net (A1.1) presented in this section provides a good basis for potential users to familiarize themselves with the CA operation through simulations, which verify all the CA claims in a convincing manner.

KEY REFERENCES

[Ip2002] Allan K.Y. Wong, May T.W. Ip and Tharam S. Dillon, M³RT: An Internet End-to-End Performance Measurement Approach for Real-Time Applications with Mobile Agents, *Proc. of the ISPAN''002,* 2002, 119-124

[Lankes2001] S. Lankes et al, Design and Implementation of a SCI-Based Real-time CORBA, *Proc. of the IEEE ISORC'2001*, Magdeburg, Germany, May 2001, 23-29

[Mitsuru1998] O. Mitsuru and K. Guenter, IBM Aglets Specification, www.trl.ibm.com/aglets/spec11.htm

[Molnár1999] S. Molnár, T.D. Dang and A. Vidács, Heavy-Tailedness, Long-Range Dependence and Self-Similarity in Data Traffic, *Proceedings of 7th International Conference on Telecommunication Systems, Modelling and Analysis,* March 1999, Nashville, USA, 18-21

[Tsybakov1998] B. Tsybakov and N.D. Geoganas, Self-Similar Processes in Communications Networks, *IEEE Transactions on Information Theory,* 44(5), September 1998, 1713-1725

[Willinger2003] W. Willinger, V. Paxson, R.H. Hiedi and M.S. Taqqu, Long-Range Dependence and Data Network Traffic, in *Theory and Applications of Long-Range Dependence,* P. Doukhan et al., Eds., Birkhuser 2003, 373-408

[Wong01B] Allan K.Y. Wong, Tharam S. Dillon, Wilfred K.W. Lin and May T.W. Ip, M²RT: A Tool Developed for Predicting the Mean Message Response Time for Internet Channels, *Computer Networks.* 36(2001), 557-577

APPENDIX B: GLOSSARY OF TERMS

Active queue management (AQM)	A network congestion prevention measure that uses a "throttle first and then drop" operation at the system/router level to prevent buffer overflow and shorten RTT
Aggregate	A collection of data points or time series sampled statistically.
Asymmetric rendezvous	The client/server interaction relationship in which the server is simultaneously serving different clients.
Average number of trials (ANT)	A measure of the number of times that a message must be sent before a successful transmission occurs.
Buffer	A finite memory space where objects are queued up.
Cache	The local memory where the proxy server keeps all the popular/hot data.
Caching parameters	Parameters (metrics) used in an algorithm to ensure there is sufficient hot data in a cache usually of static size. These may include the "least frequently used objects" and "least recently used objects."
Client	Conceptually, any service user.
Client/server relationship	In this relationship the same server may serve many clients at the same time. This many-clients-and-one-server relationship is also known as the asymmetric rendezvous. The interaction is by message passing irrespective to whether it is at the system or user level. The system/router level includes all the activities within the TCP channel, and the user level includes the client and server entities that interact over the TCP channel in an end-to-end

	manner.
Compensation measure	A compensation measure that brings any deviation back to the norm of system operation.
Convergence algorithm (CA)	An IEPM method for real-time application derived from the *Central Limit Theorem*. Its accuracy is therefore independent of the waveform type.
Deleterious effect	The undesirable consequence from remedying a spurious problem.
Dynamic cache size tuning (DCST)	A real-time technique that maintains the given cache hit ratio under all operational conditions. In the process some chosen network parameter(s) are leveraged to determine the cache size adjustment on the fly.
Dynamic buffer size tuning(DBST)	A technique that effectively tunes the buffer size on the fly, with the adjustment computed from some chosen network parameters.
Fuzzy Logic Controller (FLC)	A real-time dynamic buffer size tuner that ensures buffer length always covers the queue length to eliminate any chance of user-level buffer overflow.
Gaussianity	Synonymous with a normal distribution that has the *kurtosis* and *skewness* values of 3 and 0 respectively.
Genetic Algorithm Controller (GAC)	A dynamic buffer tuner that uses genetic algorithms as its basis.
Heavy parameterization	The phenomenon of using too many parameters, in which the computation cost outweighs the benefits.
Hit ratio	The chance of finding requested data in the proxy cache. Whenever the data is not found, the proxy has to search via the DNS of the Internet from the remote data source(s) or web server(s).
Intelligent buffer controller	The controller works with soft computing techniques that include fuzzy logic (e.g. the Fuzzy Logic Controller) or neural computing (e.g. the Neural Network Controller).
Inter-arrival time (IAT)	The time between the arrival of two consecutive objects.

Internet end-to-end performance measurement (IEPM)	A tool that monitors and gauges the Internet channel behavior through the mean end-to-end RTT.
Internet traffic patterns	Patterns include short-range dependence (e.g. Poisson), long-range dependence (e.g. self-similar and heavy-tailed) or multifractal.
Kurtosis	The sharpness measurement of a distribution.
Local service response time	The queuing and service delays at the server side excluding the client/server communication delay.
Long range dependence (LRD)	A waveform that is stationary and has a Hurst (H) effect in the range of $0.5 < H < 1$. Examples are heavy-tailed and self-similar. $H = 0.5$ is not used because it represents white noise. The LRD autocorrelation function is nonsummable.
Mean Message Response Time (M^2RT)	An IEPM approach that implements the CA at the macro level to determine RTT changes over time for a communication channel. At the macro level the tool has to be installed at the two nodes that represent the two ends of the channel. The monitoring process needs human intervention.
Micro Mean Message Response Time (M^3RT)	An IEPM approach that implements the CA at the micro level to gauge the RTT changes over time for a communication channel. At the micro level the tool exists as a logical entity that can be invoked for service anytime and anywhere by message passing.
Model for Adaptive Cache Size Control (MACSC)	A conceptual framework that uses the ratio of the two most current standard deviations representing changes in the object popularity distribution to dynamically adjust cache size and maintain the given hit ratio.
Network congestion	The inundation of the router by a large volume of incoming packets that depletes buffer capacity, causing network congestion. This leads to loss of packets and very slow or no response to clients' requests.
Neural Network Controller (NNC)	A dynamic buffer size tuner for real-time application working as a feed-forward backpropagation perceptron with supervised training.
Packet loss	The dropping of a packet by the receiver during the transmission process to prevent local buffer overflow. This is a congestion prevention measure.

Parameter tuning	Parameters are selectively tuned on the fly so that they work to produce the expected optimal effect.
PIDC (Proportional + Integral + Derivative Controller)	A dynamic buffer size tuner that implements the CA at the micro level as support.
Proxy server	The gateway for clients within a firewall to communicate with the outside world.
Real-time traffic pattern detection (RTPD)	A novel concept that aims to determine the Internet traffic pattern anytime on the fly.
Relative object popularity (ROP)	The correlation between the access frequencies and specific data objects over the period of interest. The standard deviation of the distribution changes if users shift their preference for some objects in the period.
Roundtrip time (RTT)	The interval between the sending of a request by a client and the correct reception of the corresponding answer. Retransmissions lengthen the average RTT.
Safety Margin (Δ)	The predefined minimum difference between the buffer length and queue length at anytime. When it is maintained on the fly, for example by elongating the buffer length, it can prevent the reception buffer from overflowing due to sudden surges in the number of incoming requests.
Self-similarity (S^2) filter	A statistical estimator that determines if an LRD waveform embedded in an aggregate sampled on the fly is self-similar. It also shows if the dimension of the self-similarity is static (monofractal) or varying (multifractal).
Server	Conceptually any service provider, which may be sometime a client that requests service from others.
Service response time	Synonymous with service RTT.
Skewness	A measure of the degree of symmetry of a distribution.
Stochastic process	A process that works with operational paths that are event-driven from beginning to end.

Short-Range Dependence (SRD)	A waveform that is stationary and has a Hurst (H) effect in the range of $0 < H < 0.5$. An example is a Markovian pattern such as Poisson.
Transmission control protocol (TCP)	One of the two protocols in the Internet transport layer: the connection-oriented TCP and the connectionless UDP (User Datagram Protocol).
Zipf-like behaviour	The log-log plot ($y(r)$) of the access frequencies versus the ranked positions (r) of the corresponding data objects in descending order. This plot is represented by $y(r) \propto 1/r^{\beta}$, for $0 < \beta < 1$. For the Zipf Law, $\beta = 1$.

INDEX

A

B

C

D

E

F

G

H

I

J

L

M

N

O

P

Q

R

S

T

U

V

W

X

Y